MICHAEL REPEL

THE MUSIC INDUSTRY SELF HELP GUIDE
2nd Edition

TAKING YOUR FIRST STEPS TOWARDS TRAMPLING OVER
THE OBSTACLES IN AN INDEPENDENT MARKET

Repel Media Publications

For permission requests, please email the publisher, with the subject line addressed "Attention: Permissions Coordinator," at info@themusicindustryselfhelpguide.com.

Ordering Information:

Special discounts are available on quantity purchases by corporations, associations, U.S.trade bookstores, wholesalers and others.
For details, contact the publisher at info@themusicindustryselfhelpguide.com or visit http://themusicindustryselfhelpguide.com

Cover artwork by Mike Repel
Printed in the United States of America

Repel, Michael.
The Music Industry Self Help Guide: A Guide to Taking Your First Steps Towards Trampling Over the Obstacles in an Independent Market / Michael Repel.

ISBN 10: 0991515536
ISBN 13: 978-0-9915155-3-0

1. Music—Education.   2. Music —Artist development.   3. Music Industry—Careers.   4. Non-Fiction.
 I. Repel, Michael. II. Title.

Second Edition
14 13 12 11 10 / 10 9 8 7 6 5 4 3 2 1

*This book is dedicated to the people
who won't take no for an answer,
those who refuse to be a part of the status quo,
and independent artists and musicians everywhere
who take the restless desire to succeed
and turn it into a course of action.*

For Johno Cardona

TABLE OF CONTENTS

FOREWORD AND EDITOR'S NOTES

This book's editor, Carlos Fournier, performing with his Miami-based band, On Our Own.
Photo credit: Cortney Warsh

At first glance, Mike Repel strikes an intimidating pose. You'd probably think to yourself that he's the kind of guy you wouldn't want to run into in a dark alley before you'd even consider that he's an accomplished musician, former record label owner, music and media distributor, and author.

I first met Mike in 2007, shortly after I'd first moved to Chicago. We were introduced to each other by a mutual friend, and when Mike caught wind that I'd been a vocalist for a hardcore band, he instantly perked up and handed me a business card, inviting me to rehearse for a band he was forming on the city's south side.

Little did I know that this conversation would form an instant bond that lasts to this day.

While the band ultimately fizzled out, our friendship didn't. Even though I no longer live in Chicago, Mike and I remained in touch and I was honored when he asked me to be his editor for this project.

Mike has an unparalleled work ethic, and this is something you'll pick up on very quickly once you start reading this book. Simply put, the guy won't take no for an answer, and once he sets his mind on something, he won't finish until he's accomplished it and spun off at least three other projects to follow up with. The information in this book is invaluable to any new musician that wants to dive into the waters of the music industry, but even seasoned, die-hard veterans can benefit from it. If you've been there, done that, and lived to tell the tale, at the very least you'll find yourself nodding in agreement at various points throughout the book.

What you're getting here is not your typical musician's guide—far from it, in fact. Sure, you'll get tips on things like improving your songwriting and finding gigs, but you're also getting facts, figures, and uncensored (perhaps even unpopular) opinions from a longtime music industry veteran.

One thing you can expect *not* to get from this book is be coddled or have your hand held. What follows in these pages is, at times, a form of tough love that's certainly not for everyone, but is absolutely what many aspiring musicians need.

Mike takes a no-bullshit approach to just about every aspect of his life, and this is particularly evident in his writing style. Some may even find this offensive; but quite frankly, this industry isn't for the meek and sensitive to begin with. You truly need a thick skin to be a musician, and how you handle criticism and adversity will play a big part in shaping your future. Of course, no amount of planning can leave you prepared for every possible scenario as a musician. When my old band On Our Own was on tour once, we found ourselves lost on a dirt road in Death Valley with our gas tank running dangerously close to empty, no cell phone reception, and our van's brakes even caught fire because it was so fucking hot outside. There isn't a book in the world that could have helped us get out of that mess.

Thankfully for you, however, situations like that one aren't the norm. What this book will prepare you for are the much more common challenges that you'll face as you take your first steps towards becoming a serious and driven musician.

What also sets this book apart from others like it is its emphasis on the DIY mindset. Coming from our collective backgrounds in punk rock and hardcore, that mentality can be easy to take for granted because it's been drilled into our heads so often over the years; but for those of you that haven't been exposed to it, I'm happy to report that this will open your eyes to a way of thinking that you could apply to every single aspect of your life beyond just that of a musician.

Take heed to the lessons and information that you're about to absorb, and don't hesitate to use this as a springboard to do further research on your own. As comprehensive as this book is, there's always more to learn.

Most importantly, though, don't forget to have fun as you embark on this journey. Hard work can certainly lead to success, but there's no reason why you shouldn't enjoy yourself along the way.

Carlos Fournier – Editor

PREFACE

After receiving consistently positive feedback and support for the first edition of this book and realizing its greater purpose for musicians of all genres, I am now proud to provide you with the beefed-up **Second Edition** of *The Music Industry Self Help Guide,* which I have been working on incrementally since shortly after the release of its predecessor.

I originally wrote *The Guide* because it seems that regardless of genre or region, every musician goes through identical stages of development and needs access to the same tools and information to get ahead in this industry.

Over the last three decades I have continued to see a reoccurring disparity with different musicians that don't know where to look—and don't know what to look for—which keeps them isolated with no real hope of success. I've encountered this not only in local developing music scenes but also while formally mentoring aspiring artists at music conferences across the country.

My participation in independent music scenes dates back to before I was even in high school. I have had the opportunity to take the things that I learned and the networks that I've seen function and flourish and use them to help me with the development and growth of my own bands.

Subsequently, this is the same management style and skillset that I not only used for the advancement of my own groups and to start my own independent record label, but also to self-publish, market, and promote this book by myself as an independent publisher.

In writing the original manuscript, my experience and accumulated knowledge base placed me in a unique position to provide you with information from the point of view of an artist, a manager, and also from that of a record label.

It was important in the creation of this book that all of these perspectives were taken into consideration, as they vary so greatly in how they interpret what is actually required to succeed in today's market.

I also would like to stress the fact that the views in this book are not merely comprised of one person's observations of the music industry, but includes tried and true methods of success that have been implemented by bands that have maintained relevance for more than three decades.

Following the publication of the first edition, and after my first handful of radio interviews and book reviews, I soon realized that I may have actually done something transformative, because this was not a book on one specific topic of artist development to categorize in one discipline of curriculum, but rather a well-rounded, all-encompassing guide to creating momentum and visibility for emerging artists that covered all of the developmental elements that they would need to lay a solid foundation for themselves in the independent market.

Although multiple books and publications have been written on some of the various subjects contained herein that have a cold encyclopedic reference style of providing information, what I did in writing *The Music Industry Self Help Guide* was approach as many of these topics as possible, link them all together, and present them on more of a personal and direct level.

What resulted was a brutally honest and thought-provoking guidebook written in a conversational manner that can give your career a serious head start and help you move forward if you choose to implement its information.

The first edition provided a very solid framework for this expanded edition which has additional chapters, resources, lists, and a step by step guide on how to fill out an online copyright form.

This entire book was also re-tooled to provide quick and easy reference points for easy navigation.

What you now have in your hands is a book that was designed with your success in mind and has been refined into a better product for your added benefit.

Although this book encompasses the entire spectrum of the music industry from the earliest stages of a developing artist's career to the corporate wranglings of the music industry giants, I chose to focus primarily on the independent market, because this is the place that you must pass through while earning your stripes and paying your dues in this industry.

As the title implies, this is a self help guide, so what this book also does to prepare you for success is look at one of the largest hurdles that aspiring musicians face as they try to move forward in their career: themselves.

No other key component in this book will surpass the importance of one's ability to master oneself, and this book will callously press you to take an unflinching look inside yourself to understand who you really are and attempt to identify what is holding you back.

How far you get beyond the independent market will not only rely on the quality of the music you release, but will also hinge largely on how you utilize the things that you read in this book.

Thank you for taking an interest in *The Music industry Self Help Guide*.

Remember that knowledge is power, and once you have read this you will have tools that no one can ever take away from you.

Mike Repel

INTRODUCTION

Get this through your thick fucking head:
No one cares about you, and you are not as awesome as you think you are.
So get over yourself.

In this book, I intend to pull the wool completely off of your eyes and give you a real, concise, and current look into the music industry, while dispelling many of its myths. You paid for the book, so you deserve the honesty that comes with it.

New musicians seem to have this dream that they will be instantly catapulted onto a huge stage performing in a packed arena in front of thousands of crazed fans, flying from one city to the next in a private jet, and having vast amounts of wealth and all the excessive indulgences that come along with it.

That's a nice dream, but having a dream without a plan of action is just a delusion.

The music industry is the most competitive arena in the world next to professional sports or politics. If you are not ready to commit yourself wholeheartedly to making this dream a reality then what you have, my friend, is not a dream at all—it's merely a fantasy. The artists that you see on those big stages, on the other hand, woke up one day, took that dream, implemented a realistic plan of action, and got their asses out of bed to work towards that dream every day.

No matter how talented you are, nobody is going to give you a handout, and nobody owes you shit. So get mentally prepared to do some work. This is non-negotiable; you will need to be hands-on. If you aren't, success and opportunity will slip out of your hands before you can even grasp onto them.

There are no free rides in life, not in any field. Do yourself a favor and get this fantasy out of your head now. Man the fuck up, stop putting things off, get started, and stay till the job is done.

When you see a major label artist performing in an arena, under the big colored lights and scaffolding with cameras flashing while the crowd goes wild, stop comparing yourself to that image. That is not you. That person has most likely been doing this from a very young age. That person has paid his or her dues. That act has developed a loyal fan base and following well before they ever had a chance of playing an arena and was once where you are now.

That level of success won't happen for you next week and probably not in the next few years either. It takes time. It takes work. It takes commitment, and a lot of it.

Have you exercised that level of personal commitment? Have you taken personal initiative to put yourself on that huge stage? If you haven't, and if you aren't working on multiple aspects of your career every day, for hours at a time, then you're doing nothing to separate yourself from a huge and growing number of artists that are all trying to do the same thing as you.

Do you have an ongoing, realistic plan of action that includes long- and short-term goals that can guarantee you an opportunity to land a slot on that stage? Have you realized that before you ever become a headlining act you'll need to fill a slot as a supporting act first?

What makes you think you even deserve to be on that stage? Is it your own pride? Your own arrogance? If so, I recommend you lose that attitude, and lose it quickly.

You are not a rock star, and nobody likes a rock star mentality anyway; those egocentric and arrogant pricks are the worst people to deal with and are impossible to manage.

I have recently spoken with artists who are downright angry that they aren't getting their just rewards. They name a long list of personal accomplishments that make them think that the industry owes them something due to their so-called "grinding."

If you are one of these artists and have a gripe, you need to stop and ask yourself these questions:

- *Throughout all of my activities as an artist, am I doing the same amount of work as the artists that I aspire to be like or that I am comparing myself to?*
- *Am I performing as often as they are?*
- *Have I created the same track record and ongoing amount of visibility for myself as they have for themselves?*
- *In all of my activities as an artist, have I remained consistent in these endeavors?*

If the answer is no, then you should now clearly realize that you have more work to do.

A lot of this industry is based not only on strategy, but also on personal relationships with people. So if you're walking around with a huge chip on your shoulder because fate hasn't dealt you the fame and fortune that you think you deserve, I strongly suggest that you knock that shit off.

People do not want to deal with your drama or your negativity. Period.

Remember that.

It also seems like some of you hopeful artists are under the impression that new artists just magically pop up on your television or on the radio overnight. This didn't happen to your idols and it sure as shit isn't going to happen to you. There's a long continuous story of making the right decisions that led them up the ladder to where they are now. They seized opportunities and worked through all the potholes and pitfalls that nobody ever seems to acknowledge long before they ever found their way down the road of success.

Furthermore, that artist's lifelong history of upward mobility, extensive presskit, and proven sales record as an independent artist were most likely the factors that attracted a major label (who under most circumstances do not accept submissions from unsigned artists) along with management, sponsorships, and investors to spend a lot of money in his development,

3

exposure, and success because in him they see the potential of receiving a positive return on their investment.

The flash that you see on television and in magazines is the end result of a label's marketing campaign. Everything is polished to the hilt in an effort to create an image of success so you'll buy this artist's records. Even though most of the jets, jewelry, limousines, and even wardrobe are rented, the fact that the artist has even gotten his label to pay for this type of mainstream visibility is due to a great deal of discipline, hard work, and dedication. Yes, some mainstream artists do eventually reap the benefits of this success and are able to afford some of these lavish things, but only a very small number of them will ever see this amount of success in their lives.

These superstar artists are human and are prone to mistakes just like anyone else. They may not freely admit them, but under that glamour and pizzazz is someone who underwent a learning process that involved some challenges—and at one point in time, some sort of failure.

Let's look at some of the common reasons for failure:

- The inability to follow instruction
- The inability to care or commit
- Social ineptitude or the inability to interact or communicate with others
- Failure to plan in advance and follow an itinerary
- Failure to meet deadlines
- Failure to complete tasks
- Failure to be consistent

In some cases, failure is a necessary step in becoming successful. When it happens in nature it's called evolution. It's the only natural way for you to learn on your own without outside influence. Even the most stubborn of people will learn from their mistakes; this in fact may be the only way they're able to learn. You'll meet a lot of egotistical, self-centered people in this industry that need to go through this process, and you yourself may very well be one of them.

There is about a 97 percent failure rate amongst musicians because they just don't have all the pieces of the puzzle and don't know how to put together the pieces that they do have.

It takes some hard and embarrassing lessons, gut-wrenching moments of clarity, and—most of all—failure before the industry chews you up and spits you out as a seasoned artist.

Keep in mind though:

If you fell flat on your face it was because you were moving forward.

The higher you set you set your goals, the more times you are likely to experience failure before you achieve success.

The reality of the music industry is that you'll play in shitty bars, have scumbag promoters try to fuck you out of money, and your personal relationships will suffer while you spend long hours on the road, cramped in a van with no air conditioning, bulky equipment, and people who haven't bathed before you ever find yourself on a big tour bus, much less a private jet.

Success is a process that you need to work towards in stages, similar to education. Just as there is kindergarten, grade school, high school, and college, so are there many consecutive levels of success that you must go through in your music career. One stage must happen before the next; this is a natural process.

Success is a work in progress, not a handout.

If you are looking for a handout, please put down this book and apply for public aid; you will receive better results.

If you're seriously considering this field as a profession, or any other one for that matter, ask yourself this one very important question—and this may be the most important question that I'll have you ask yourself in this book.

You will need to ask yourself this question repeatedly, and constantly think about the answer that you're giving yourself. That question is:

What is my own personal work ethic?

How you answer this question will sum up how successful you'll be, not only in the music industry but in all aspects of your personal life as well. The sooner you come to realize the critical importance of hard work and dedication, the more comfortable and financially secure you'll be later in life.

Some of the most successful people that I've met in my life had tunnel vision. They stayed on one narrow path, dedicated themselves to one goal, and didn't let things distract them. Every last one of these people has reached the pinnacle of their respective career. They're seated at the top of their field and are sought after for their knowledge and experience. This is a direct result of an entire lifetime of continual self-improvement and upward mobility in their field.

It is true that some young and brilliant people will skyrocket past others in their discipline, especially in this industry where the creative side of the brain drives so much of the field itself.

That being said, you should know that even if you went to school to learn graphic design or music, that doesn't necessarily mean that you're an artist or a musician. Your school can teach you techniques and concepts in music and art, but it can't teach you how to be creative.

The ability to regurgitate information on cue does not make you a creative person; all it means is that you're receptive to programming. You can obtain countless degrees and certifications through formal education, and even though you may become referred to as an expert for your learned knowledge within its applicable field, there's nothing in any certification or degree that means that you're a natural, have a gift, or are special in any way.

If your certifications place you in the same category as everyone else with your skillset, this isn't a sign of brilliance; it's a sign of mediocrity.

Unless you can apply what you've learned and actually create something innovative, you'll just be another face in the crowd.

As Albert Einstein said, "The true sign of intelligence is not knowledge, but imagination."

You may have been referred to as "special" or "gifted," as people with an imagination often are.

It seems that because of the way that imaginative people's brains are wired, they have a tendency to pick up on things quicker than others do, or they just seem to "get it," and some of them show an ability to do difficult things effortlessly. But even though they get it, and it seems that they have all the pieces of the puzzle, they still have to put in the work.

Nothing is as disappointing as seeing people with this kind of natural God-given talent not focus and apply the skills that they have.

The common denominator here is *work*. *You have to do the damn work*.

I cannot overemphasize how important it is to learn how to take your career into your own hands from the very beginning and develop a clear understanding of each of the building blocks you obtain as you lay your foundation. This solid footing will give you more of an understanding of the other aspects of the business that will get thrown your way.

It takes time, it takes the desire to learn, and you have to do the damn work.

Due to the demands that others will make of you and that you'll be required to make of yourself, I hope for your sake that you're embarking on this long arduous journey because you understand that it's really all about the music and that your success may one day only be measured by the culmination of the small accomplishments that you have made over a lifetime.

If you are in this strictly for financial gain and the music itself comes secondary, then you may want to take a step back and really reconsider what you're about to get yourself involved in. Ask yourself if you have the personal fortitude to deal with the frustration that comes along with this lifestyle, and if you even possess the energy and the patience that it takes to chase a dream.

If you manage to persevere, you'll eventually find yourself among more and more people that can help you along on your journey and a lot of them are extremely experienced and have been doing this all their life. If you know where to look, there are some very decent people out there who care about their reputations and stand behind what they do.

On the flipside of this coin, a large portion of the music industry is filled with bottom-feeding leeches who care nothing about you and want you only for your money. They charge you for services that they'll do ineffectively because of their own lack of experience, lack of professionalism, and lack of concern for your personal career. Once you figure these two-bit hustlers out, they'll simply move along to the next naive artist and perch themselves upon that artist's back with their beaks in his wallet. These people are vultures, nothing more. Many of the services for which they're charging fees you can actually do for yourself more effectively, because no one will ever care about your personal success more than you will.

Unfortunately these opportunistic feeders only exist in today's market because we have entered into the era of the lazy and uninvolved artist. Had it not been for the fact that many artists are constantly looking for someone else to do the work for them, these people would not have a job in the first place.

In this book, I intend to give you a head start on what you need to do to gain momentum for yourself while also giving you some insight on the people that you'll come across in this industry. You'll meet productive people with good intentions and dishonest ineffective people as well; hopefully you can differentiate between the two. I'll try to help you avoid some common mistakes that artists make and maybe even some fatal ones. At times I'll provide you with a series of questions that are directed at you personally.

You may want to highlight the questions I'm asking you in this book; although this book provides many solutions for independent artists, some of the questions I've placed here are strictly for you to gain some insight as to who you are and where you're at in your career. Seeking the answers to these questions will empower you to become better at your craft and will teach you an exercise in being independent. The less you rely on others, the more self-sufficient and successful you'll become. Remember, no one cares about your personal success more than you do.

Whether you're a musician in a band, a solo artist, or a rap artist, this book is designed with your success in mind.

However, if you are the kind of person who gets butthurt over some strong language like that of my introduction, then maybe this book and this career move are not really for you.

Perhaps you should consider a less aggressive field and do something a little more placid, because you may not be cut out for this lifestyle, and if you're not an aggressive person you will be looking up the next person's ass on the corporate ladder for the remainder of your days on this earth; this, my friend, I promise you.

Man the fuck up, kid,

because life's about to get ugly.

CHAPTER ONE

BE PREPARED TO DO IT YOURSELF

The best place to find a helping hand is at the end of your sleeve.

So you want to play a show, huh? And somebody knows a guy, who knows a guy that can get you a show.

Yeah, well good luck with that.

Waiting around for others to do things for you is the wrong approach for your career and for your life in general. If you want something done—and done right—get off your ass and do it yourself.

As I've mentioned before, no one cares about your personal success more than you do.

Furthermore, it's very unlikely that anyone is going to help you out unless you're actively doing things for yourself already. Any good promoter will know if you're being proactive in your own career; it's really the one main thing they look for.

If you have a buzz, and people are talking about you and coming to see you, promoters will be contacting you. If you're doing nothing, nothing will happen for you and no one will contact you.

This entire book emphasizes the DIY (*do it yourself*) approach to managing your career. By doing things yourself, you can eliminate several factors that are directly related to failure when relying on other people. Unnecessary delays, missed opportunities, and miscommunication are some of the common things you'll encounter if you ask anyone other than yourself to get something done.

Underground bands and artists have a rough time getting off the ground and are widely ignored by the mainstream media and club promoters in general; the attitude today that most new acts have to contend with is that if you don't have a large following then there's no money in it, so therefore it must not be worthwhile.

The music industry seems polarized due to the fact that it's occupied by two completely different forces that can't work or even exist without each other. The sometimes free-spirited views of the artists and their desire to write, create, and just get out and play sometimes hits a wall because of the business side of the industry. Some musicians wonder why they aren't able to get on the shows they want to play and they look at the people involved in the business side of things as oppressive because everything revolves around the cash register.

Staffing the large tours, the big arenas, and any nightclub or bar, for that matter, involves employment for bartenders, club security, live sound engineers, record label employees, promoters, photographers, lighting and scaffolding riggers, electricians, and many more people in many different positions. There are also many supporting industries directly tied into the field of music and live entertainment such as liquor companies, radio stations, magazines, compact disc manufacturers, advertising and marketing firms, T-shirt and merchandising companies, and many more.

The bottom line here is that this is a cash-driven business.

You need to start taking steps to ensure that your act can bring enough people into a club to justify your placement on the show bill.

If you want to have any chance of getting paid, you'd better be able to bring people through the door.

If you want to be able to successfully pull off a tour, you'd better have people interested enough in your band to buy your music and your merch. It costs money to put fuel in a van and to feed people. Exactly where did you think that money was going to come from?

Do you want sponsorships, endorsements, and placements? None of this will happen unless your music is moving units.

Starting a career in music involves creating revenue streams— several of them in most cases. This is vital to your sustainability as an emerging artist. Unfortunately, many artists completely miss this concept altogether.

Many of you believe that your music is hot and that your career is worth an investor's financing. However, if you can't provide a detailed record of any viable sources of income related to your music, then what do you think will convince this potential investor that you're a worthwhile investment and have the ability of creating a return on the capital he's contributed to your venture?

For many of you, the problem is that you want to ask for money and help instead of getting your hands dirty and just doing the groundwork.

I've met many people that tell me that they're talking to sponsors, crowdsourcing, crowdfunding, and employing other methods of getting a helping hand. Some people are trying to start companies by way of applying for a grant. They spend more time shooting at angles and looking for someone to help them along than they do to facilitate their own success with their own two hands. I do understand the mechanics of these programs, but if they're your sole focus then you need to re-evaluate your approach. If you haven't learned to manage your group or your business on the most micro-economic level, what makes you think that money will really make a difference in your success?

If you haven't shown that you can successfully create revenue streams and manage accounts and money, your chances of getting a business loan or having a grant approved are slim to none. People want to see that you'll be successful before they decide to invest capital into your project. In mostly all of these cases you'll be required to submit a business plan. Do you have a business plan to present to someone? Do you even know how to draft a business plan?

It's almost just as easy to ask for $100,000 as it is to ask for $10,000, so what are you going to say that's convincing enough to get approved for these funds?

Oh, I'm sorry, I forgot. Your music's hot; that's right. Well in that case, let me just write you a check right now.

In the occasion that you may succeed in getting a loan or a grant early in your career, all you've done is circumvent the natural growth process and place yourself in a financial position that you may not be qualified to handle. Your ambition to jump headfirst into the action will result in the arrival of an abundance of questionable people in your life who are eager to relieve you of your funds in a short period of time. They'll remain on your side until your funding runs out and leave you with no established long-term avenues for you to make an ongoing return on your investment.

A fool and his money are soon parted.

If some of the people I've met along the way spent as much energy doing the work as they did looking for a way to get around it, they'd already be reaping the benefits of their efforts. This in itself is the biggest problem with people in this industry; they're so focused on the finish line that they don't focus on their immediate priority, which is where they need to place their next step on the path beneath them.

If you are a person who is always looking for shortcuts, the only thing you will be cutting short is yourself, your potential, and your future.

There's an abundance of stubborn people that enter this field. They don't know the first thing about what they're doing or what they're supposed to do, yet they won't or just can't bring themselves to listen to the advice of anyone around them.

It's okay if you are new to this industry and you don't know anything, because eventually you will learn; but if you don't know anything and can't listen to others or follow instructions either, well then you're a detriment to yourself and you are just hopeless.

It is always the most inexperienced, unprepared, uninformed artists who are unequal to the task that feel predisposed to success as if it was their birthright. I meet delusional acts like this every day. They want it all, want it now, and don't want to do anything to get it. Yet they feel that they are entitled to it.

This may be the result of a psychopathological condition such as megalomania, which is characterized by unrealistic fantasies of wealth, grandeur, or unlimited power. Or it may be an unrealistic, inflated, or firmly held sense of entitlement which in clinical psychology and psychiatry may be considered symptomatic of narcissistic personality disorder

I guarantee you that if you don't have a musician with one of these Cluster A- or Cluster B-grouped personality disorders in your band already, you'll meet one of them soon.

That is, if you are not indeed one of these people yourself.

The music industry appears to be a magnet for misfits of all shapes and sizes.

That being said, welcome home.

Whether you feel entitled to success or not, I challenge you to provide me with an example of a person that was handed fame and fortune on a silver platter without working for it.

It has never happened, not to any one person in the history of the world.

Once the big dream or fantasy of being on Easy Street is replaced with an actual list of things to do, a great majority of people will fail to proceed any further and will fail simply because there's work involved.

There's an absolutely mind-boggling amount of lazy people who are just mentally incapable of doing work, that feel entitled to success, and are convinced that they have a chance to make a break in this industry.

So in an effort to shed some light on the actual amount of recording artists in this industry who will achieve some level of success, here's a reality check:

By looking at Nielsen statistics provided to us in the May 2010 *Fordham-CMGB Music Industry Overview* by Rich Bengloff, we see that in 2008

- Only 5,945 artists sold more than 1,000 copies of their album
- Only 1,515 albums sold more than 10,000 copies
- Only 110 out of 105,575 albums released sold more than 250,000 copies

Hopefully these numbers will help deflate any delusional visions of grandeur that you may have had and bring you back down to a point where your expectations now coincide with reality.

So with the assumption that you still don't have your head in the clouds, let's approach the industry from a realistic point of view and see what it will take to make a name for yourself, one step at a time.

Working on your career is something that should be embraced, and it's not that daunting of a task if you have the desire to do it, along with the motivation to *do it yourself*.

If you look around, you'll find that the *DIY mentality* has been one of the largest driving forces within the music industry for a very long time.

If you take the time to actually study the humble beginnings and chronological history of your particular music genre, you'll gain a technical perspective of the incremental stages of development that it passed through before it developed into the systematic machinery that it is today. Having this understanding of the bigger historic picture of your scene and applying it directly to your career will accelerate your own personal development overall.

KNOWING YOUR HISTORY WILL HELP MOLD YOUR FUTURE.

Take rap music, for example; just about every underground rap artist that I meet is convinced that they are headed for the top. These new artists all believe that they have the inner workings of the rap game figured out but don't even know who Sylvia Robinson is. Were they to study the strides and individual moves this woman made while at the helm of Sugarhill Records, they would understand what it took to launch the entire genre of rap out of obscurity in the first place.

When you take this historical disconnect from the facts and combine it with the media-manufactured images of successful artists, you discover the root of the entire illusion that this book was written to remove from your mind.

I've been watching the functionality and structure of DIY music scenes since 1986. The bands I grew up watching spurred a musical revolution and created an international network long before any major label was even aware of what they were doing.

A prime example of the DIY mindset and the music scene that I am referring to is that of hardcore. The name of the genre was taken from the content classification used in the porn industry and used to describe the music. Just as there is hardcore and softcore porn, there are also softer forms of punk rock which were originally characterized by such bands as the Ramones and the New York Dolls. As a way to differentiate the softer punk acts from the newer and harder bands that were springing up in New York, D.C., and LA, the term "hardcore" was applied to this newer and more aggressive sound that was being churned out from these new bands.

The bands in the hardcore music genre took their career into their own hands and created a movement that thrives to this day. In the early days, young bands such as Agnostic Front, The Cro-Mags, Murphy Law, Sick of it All, Breakdown, Judge, Youth of Today, Bold, Gorilla Biscuits, and the Beastie Boys (which were also a hardcore band before they started their rap career) with their primarily underage following played Sunday matinee shows at CBGB on Bleecker and Bowery Streets in the Lower East Side of Manhattan. Any club is going to reserve its Friday and Saturday nights for larger bands and make every effort to capitalize on alcohol sales to its *of age* clientele, but not having a prime spot did nothing to suppress this movement's growth. People from across the world were becoming aware of the Sunday hardcore matinee shows at CBGB.

Grassroots scenes were developing from city to city. Los Angeles was known for its shows (and riots) at the Whisky a Go-Go on Sunset Boulevard with bands such as Black Flag. The San Francisco Bay was birthplace to the Dead Kennedys. The D.C. punk scene, which is well known as the birthplace of Bad Brains, had the Dischord House (home to Dischord Records), the Teen Idols, Minor Threat, Government Issue, Youth Brigade, and S.O.A., which featured a young Teen Idols roadie named Henry Garfield on vocals who was later to become known as Henry Rollins, front man of Black Flag and then the Rollins Band. For those of you readers unfamiliar with Rollins' musical background, most of you have probably seen him recently as the antagonistic character A.J. Weston in the "Sons of Anarchy" TV series.

These primarily young, under-the-radar bands snubbed the mainstream music establishment and created a national and international network with each other out of necessity without the use of booking agents, touring companies, or major labels. They also managed to pull this off long before the Internet, email, or cell phones ever existed. If they were able to do this in their time, then there's no reason that you can't do this now in the information age.

Small grassroots labels on shoestring budgets such as Alternative Tentacles, Dischord, SST, and Revelation sprouted up in these cities and saw enough money coming back from their early releases to expand their rosters. Then with the advent of having physical distribution in place, which made these bands' music available in the cities in which they were touring, the movement not only began to spread, but it began to flourish and thrive.

Many of the New York hardcore (NYHC) bands were touring with members that were 16 and 17 years old. The first time I saw Freddy "Madball" Cricien perform live, he was on tour with Agnostic Front at 12 years old.

These bands created a loyal cult following that supported the music scene. "Music scene" is actually not even the right way to describe this; it's actually more of a music community than anything else.

The movement functioned and grew not only because its members took matters into their own hands but also because they understood, embraced, and preached a sense of unity and pride. It wasn't about fashion; it was about a genre of music and a way of life, and remains so to this day.

This sense of unity and inclusiveness is what sewed up a vast network of bands and people across the globe that created the independent market that we know of today. There are bands, genres, and labels we know of today that would not have come into existence had it not been for this movement including Biohazard, Hatebreed, Green Day, Dropkick Murphys, and Victory Records. Had it not been for my own involvement in this scene, this book would not be possible.

Creating a network of bands from within your genre to consistently work with will help you create your own music scene and community. If you can get other groups to share your vision, you can be responsible for creating the next viable music movement in your city. It may start out small, but just like anything else, things will grow over time if they're maintained properly.

In order for you to be able to pull this off, you'll need to implement a few things:

- *Mutual support* – Purchase music and merch from the bands that you work with, wear each other's shirts, and help promote their music and their upcoming dates. When you play with other bands, you and your guests need to stay and watch them perform after your set, not only as a show of support, but to ensure that their music gets heard by as many people as possible. It's very rude to walk out on a band right as they get on the stage or before they have a chance to perform, especially if they stayed and watched your whole performance. By working together, you'll help each other maximize each other's fan base.
- *Build bridges and maintain relationships* – Connect with other labels and promoters in other cities and countries that are doing what you're doing. Share ideas that will nurture growth and sustainability, perform live in each other's cities, and become a deeply rooted part of each other's music community.
- *Cross promotion* – If one of the bands from your network has a new release, whether they're local or from out of town, pass out their flyers, hang their posters and slap their stickers on bus stops and street lamps, and play their music in your clubs and at your social gatherings.
- *Share your resources* –These music scenes start small and so do the businesses that develop with them. If there's a kid in the audience who is silk screening shirts, let all the bands know who he is and support him, because he's supporting you each time he pays admission to your show.
- *Network with people like yourself and remain united to a larger cause* – Just as any community needs to work together, and as any business district needs to keep businesses thriving within its own chamber of commerce, you need to keep working with each other and doing business with each other. Keeping all of your business and promotions active within a small sphere or centered around a small scene or community is what will make it function and flourish.
- *Nurture your community* – Create support systems to help members of your community. Do benefit shows to fund a band's next recording or fundraisers for people in your music scene who

are having a hard time financially or medically. If you treat your whole network as an extended family, you'll be making your music scene a home that people can be proud to call their own.

- *Remain accessible and available at all times* – Having a network and a community can't happen without communication. You can't really be involved without being physically present. People come to these events to see each other as much as they do to see the bands. Learn the importance of face time and be a part of the fiber that holds your scene together.

Everybody these days seem to have their own clique. Yours should be your music scene—and your music scene only—if you plan on doing this for an ongoing period of time.

This is the essence of the grassroots, underground, *DIY* way of making it happen.

Stand united,
Kick down all of your barriers,
Recognize no boundaries,

AND FUCK THE STATUS QUO.

CHAPTER TWO

WHAT IT REALLY MEANS TO BE INDEPENDENT

In today's music industry, the lines have been blurred on what clearly defines an independent artist or label.

This term seems to have exceeded its usefulness as it is not only used to describe the lowest tiers of underground artists, but also to describe the largest of the independent labels that are dominating the market.

Over the last 20 years, independent labels have gained a strong foothold and market share of this industry. This didn't happen as a fluke, either. The timing of new emerging genres, the introduction of the Internet, and the rapid globalization of the independent sector of the music industry have created sustainability for indies in what was once a market dominated only by the majors.

Independent labels have shown massive fiscal growth. Some have been offered (but rejected) buy-outs by the majors, some have sold out to the majors, and many also rely on the distribution chains of the majors.

However, in today's music industry, distribution with a major label has become unnecessary for independent artists and labels due to the advent of independent distributors and aggregators who are willing to distribute any and all music that comes their way.

THE BIG DIFFERENCE

One thing is for certain, though; there still is a clear and definitive line between a major label and an independent label, and a major label recording artist and an independent label recording artist.

Although the independent labels have fought their way in, the majors still control a majority of the available investment capital to fund a new artist, along with the clout, influence, and connections to place their artists at the forefront of a media blitz.

For all you hungry artists out there, this fact should be of no consequence to you, because at the end of the day, MAJOR LABELS ARE NOT SIGNING UNPROVEN AND UNSOLICITED ARTISTS.

For you to see this in black and white, there is a directory you can purchase called the *Billboard Magazine Guide to Touring and Promotion*, and in the section for record labels you will see under every major label listing a phrase that states *"We do not accept unsolicited material."*

Case in point: major labels are no longer doing artist development. They want a proven artist to walk through the door because it lowers their risk threshold. It's much safer for a major label to approach the final contestants of "American Idol" or "The Voice" and offer them a contract, because by the time that artist has made it to the final rounds, he or she has already become a household name and has developed a fan base that roots for him or her on a weekly basis. In a scenario like this, the development and branding is done already; the artist can walk right in and sell records to the people who have been glued to the TV since the beginning of the season.

Grasping this concept is a huge problem among emerging musicians, and when you attempt to explain to them that they need to undergo a development cycle their eyes glare over as if you've just told them for the first time that there's no such thing as Santa Claus or the Tooth Fairy.

There are many reasons for a label's lack of interest in unsolicited artists. Besides the label's obvious desire to only sign acts that have the ability to create revenue through an established fan base, I believe it's also to ensure that they are dealing with artists who have already had their delusions previously removed. Artists who have been broken through extensive road work have a much more realistic perspective of this industry and therefore their expectations coincide with reality.

That being said, one may begin to ponder what the exact definition of *broken* really is.

Does it mean that the artist has finally broken out of obscurity? Or does it mean that now that this artist has had his hopes and dreams broken, shattered, and destroyed beyond recognition by a series of shows with bad attendance, pay-to-play promoters, and decimated artist revenues resulting from streaming and piracy that the reality of hard work and dedication to one's career has finally set in?

Perhaps the answer is that one must be *broken down* before one gets *broken out.*

This entire topic makes it increasingly evident to me that the wool of self-deception can't really just be yanked off of an emerging artist's eyes. The fibers of that cloth run thick and seemingly need to be worn down over time by the negative experiences and moments of clarity that they must endure on their own as they blunder through this overpopulated fools' paradise.

It was my intention to help you avoid this path when I wrote this book, and there is no doubt that this book will provide you with plenty of direction, but unfortunately some of you stubborn, know-it-all motherfuckers will still need to be drug through the gutter by the hand of your own personal mistakes before any of this even begins to make sense to you.

If you have any intention at all of becoming competitive in this industry, it is imperative that you read this book chapter by chapter and cover to cover if you truly want to learn something.

If you cannot do this successfully then you have just failed the first test in your own development and taught yourself a valuable lesson in your ability to commit to a single task and complete it successfully.

CHAPTER THREE
BRINGING THE GOODS

Artist – (art-ist) a person skilled at a particular task or occupation.

The competition starts early. One out of every three adult males plays guitar, everyone thinks they can sing (a trip to any karaoke bar will provide plenty of evidence to the contrary), and it seems that just about everyone is a self-proclaimed rapper. That coupled with the readily available amount of recording equipment and high-end audio software from retail stores including all of the cracked software out there creates an environment where just about anybody can record just about anything; whether it's good or it's bad will depend on a great number of things.

Whether you're playing guitar or bass in a band, or have a keyboard in front of you and are producing compositions for rap music, what is your proficiency level with your instrument?

Just owning a guitar or a program such as Fruity Loops or Reason doesn't mean that what you're writing is actually music.

Yes, the computer software you're using will make the process of writing music easy, but it still takes the individual composer's understanding of music to make it brilliant.

Contrary to what you may believe, there are rules and guidelines that you must adhere to when writing music. Understanding these concepts will separate you from either being able to actually compose music or possibly just playing garbage.

So in an effort to provide you with a basic understanding of music theory, I'm including some information in this chapter that is absolutely critical to your development as a singer, poet or rap artist, percussionist, composer, or musician.

I wouldn't feel that this book would be complete without an introduction (or in some of your cases a review) of this material, so let's jump right into a brief but comprehensive and necessary section of this book.

CRASH COURSE IN MUSIC THEORY

Do you know your chord structures? Do you know your scales, modes, and general theory? Are you incorporating harmonies and melodies into your writing?

The building blocks of all music are found within 12 individual musical tones.

Seven of these 12 tones have been deemed to have "major" importance and are also referred to as whole tones. The other five tones—which are classified as "minor"—are designated as *sharps* or *flats* and are also referred to as semitones or halftones.

Sharps, which are created by raising the pitch of any major tone by a half step, are denoted by a "♯", while flats are created by lowering the pitch of any major tone by a half step and are denoted by a " ♭ "

These 12 individual tones make up the 12-tone scale, which is also known as a chromatic scale.

These 12 tones are **C**, C♯ or D ♭ , **D**, D♯ or E ♭ , **E**, **F**, F♯ or G ♭ , **G**, G♯ or A ♭ , **A**, A♯ or G ♭ , and **B**.

As you can see above, C♯ and D ♭ are actually the same tone. This is called an enharmonic spelling, which simply means that the particular tone in question will be named as a sharp or flat depending on its role in the progression in which it is found. This also occurs with the other minor keys such as D♯ and E ♭ , F♯ and G ♭ , G♯ and A ♭ , and A♯ and G ♭ .

You'll also notice above that there are no sharps or flats between **E** and **F** or between **B** and **C**; this is known as a natural half step.

I realize that this is a lot of information for you to digest, and it may not make a lot of sense to some of you, so I'm going to simplify this for you in way that you can easily remember it.

On a keyboard, all of the major tones are assigned to the white keys and all of the minor tones (or the sharps and flats) are assigned to the black keys.

The seven major tones are the foundation of the Major scale, which is also referred to as the *Ionian* scale.

Combining several of the notes that occur at different intervals (or degrees) within a scale pattern and playing them simultaneously is how we create a chord structure; on sheet music, this simply appears as a bunch of stacked notes. *(Figure 1)*

Figure 1 - C Major Triad

The notes of a basic chord are made by combining the first (or the *root* note), third, and fifth degrees of a scale. This is also known as a triad, but there are many other chord structures as well.

To create a C Major Triad chord you would simply take a C major scale (C, D, E, F, G, A, B) and play the root note of **C**, with the third degree of the scale or **E**, and the fifth degree or **G** and play them together at the same time.

Figure 2 - C Major Scale

Playing the C Major Triad chord on a keyboard is done simply by playing three keys at once. The dots located on the keys represent each of the notes (*or degrees of the scale*) you will be playing.

Figure 3 - C Maj Chord Keyboard Diagram

The root note of the chord is the note that dictates what key the chord is in. Since all of the other notes in the chord are different intervals or degrees of the scale created by the root note, they will all share this key and result in a thicker, bolder sound when played in unison.

Playing the individual notes within any scale in any random sequence is what creates a progression, and by using each of these notes as a root note to build a chord from, you'll create what's known as a *chord progression,* which is the foundation of every song.

There are rules that music theorists adhere to when writing chord progressions, ultimately because research shows that following these rules will create music that sounds better; but as a composer you do have some flexibility on if you want to follow these rules when writing your progressions.

How a progression is played in relation to time, tempo, and phrasing is how we create and define *rhythm*.

Overlapping these progressions at different *steps* or *octaves* changes the *pitch* and is how we create the *harmony* and the *melody*.

To understand the notes that these progressions are based on, let's look at the seven-tone scale such as the *Ionian* (or *Major*) scale. To remain consistent, we'll once again use the C Major scale; which has a natural tonal progression of C, D, E, F, G, A, B, and then the scale repeats itself, beginning again with the C (also known as the tonic).

With the C being a repetition of the first tone, this eighth tone then creates a different octave, which is a higher or lower pitch of the same key depending on if your scale is ascending or descending.

C D E F G A B C

C Major Scale with tonic (or next octave)

The major scale also has several variations, which are known as modes. The modes for the Major scale are the *Dorian, Phrygian, Lydian, Mixolydian, Aeolian* (or *natural minor*), and *Locrian*.

Each of these modes begins on a different tonic of the major or Ionian scale and continues their sequence of notes from the order from which they begin.

For instance, in the case of the C Major scale:

- The Dorian mode of this scale would read D, E, F, G, A, B, C, D
- The Phrygian mode would read E, F, G, A, B, C, D, E
- The Lydian mode would read F, G, A, B, C, D, E, F
- The Mixolydian mode would read G, A, B, C, D, E, F, G
- The Aeolian or natural minor mode would read A, B, C, D, E, F, G, A
- And the Locrian mode would read B, C, D, E, F, G, A, B

Even though these modes utilize the same notes as the C Major scale (or the Ionian or parent scale) they all have their own tonic and therefore their own unique sound.

There are 12 different Major scales. The 11 others include *sharps* or *flats*. The major scale listed above has no sharps or flats, four of the others have sharps, four of them have flats, and three of them have enharmonic spellings.

There are many other scales from many different regions and cultures and for each and every scale that exists, there are also modes for those scales as well. All of these other scales come from the seven-tone scale, and this is why it's been the main focus of this section.

TABLATURE

Tablature is a form of musical notation that is used to complement the traditional music staff and notation format. It is best described as a translation of the musical staff and notation into a format that represents where the notes and finger positions are located on a guitar fretboard or a piano keyboard.

In traditional sheet music, notation is placed on a five-lined staff preceded by a treble clef (*see Figure 4*). Tablature explanation is a separate musical staff that appears below the music staff and is preceded by the word "TAB."

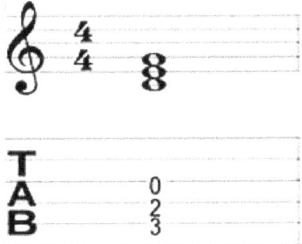

Figure 4 - C Maj Chord Tab

The tablature staff in *Figure 4* is meant for guitar. Each line on the staff is representative of one of the six strings on the guitar. The lowest string in pitch (deepest sounding) is on the bottom of the Tab staff, yet it is on the top of your guitar. So you must keep in mind when reading tablature that the strings are inverted. You will also see that the notes stacked in the C Major Triad chord in *Figure 4* are replaced with numbers on the tablature staff. This is because each number represents a fret on the guitar. The frets are the spaces on the guitar's fretboard that exist between the metal fret bars.

So to play the C Major Triad chord as shown in Figure 4, you would simply take your middle finger and place it on the fifth string over the third fret. While doing this you would also place your index finger on the fourth string over the second fret. Because there is a zero located on the fourth string in the chord diagram, you would play this string "open," meaning that you do not rest a finger on this string at all. When these three notes are strummed simultaneously you have played the C Major Triad chord.

REFERENCING THE FRETBOARD

There are several dots on a guitar fretboard that are used as reference points. The third, fifth, seventh, and ninth frets all have a single dot embedded into the guitar's neck. These single-dot reference points also continue on the 15th, 17th, and 19th frets. The 12th fret, however, has two dots. The 12th fret is also the octave or tonic for each open string. This is based on the 12-tone chromatic scale, which includes sharps and flats, that we discussed earlier and is not to be confused with the seven-tone major scale.

SCALE DIAGRAMS

Scale diagrams and chord diagrams are made up of a series of dots displayed over their respective string and fret location.

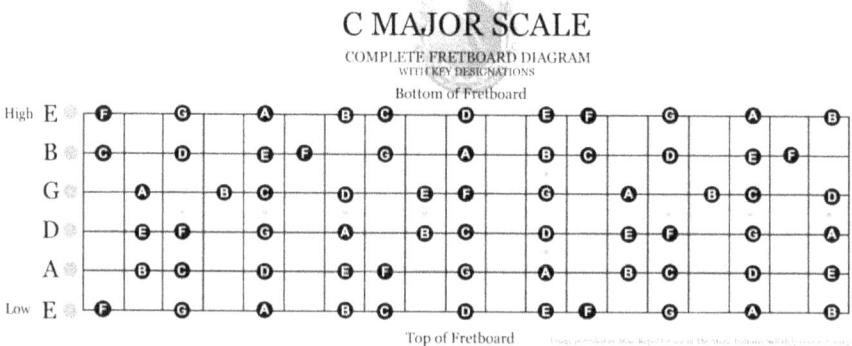

C MAJOR SCALE

COMPLETE FRETBOARD DIAGRAM
WITH KEY DESIGNATIONS

Bottom of Fretboard

High E	F		G		A		B	C		D		E	F		G		A		B
B	C		D		E	F		G		A		B	C		D		E	F	
G		A		B	C		D		E	F		G		A		B	C		D
D	E	F		G		A		B	C		D		E	F		G		A
A		B	C		D		E	F		G		A		B	C		D		E
Low E	F		G		A		B	C		D		E	F		G		A		B

Top of Fretboard

As you can see in the previous image, all the notes that fall within the C Major scale are represented as black dots on the fretboard. This is essentially a road map for guitar players to use when writing music or guitar solos.

By using these diagrams as a reference when composing music, you can obtain theoretically correct results quite quickly.

What I've listed above are just some of the basic fundamentals of music theory, because as you can see, this can get complicated rather quickly. I strongly urge you to learn as much about music theory as you can because incorporating this knowledge into your composing will increase your writing ability and make you a much better musician overall, and in most cases you'll hear a noticeable improvement in your playing immediately.

PHRASING

Having now covered some of the basic fundamentals of music, let's talk about *how you're playing* these notes.

Accentuating your playing with pitch bends, vibrato, slides, trills, (and in the case of guitar) hammer-ons, pull-offs, tapping, harmonics, pinch harmonics, string muffling, pick scraping, palm muting, and vibrato bar dives is known as phrasing.

If theory is the body of your music, then phrasing is without a doubt its soul.

Phrasing is how you express yourself. Adding a hard bend and holding it in the right place in a song can grab the listener's heart on a hook and drag them around for an entire solo or musical passage.

Developing your playing skills by combining musical theory and utilizing phrasing in your writing is how you'll develop your own personal technique and put soul in your playing.

This, just like everything else in this book, will not happen overnight. It will take time to develop and refine itself and it is the result of patience, hard work, and dedication.

Some guitar players have an advanced technical understanding of soundscapes because their writing encompasses advanced theoretical techniques along with several layers of ambient sound which they create and manipulate with a varied menu of effects such as delays, reverbs, chorus, flangers, and wah pedals. If you're a guitar player, have you dialed in your tone? Do you have a smooth transition when clicking these effects on and off? If your lead or solo settings are accentuated, are you oversaturated at loud volumes?

If you're producing whole musical compositions for EDM or rap music, please tell me that you're using a keyboard with your software and not writing everything with your mouse. If you haven't stepped up to buy a keyboard, you're extremely limiting the amount of artistic expression that you can achieve in your writing. Are you layering instruments? Do you know the voicings of the instruments that you're using? If you do, then are you using counterpoint theory in your orchestrations?

COUNTERPOINT THEORY & CLASSICAL INFLUENCE

Counterpoint theory is quite advanced in nature and adheres to a strict set of rules that generally involves the writing of musical lines that sound very different and move independently from each other but sound harmonious when played simultaneously.

Counterpoint, which developed in the 12th century, grew increasingly more complex through the Renaissance, Baroque, Classical, and Romantic periods, and is seen most often in classical music.

Past composers such as Beethoven, Mozart, Tchaikovsky, Pachelbel, Dvorák, Liszt, Handel, Palestrina, Schubert, Schumann, Wolf, Verdi, Wagner, Strauss, and Stravinsky all utilized this method. Through the use of counterpoint, these composers wrote the greatest masterpieces known to humankind. The works of these composers still fall short of the music created by Johann Sebastian Bach, who was probably the cleverest composer who ever lived; the mind-boggling complexity of much of his late music has yet to be matched by any composer to this day.

Even though we live in modern times, classical music influences still permeate the industry today and include the impeccable guitar work of

Randy Rhoads on Ozzy Osbourne's first two albums including the song *"Crazy Train,"* which was placed ninth on *Guitar World*'s 100 Greatest Guitar Solos reader's poll. Muhammed Suiçmez, who was influenced by Prokofiev and Beethoven, has written some insanely technical and emotional guitar solos on the Necrophagist album *Epitaph,* which is quite arguably some of the best guitar work of the millennia.

In today's pop music some of these classical compositions were actually not just the influence, but were actually sampled into the song.

- *"Karma"* by Alicia Keys contains a sample from Johannes Brahms's Violin Concerto.

- *"I Can"* by Nas contains a sample of the classical piece "Für Elise" by Beethoven.

- *"Coming 2 America"* by Ludacris contains Mozart's "Requiem," 3rd movement and Antonin Dvorak's Symphony No. 9, "From the New World", 4th movement.

Classical music compositions that incorporate counterpoint theory are the types of well thought-out orchestrations of individual genius that you should aspire to write. Even though you'll obviously be writing music indigenous to your genre, it would benefit you a great deal to study and understand what these composers were doing because these *masterpieces* are sonically flawless, and incorporating this theory into your writing will place you well in front of many songwriters that you may know.

This is, after all, the stuff that hit songs are made of.

To reiterate my point with absolute clarity, I said to incorporate this theory into your writing.

I did not say incorporate samples of other composers' music into your writing.

Although commonplace in today's industry, this is a practice that many musicians who have grown up playing organic instruments do not support, endorse, or agree with; their consensus is that engaging in this practice shows that you're lacking in originality and skill. I recommend that you push yourself to your mental limits and rely solely on your own talent to create the foundation of which your songwriting merits will be based.

However, and as unfortunate as it may seem for music aficionados the world over, this brings us to our next section:

ROBOTS ON THE RADIO AND THE GRAMMY FACTORY

As I have just alluded to, pop music is despised by almost every single formally trained and self-taught musician that I know.

In today's Grammy Award-winning studios, the dynamic of songwriting has changed immensely.

No longer does the status quo dictate that a few musicians write and rehearse an album for months on end and then sit in a studio and hash out an entire full-length album.

Instead, you are more likely to find a revolving door of high power talent cycling through the production of a performer's album.

Hold on, please.

I would like to re-emphasize what was just stated.

I used the word *performer* in lieu of the term *artist* or *musician* for a very good reason.

It not only more accurately describes the person whose name will appear on the album, but also provides a clear indication of what this person is doing on the songs. Without the ability to play an instrument, one has no ability to compose the music for a song, and if the performer has a ghostwriter for the lyrics, then he or she is merely performing other people's creations and no artistry is involved at all.

It is not uncommon for performers to find themselves in a position where the label that is funding their success takes creative control over their project. The performer, who is often adored by the public, may be someone with limited musical abilities who has music publishers handing him lyrics that were written by other songwriters which he will perform over music written by people who aren't directly involved with the album production.

Then the producer will add Auto-Tune and auto correction to the performer's voice until it sounds nothing at all like his actual voice and sounds more like a robot than a human. Almost every song on the radio today has a vocal track on it that sounds like the performer swallowed a throat cancer patient's electric voicebox.

Now add bits and pieces of catchy melodies from enjoyable songs from eras gone by, and you have created a song that you can sell to massive amounts of young impressionable people who haven't been exposed to the original works. Meanwhile, you have simultaneously and completely alienated a sizeable portion of the older populace because they can clearly identify these sampled melodies and immediately realize how bad you fucked up a good song from 30 or 40 years ago.

Drop in a mindless and repetitious computer generated 4-on-the-floor beat over the whole thing and you have just completed your latest club hit.

This happens for each and every song on the album and by the time the album is finished, it may have multiple songwriters and producers. If you are curious to see who is actually involved in creating an album in this category, just look at the credits or liner notes on the album or CD; you may actually find out that your favorite artist hasn't really written much at all.

This is pretty much representative of every Top 40 hit in today's market, where the same production techniques are employed and oftentimes the same featured artists are used. This leaves the radio airwaves filled with robotic sounding cacophony of monotonous programming with little or no individuality between artists.

On the rare occasion that I listen to the radio and am forced to listen to a Top 40 hits station it becomes more and more apparent that the amount of actual musicianship in this industry is at an all-time low.

Music itself is going through a de-evolutionary process at this time. The beat or the pulse of the song is all that the youth are interested in, and the fundamentals and discipline of music theory are getting thrown out of the window and replaced by a computer program.

"I'm all about the bass, bout the bass, no treble" – Yes, of course you are, and it's because you don't have the slightest fucking clue about music theory.

With that being said, back to your lesson.

PERCUSSION

Musical compositions are not only based on the theory behind the sequences of their musical notations, but also on how these notes are played rhythmically and in time with the percussive measures of the song.

In the percussive sections of your writing, are you changing the time signature or the beat during the choruses (hooks) or is it the same beat running through the entire song? If that beat doesn't change then you need to work on that, songs that have the same beat throughout are dull and boring. What kind of tricks do you have in your arsenal as a percussionist? Do you have several techniques to change up to? How are your offbeats and your fills? Are you breaking your patterns with rests and adjusting your sticking?

I have heard many bands with drummers who have limited skills, and although they can pull off a decent amount of songs due to the writing skills of the other members, every song has the same drum pattern and predictable rolls. It is very easy to become bored with this quickly.

On the other hand, an awesome drummer can easily transform a band with a mediocre guitar player into a force to be reckoned with. These drummers are actually somewhat hard to find, so if you find one you had better keep him around, even if he is in three other bands. Drummers in general have always been in limited supply and high demand, so if you're a drummer, learn as much as you can and you will always have a job.

As a drummer, even though you're stuck in the back of the stage and are staring at the singer's back, you have the most important job in the band: you keep the time and set the tempo.

You, sir, are a clock.

To help you build upon this, and to help you break out of any mundane and predictably repetitive patterns that you may be creating, you should take the time to research and develop a clear understanding of the actual elements that rhythm consists of.

These are:

- Pulse, beat, and measure
- Unit and gesture
- Alternation and repetition
- Tempo and duration
- Metric structure

Although I'd like to go into a more in-depth description of percussive techniques, this isn't my specialty area. So I encourage you to research and develop your craft.

However, I would like to say that in an age where a good portion of music is computer-generated and mostly everything is robotically quantized, I think that it's important for you to think outside of the box. Breaking away from the mold is what creates innovation. As a way to facilitate and encourage this, I'd like you to consider approaching your songwriting using the Claude Debussy philosophy of composing music. This is defined by *understanding that music is not made up of the beat and the notes*;

It's made up of the spaces between the beats and the notes.

Music itself is this interwoven soundscape created from the feeling and ingenuity of all the musicians in the group working together. Utilizing rests will create space for which the other musicians will express themselves through their accents and phrasing.

Watching a good jazz band with musicians who know when to hold back and when to express themselves will show how these spaces are exploited by improvisational techniques.

This all funnels into another absolutely critical fundamental building block of music: timing.

TIMING

Everything in music is based on timing. Some musicians play by "feel" and have problems when playing with "metered" musicians that play to a "click track" or metronome, which is a device that counts the pulse or the beats per minute (which can be set by the device).

For you electronic musicians and *beat composers* (a term incorrectly dubbed as "*producers*" in urban music), this can be best described to you as "quantized playing."

Software such as Fruity Loops and Reasons' REDRUM offer easy ways to lay beats down at any time interval within a measure. This unfortunately often creates a repetitious beat (often the hi-hat in rap music) that never changes and is constant throughout the entire song.

In many electronically produced songs, this repetition becomes monotonous and makes it difficult to differentiate where a chorus starts and a verse ends because it is just one beat from the beginning to the end of the song. Furthermore, if it is based on a common 4/4 time signature that many programs use by default—it adds to the monotony and the loops become anticipated and predictable. Changing the time signature or the entire arrangement of the beat and the supporting instrumentation in different parts of the song will liven up your composition and keep it from getting boring.

Although many rock songs were also written in a 4/4 time signature, some more memorable compositions actually deviated from their time structure several times during the song.

Pink Floyd's "Money" is a famous example of the use of odd time signatures. It was written in a 7/8 time signature that then changes to a 4/4, returns to 7/8, and goes back into 4/4 while the saxophone is playing a 7/4 time signature *(It is argued that this song is actually all in 7/4 time, but Roger Waters and David Gilmour have stated that it was composed in 7/8 time)*.

Time signatures which are referred to as "odd" can be described as any meter that doesn't maintain a feeling of two or four pulses per measure, or three in a waltz because they aren't smoothly repeatable. However, these times signatures eventually resolve themselves within the song structure, which the listener will still find rhythmic.

Time signatures and tempo changes are also common in modern genres of music where hard and fast changes occur or the song suddenly slows down to a heavy groove. This can sometimes be described as adding a "drop," a "breakdown," or a "beatdown" into a song.

There are some musicians who insist that a metronome should only be used to set the tempo.

Some musicians can get caught in a mold where they are unable to break out of that robotic timing and have difficulty catching a groove based on the feel and emphasis of a time signature change or of free time. There is a certain consciousness and connectivity to the other members of the band that really should be there at all times. This is what adds a human element to the song. Then there is something known as *free time*, which has no meter at all; it is often implemented by jam bands and jazz improv bands.

Yet, as a musician, you should start using a metronome if you are not already. Professional studio musicians are all metered and can sit in any jam session and play competently and in time, resulting in a tight sounding performance.

CRESCENDO AND DECRESCENDO

Another way to approach songwriting is to build everything up to a crescendo.

The crescendo is also known as the climax of the song. This is the point that every other section of the song is building up to, be it instrumentation, volume, tempo, intensity, or a combination of them all.

Once this climax is reached, it's then common to implement the decrescendo, or as stated in the previous section, the drop, breakdown, or beatdown as the song dissipates in minimal instrumentation, volume, tempo, and intensity.

VOCALIZATION

Now I have saved the one position that everyone aspires to fill at one point or another for last. I have postponed any discussion about this until the end because this is the person who really should know all of the dynamics of the other band members that create the music over which he writes.

The front man, the vocalist, the solo singer, or the rap artist.

If this is you, I purposely wanted you to read everything I have laid out about the actual music before I got to the section pertaining to you.

The brief interpretation on music theory that I gave you was not meant just for musicians who play instruments. It was meant for you as well because you yourself are also an instrument.

Having this understanding along with the ability to visualize yourself as an instrument in a larger ensemble will allow you to become better at your craft.

VOCALS ARE THE FOCAL POINT OF THE SONG

You need to understand the dynamics of the music that you're singing over so you can complement the arrangement or work with the other musicians in your group to tweak it to fit your phrasing. No matter what genre of music you perform, your vocals are the focal point of the song; you need to know your talent and what to improve upon as well.

In actuality, your voice and the parts of your body that make it function combine to form a complex instrument that you need to learn how to use just as if you were learning piano or guitar.

A good vocalist has the ability to go from a narrator, to a singer, to an actual instrument at will. To do this effectively takes skill, conditioning, and strengthening of the lungs and diaphragm, along with breath control, pitch control, and diction.

You should also learn music theory because vocal passages can become as complex as layered instrumental passages and singing will at times incorporate melody, tenor, baritone, and bass along with two- or three-part harmonies and at times more complex techniques such as counterpoint theory as well.

I hear singers and rap artists singing to themselves with no emotion, no emphasis or dynamics, and no passion. Some of these monotone and out of key passages sound so horrible that they become even worse when put through Auto-Tune or an auto corrector.

Keep in mind that shit is shit, and that you cannot polish a turd.

So in an effort to avoid falling into this category, you need to ask yourself the following three questions:

- Can you stay in key?
- Are you utilizing phrasing techniques in your singing?
- Are you breathing correctly and at the right times?

Developing perfect pitch hearing and practicing audiation are two very powerful tools that will enable you to do this and help you grow as a singer.

SINGING IN KEY

If you listen to any choral passage, you can hear the different inflections in the singers each time the key is changed. Being able to identify and anticipate these notes is critical to your singing ability, and is known as audiation.

Audiation is a word that is used to describe the auditory equivalent of imagination. Since imagination itself is visual, the term audiation was coined to describe how the brain interprets music that's not there. Utilizing audiation will help you integrate your singing into a progression that you have just heard or what you are anticipating to hear.

An example of how audiation is used when anticipating key changes in a song can be seen below in the notation for "Amazing Grace."

Notice how the lyrics of the song in the music staff coincide with the notes above them. By looking ahead of the word or syllable that you are singing, you can see the following note that you will sing next and anticipate if you will go up or down in pitch, as well as identify which key you will be singing in next.

The previous figure is the way that every song in every church hymnal is laid out. It's no surprise that gospel and R&B singers with a church choir background that involved the *sight reading* of music notation have superior singing abilities when compared to artists that don't.

Many singers who have this background have been singing since they were children. This is important to mention, because talent and skill come with constant practice and dedication. No one is an overnight success (not unless they were a lifetime in the making first).

Another acquired skill is called perfect pitch. Perfect pitch teaches you how to identify a note by hearing it, and several relatively inexpensive training courses are available online that will help you develop this skill.

SOLFEGE

Teaching one how to sing in key and how to sight read music is known as solfège (or "solfeggio" in Italian). This method is based on the sol-fa method, which utilizes a seven-tone major scale represented by the syllables *do, re, mi, fa, sol, la, ti* that all of you should be familiar with from the 1965 classic movie "The Sound of Music" with Julie Andrews.

The sol-fa method is taught the world over to create vocal pitch fluency and intervals and is the fastest way for you to learn how to sing a major scale.

The first system in solfège is called the *Fixed Do*, which named for the first interval in the scale; which is subsequently always the equivalent of the key of C (or *Do*). So once again, we will revert to the C Major scale as mentioned earlier in this chapter to show you how the syllables in the sol-fa method are assigned to the different scale intervals. They are:

Do = **C**, *Re* = **D**, *Mi* = **E**, *Fa* = **F**, *Sol* = **G**, *La* = **A**, *Ti* = **B**

There are two other systems in solfège: *Moveable Do* and *Numbers.* Feel free to research these others on your own, keeping in mind that this chapter is just a crash course of the basics and that this condensed material is not only here to teach you, but to also help you determine what kind of actual foundation you have in your craft as well as where your shortcomings are so you can develop them.

Once you develop the ability to sing in key, if you aren't doing so already, please keep in mind that you also need to develop your phrasing techniques. By adding accents to your vocals such as sustain or vibrato you will make a huge and immediately noticeable positive impact on your singing.

RAP AND POETRY

If you're a rap artist, are you familiar with the building blocks of your craft? Have you heard of Prosody? Prosodic units and their phonetic cues? Do you know the difference between qualitative and quantitative meter? Do you understand iambic pentameter or other meters? Are you familiar with the rhythms used in poetry such as Trochee, Spondee, Anapest, Dactyl, or

Pyrrhic stress patterns? Are you incorporating rhythm, form, metaphor, and other poetic techniques into your songwriting to enhance your work? Do you start a verse with your poetic feet in the right place but fall out of syncopation near the end of the passage?

The analysis of how rhythm, stress, and pitch are used in speech is referred to as prosody; it's defined by the number of lines in a verse, the number of syllables in each line, and the arrangement of those syllables as long or short, accented or unaccented.

Prosodic units are marked by phonetic cues. Phonetic cues can include aspects of prosody such as pitch, pauses, and accents, all of which are cues that must be analyzed in context, or in comparison to other aspects of a sentence.

Pitch, for example, can change over the course of a sentence. In English, falling intonation indicates a declarative statement while rising intonation indicates an interrogative statement.

Pauses are important prosodic units because they can often indicate breaks in a thought and can also sometimes indicate the intended grouping of nouns in a list. Breathing, both inhalation and exhalation, seems to occur only at these pauses where the prosody resets.

Prosodic units, along with function words and punctuation, help to mark clause boundaries in speech.

Accents, meanwhile, help to distinguish certain aspects of a sentence that may require more attention. English often utilizes a pitch accent, or an emphasis on the final word of a sentence. Focus accents serve to emphasize a word in a sentence that requires more attention, such as if that word specifically is intended to be a response to a question.

Prosody may reflect various features of the speaker or the utterance; the emotional state of the speaker; the form of the utterance (statement, question, or command); the presence of irony or sarcasm; emphasis, contrast, and focus; or other elements of language that may not be encoded by grammar or choice of vocabulary.

Prosodic phenomena are considered the suprasegmental features of intonation, stress, rhythm, and speech rate, and can be classified in two separate groups: linguistic and phonetic.

An excellent example of where you can pretty much hear every single one of these prosodic features being implemented is in the song "*What's Your Fantasy*" by Ludacris featuring Shawnna (*Def Jam South. December 31, 2000*).

Qualitative and Quantitative meter

More basic to poetry than rhyme is rhythm. In poetry, rhythm is based on syllables, and it is called *meter* (from the Greek word to measure). In English, meter is based on stress, and the types of meter are arrangements of stressed and unstressed syllables into patterns. This is qualitative meter. Quantitative meter is something you'll rarely encounter in English. It is based on the length, not the stress, of a syllable and is the basis for meter in the Greek and Latin traditions. In languages like Japanese, simply counting syllables may provide the rhythm.

The basic unit of meter is the *foot*.

These are the standard feet:

- *Iamb.* An iamb is an unstressed syllable followed by a stressed syllable. Words like *become* are iambic. This is the normal foot for most English poetry.

- *Trochee.* A trochee is the opposite of an iamb: it is a stressed syllable followed by an unstressed syllable. The word *poet* (and the word *trochee* itself) is trochaic.

- *Anapest.* An anapest is two unstressed syllables follow by a stressed syllable ("in a word" is an anapest). It tends to be used in comic verse, such as limericks

- *Dactyl.* This is the opposite of an anapest. It is a stressed syllable followed by two unstressed syllables (Benjamin, for instance). The Greek word *dactyl* means *finger*, and if you look at your finger it has one long joint followed by two short ones (Greek meter was based on long and short syllables, not stressed and unstressed syllables).

- *Spondee.* This is two stressed syllables side by side. Very rarely is a whole line spondaic; this foot is used for contrast—it slows a line down and provides emphasis.

In describing poetry, one gives the standard type of foot and then counts how many feet are in the line. Thus iambic pentameter means the standard 10-syllable line is constructed out of five iambs (this is the standard English form); trochaic hexameter is a 12-syllable basic line made up of six trochees; and anapestic tetrameter is another 12-syllable line but constructed out of four anapests (for those who can't count in Greek, you get monometer, dimeter, trimeter, tetrameter, pentameter, hexameter, heptameter, octameter).

To determine the meter of your lyrical content, you'll need to scan it, which means marking where the stressed and unstressed syllables fall. Making an effort to analyze your writing like this will give you a concise view into where your rhythmic pattern is becoming compromised and where you may need to interject alternate monosyllabic or polysyllabic synonymous words into your writing to maintain your meter.

If you aren't able to maintain your timing and stay in meter during a *stanza,* your lyrical delivery will go from good to garbage.

Most rap artists I hear that can't keep their meter end up relying on adlibs such as "ugh's" and "ahh's" near the end of their stanza to make up for the fact that they have gotten lost rhythmically and they appear to be just grabbing onto anything to keep them afloat until the end of the passage.

I implore you to consider the information that I'm providing you here because I've heard a lot of what's currently out on the independent market and many of you would benefit greatly from taking a step back and developing more of a solid foundation by fully understanding the basics of your craft.

There's a methodology for each instrument and each vocalist in each specific genre of music that can be studied in great detail. If you have

the desire to truly excel in your field, you'll seek out and research this information and learn as much of it as you are willing to study and able to comprehend.

I've provided you with this information to shed some light on the basic principles that you should be studying that will allow you to enhance your ability to deliver what's even more important:

The content, or the message of your song. Does your songwriting or energy complement the mood set forth by the music? What is your lyrical content about? Is it thought-provoking? Does it tell a story? Can you connect with people through your own life experiences? What is your message?

SONGWRITING TECHNIQUES

It has been said that the best songs ever written are the ones that tell a story. Whether you agree with this or not is entirely up to you. However, if you can touch the actual soul of your listener through your songwriting then you've made a fan for life and have done what so many other songwriters fail to do.

Some of this is directly related to your choice of words and how you paint a picture with your lyrics. Do you own a thesaurus? If not, I recommend you buy one now. Having one will definitely enhance your songwriting ability.

A thesaurus will not only help you find more colorful and descriptive synonyms for the words you're trying to use, but will also give you options that may vary in syllabic structure, allowing you the ability to get your message across as you originally intended without wavering from the rhythmic pattern or *feet* that you established in the beginning of your stanza, which makes this a must-have if you're a rap artist since your craft is dictated in such a large part by meter and time.

Combining the use of several of the following *poetic devices and techniques* will also enhance your lyrical landscape along with giving it added variety.

- Alliteration - Alliteration is the repetition of consonant sounds at the start of a word and the occurrence of the same letter or sound at the beginning of adjacent or closely connected words. An example of alliteration that every reader should know is embodied in the phrase "Peter Piper picked a peck of pickled peppers."

  This poetic technique is not only the simplest to learn, it's also an effective way to train your ear to pay closer attention to the way a poem sounds. Like a good musician must take care to notice when a song is out of key, so must a poet learn to listen for words that create discord, or phrases that don't produce the musical quality poets often look for in their work.

  Alliteration can be a simple and effective tool for new poets to employ in their writing, giving them the freedom to express the music they hear in their head when composing. Try reading a poem out loud and really listen to the words. Don't concentrate on anything but the way the poem sounds. How does it create a mood, or provide tension and release in the poem? Read your own poems aloud, and you'll notice when the poem sounds as though it's losing its fluidity or its internal rhythm. Developing an ear for poetry is largely instinctual, so trust your gut feeling when composing your poems.

- Assonance – Assonance is similar to alliteration but repeats vowel sounds instead of consonants. For example, "The man with the tan was the meanest in the land."

- Anaphora - The repetitive use of words or phrases at the beginning of a statement, paragraph, or verse. This technique emphasizes repetition to create a sense of vibrancy and vitality in the words being used. It's often used to create an emotional response in speeches and sermons, by utilizing a passionate delivery of your content your entire passage will be much more memorable to the listener. A good example of this technique was used in the 2008 presidential campaign for Barak Obama, where the words "Yes, we can," were used repetitively throughout his speeches.

- Cliché - A recognizable word, phrase, or a concept that has been so overused that it has lost its impact.

- Colloquialisms - Colloquial language is language that is informal. This can include words as well as phrases and can be used by writers when speaking through a character or person in their song such as when a question and answer dialog is presented.

- Consonance - The repetition of the same consonant two or more times in short succession.

- Diction - Every poem or song relies on the words it contains to convey meaning, emotion, and to shape the way it is read. Diction simply means the words you choose. So choose your words with care, using the best words for each poem, rap, or song, and you'll develop your style over time. Always employ these techniques to the best of your ability.

- Emotive language - Adjectives or adverbs that convey emotion.

- Hyperbole - the use of excessive exaggeration to highlight a point.

- Imagery - Writing without vivid images makes for easily forgettable content. By choosing the right words to create a colorful image in the listener's mind you'll be captivating his imagination and drawing him into your song, story, or poem until the end.

- Jargon - Particular words that are used and understood only by people who are experts or specifically involved in different groups or fields of expertise.

- Metaphor - These are similar to similes, but instead of comparing things, they go as far as to say the objects are the same. For example, "Life is a rollercoaster."

- Narrative – A verbal account of connected or sequential events.

- Onomatopoeia - A word that imitates or suggests the source of the sound that it describes. It is common with animal sounds but has expanded to include sounds made by other sources, such as "boom goes the dynamite."

- Personification - Giving human characteristics to something non-human, be it a living thing such as a plant or animal or an inanimate object.
- Rhetorical questions - Questions that do not require or expect an answer. They can be used to make the reader think about a point being made in the question.

- Simile - This descriptive writing technique compares one subject to a different subject even though they are not normally related. An example of a simile is, "Bobby smokes like a broken stove."

- Slang - Informal (or casual) words that are made up and used by different cultural groups from region to region.

Songwriting and poetry pull depth and value from the words that the writer chooses to paint his lyrical picture. Using poetic devices to allude to what your subject matter is can oftentimes be more powerful than if you describe things directly. Sometimes it's not the things that you say that make your song have an impact; sometimes it's what you aren't saying that conveys the most powerful imagery to the listener. It's ultimately your decision as a writer which of these techniques you choose to use or how and when you will choose to combine them.

"Proper words in proper places, makes the true definition of a style." - *Jonathan Swift*

I've included this information in an effort to bring the best out of any future songwriters that may be reading this book. Lack of imaginative songwriting unfortunately pervades the independent market and even part of the mainstream. Nothing is worse than a song that has a mind-numbing, monotonous, and repetitive chorus/hook where the same line is repeated over and over and over again.

Learn the concepts and follow the rules that have been laid out about songwriting in this chapter. If you want to have the ability to compete on a professional level, you'll need to bring with you a solid foundation and a wide arsenal of tools.

Make every effort possible to prepare yourself for success as a composer and as a songwriter, because no one else can do that for you, and once you've developed it on your own this is something that no one can ever take away from you.

Once you obtain this foundation and education, it will still take long hours of consistent rehearsal to make you truly proficient at what you're doing. Being a musician is really a lifetime practice, so the earlier you get started, the better.

However, it never is too late to start something new.

CHAPTER FOUR

THE LINEUP

WELCOME TO A FOUR-WAY MARRIAGE

So now we have a little background on what it takes to be a better performer, or at least you now have a few terms that you can research in an effort to become one.

Now let's delve a little deeper and see what it's going to take to get everyone to function together as a unit.

FORMING THE BAND

Putting together a lineup can prove to be somewhat of a daunting task, and is extremely frustrating for a musician who has made up his mind to strike out on his own and form a new band.

Starting out a search for the right band members can be as easy as talking to your classmates or as difficult as trolling Craigslist and other postings trying to find someone who not only plays your genre of music, but is also well-networked within that genre. Posting want ads in Guitar Center, Sam Ash, and other music stores along with posting classifieds in your city's music periodicals is a standard practice and waiting to hear a response from these ads is always met with anticipation and excitement. Quite often, it also results in an equal amount of disappointment.

If and when you do get a response, the person may not play your style or genre of music, his playing may not be advanced enough for your liking, or there's a possibility that he may actually be too advanced of a musician for your band.

Perhaps he doesn't have the right persona or image.

Maybe he isn't motivated enough, or on the flipside of that coin, maybe he's an accomplished musician and is looking for a band that can immediately start touring and your band is not yet at that point.

Any number of scenarios can come into play, and finding the right musician for your band is the equivalent of guessing which card in a magician's deck actually belongs to you.

Musicians have a certain read on each other when they play; as a guitar player it's very easy for me to see if I can work with a drummer or not. The ability to "gel" with the person who is auditioning is usually immediate, and if you can't lock in with each other after a few short takes, it really isn't worth pursuing.

Dealing with this, along with the excessive amount of cover band musicians out there, combined with the limited supply of qualified and available drummers in certain genres can drive you insane.

In some cases, you may have to make the best out of who's available to start moving forward in the pursuit of your vision.

What this all falls back to is how well-networked you are and how big your network is. If you're active on your music scene and attending a lot of concerts, whether it's touring national acts or local underground shows, you WILL run into other musicians.

You have to be involved, because you aren't going to successfully create a lineup from your sofa cushion.

Ideally, you'll want to get a group of guys that you're already friends with from your own music scene. This will add to the possibility that they'll have the same musical influences as you, and perhaps they may even be established within your genre's music scene from the prior bands that they were in.

This is important, because if you start off seeking musicians that are accomplished already and have a small following of friends and fans, that is great. People talk, and if they are saying good things about your shows and who your lineup consists of, then they will get more people to come see you. There's also a possibility that this potential band member may have a contact list that includes promoters, booking agents, or press contacts that can further the growth of the band.

Just because someone can play well, has a deep contact list, or is part of the in-crowd doesn't necessarily mean that he's great for the band.

Which brings us to our next topic;

RELIABILITY

Does this potential band member have gear and transportation? Can you get along with him? Has he ever scolded or criticized his prior band members in public or while on stage? Is he going to be proactive in the growth of the band? If you hand him a stack of flyers, will he get them out? If you see the same flyers you gave him six months ago sitting in the trunk of his car, then don't even bother giving him more. He doesn't get it, he doesn't see the big picture, and he most likely never will. Save your promotional material for the guys in the band that understand the importance of creating visibility and awareness.

If you hand a band member 30 tickets for your show, will he be able to sell them and return the money to you or the promoter without it accidentally turning into alcohol and narcotics first?

Having a drug addict band member can be a disaster waiting to happen. Does he have his own keys to your rehearsal studio? Did he start living in the rehearsal spot? Once heroin starts calling his name, so will the pawn shop. Think about this for a second when you leave him there for the night with your equipment, because a junkie knows no other loyalty but than to the needle and the spoon.

Who you decide to surround yourself with in life can measure the level of success that you can potentially achieve. More importantly, the people you hang around with are also an exact reflection of who you are as a person.

Are most your friends dropouts, convicts, drugs users, degenerate gamblers, or unemployed? Well then I'll be willing to bet my hard-earned money that you are too, my friend.

If your lineup is filled with chronic underachievers, then you won't need to do any additional reading to predict the obvious future of your group's lack of success.

In your quest to find reliable members for your group, reflect inwards as well. What can you improve on? Do you have a history of being dependable? Can you be trusted to deliver results when people are counting on you? Are you known for being on time when people are waiting for you? Do you even show up to your own court dates on time?

If you're at least 15 minutes late for everything that you do in life, you have a serious fucking problem and until you correct this your success is doomed and failure is inevitable.

This is a hyper-competitive field. High demands will be made of you and people will expect you to be all in. More often than not, if you fail to meet a deadline or make an appointment, the person who was depending on you in that matter will most likely not bother contacting you a second time.

You may want to align yourself with people who are not only successful in music, but are successful in other aspects of their life as well.

These people bring something more to the table than just talent. They have a tendency to be goal-oriented, they have their priorities in order, and more importantly, they most likely also have a job. These are the kind of people who can follow through on instructions. They're committed, they care, they work well with others, they can formulate a plan and stick to it, they meet their deadlines, and they consistently deliver results. These are the qualities for success, these are the qualities you should adopt in your personal life, and these are the people you should surround yourself with.

Guitar strings, drum heads, cymbals, cables, rent, studio time, and transportation all cost money. Set yourself up with a lineup that can afford the things that they need as individual musicians and you will have a band that is more prepared, which means more productivity, more songs, more gigs, and more success.

COMMUNICATION

The center of all interpersonal relationships is communication. Some people are just generally fucking lost in this category. Whether they are timid, introverted, apathetic, or just too fucking stupid to get their point across, it does not matter. When you are in a situation that involves multiple people who have their own lives outside of this project, the line of communication needs to remain open. If you have a member that doesn't have the common courtesy to notify you in advance if he is not coming to band practice or he has developments that will conflict with the band's scheduling, then this person is a fucking stroke and needs to get cut loose.

COMMITMENT

There will also come a time in a group's lifespan that you may have the big opportunity you have been waiting for. Whether it's your first opportunity to open up for a national touring act or the ability to go on a tour or even get offered a record contract, make sure you are 100 percent committed to this group and that you can actually move forward.

A group itself has multiple people who depend on each other as much as than they depend on their own family. Your family can provide you with food, clothing, and a roof over your head, but the people in your group depend upon you and upon each other for the facilitation of making their dreams come true. This isn't to be played with.

JUST GOING THROUGH THE MOTIONS

If you know deep down that you're not going to be there for the long haul, you owe it to yourself and the rest of your group to discuss this early on. It is better to be up front and honest so adjustments can be made in advance than to lead everyone on and pull the plug at the last minute. If you just quit abruptly at that critical moment, you will stir up long-term feelings of resentment between you and your group, and that just isn't fair to anybody.

If you are this guy, do everyone a favor and just get out of the way.

Sometimes doing the uncomfortable thing means doing the best thing.

If everyone is pouring their creativity and their hearts into this project and if you are just doing everything half-assed then you should seriously rethink your position in this band and perhaps tell them that you are leaving but will stick around until they find a replacement.

The group as a whole is only as strong as its weakest link. Just like in any company, people who don't perform should be and usually are terminated. Dead weight will keep your project from taking off.

RELATIONSHIPS

Since this entire industry—and basically most of life itself—is based on relationships, let's focus on the one that hits closest to home: the relationship with a girlfriend, wife, or significant other and how it fits into the scenario of your band.

Ladies, feel free to swap out the female references for their male counterparts as you read this section.

As you read this book, you will come to understand that all people have a distinct psychological profile that explains their behavior. This can be a good thing at times, or it can be bad and horribly fucked up as well. What's important is that you learn to understand the idiosyncrasies of the characters around you so you are better equipped to handle any situations that may arise.

So let's start with the good.

THE PARTNER IN CRIME

If you or any of your band members are lucky enough to have a supportive girlfriend who believes in your band, you basically have a partner in crime. She's into you and into what you are doing and you click on several levels. She's the first person to volunteer to fill in as your merch girl, and she may act as your booking agent or maybe even your tour manager. She's awesome, and she's basically a part of the band, so don't fuck it up.

In the middle of this is the complacent or indifferent girl who doesn't share your passion for music. You get no emotional support or encouragement from her, and she doesn't push you forward. If this explains your relationship, you may want to consider being single because she's not helping your spirit fly.

Now, let's look at the bad side of musicians' romantic relationships and how they can derail everything that you are trying to build up and get accomplished.

THE PRISON WARDEN

Whatever it is, the answer is no, it's not happening. This person will go through great lengths to interfere with your plans. If the guys call, you won't get the message. If they stop by, she is going to make a scene and prevent you from going out, even if you have a show booked that night.

Thinking about going on tour? Fuck no, that's not going to happen, not over her dead body; and if you think you are leaving she will burn your fucking clothes, let your cat or dog go free, and change the locks on you.

You will never reach your full potential and never be happy if you are dating a prison warden.

THE ARCH-NEMESIS

Even worse than the Prison Warden is The Arch-Nemesis. This is the one person in the universe that you should not have gotten involved with, yet by some sick and horrible twist of fate, here the two of you are in a relationship.

This is the person who instinctively and psychopathically sets out to create misery for you and seems to thrive on it. Every word out of your mouth becomes twisted into something other than what it was intended to mean, and no matter what kind of rational explanation you give for any of your actions you will not win a dispute or an argument.

Why is this?

Because she is Thundercunt and arguing is the only form of communication that she can engage in.

The stress levels created by this type of relationship are the grounds for prescribed psychotropic medication and domestic violence and are just bad news all the way around.

Why would anyone stay with a person that exudes this kind of behavior?

I don't fucking know, but it is a somewhat generally accepted opinion that people who are mentally unstable are better in the bedroom, so if I had to guess, I'd put my money on that.

If anyone in your band is dating someone like The Prison Warden or The Arch-Nemesis, you may need to make an executive decision and consider getting rid of this member so he can enjoy his own custom-made spiritually draining corner of hell on his own, and not drag you and the band down into it with him and Satan's little princess.

Don't waste any time; just go ahead and do it before the inevitable happens.

YOUR LIFE IN THE PUBLIC EYE

Any publicity you get, any shows you perform, and your daily life in general may become documented and even under the microscope. This is your public image. To keep this up you need to have all of your individual band members functioning as a whole at all times. Personal distractions hinder forward movement. Keep in mind that you are a representative of your group; you should put the best interests of that group ahead of your own personal agenda. You are now a part of something greater than yourself; embrace that.

As Aristotle said, "*the whole is greater than the sum of all its parts.*"

As a band, you will spend a lot of time together. You will come to know each other's most intimate and darkest secrets. Keep this information amongst the band members. There will be times when one of you gets completely shit-faced and does something completely off the wall. These incidents are not meant for social media. I once saw a guy start his own naked mosh pit in the parking lot of a venue, and believe me this does not qualify as an Instagram or YouTube moment.

Only use social media to shed a positive light on yourselves.

Also, be sure to avoid letting the general public know your inner conflicts. Don't put your dirty laundry on social media; that's just an all-around bad move. God forbid someone important is doing research on you and finds some self-incriminating rants about your act. Nobody wants to get involved with your controversy. Record labels, sponsors, and investors will not want to endorse a group that shows signs of instability. If a band's inner problems don't subside, then it may be time to replace someone. Negative energy will hinder growth and the overall health of the group. Just as any botanist will tell you, sometimes you will need to cut off a stem to save the plant.

ZERO TOLERANCE FOR BULLSHIT

To many of you reading this chapter, it may seem like I am overbearing and that my only solution is to fire everybody. This is because it's been my life experience that everyone is programmed differently and that their overall behavior is redundant and predictable.

My point is that no matter what kind of stern talking to you are going to give someone during a band meeting, it doesn't matter and wont resolve shit. Why? Because you can't fix someone with a conversation; it just doesn't happen.

Although compromises do need to be made in life, try to surround yourself with positive people you can work with. You stand a much better chance of growth and sustainability if you distance yourself from any scenario that creates negative energy.

However, you also need to keep in mind that this is a two-way street and at times—or all of the time—it may actually be *you* who is the source of the bullshit.

YOUR BAND AS A BUSINESS

This brings us to the subject of how your band is actually managed internally. You should have some type of agreement in place that outlines everyone's job in the band, such as who handles public relations and who the band leader or manager is. This should also cover such important topics as how earnings are dispersed and at what percentage, who the name of the band will belong to if the band breaks up, and songwriting and copyright provisions should one band member leave or get fired. You can have an operating agreement drafted by a lawyer and file your band as a business such as a limited liability corporation. This makes sense if your band is creating enough revenue to cover the initial filing fee (about $500) and the annual renewal fee (about $250) associated with this business classification. Should your band ever evolve into a corporation, this status will also give you an opportunity to offset your taxable revenue by allowing you to place up to 20 percent of your income in a pension account.

Financial planning is something that you need to take into consideration, because if you do actually make it, there is no way to determine how long that success will last, and if you don't manage your money correctly you may one day become a person with champagne and caviar tastes who's living on a Miller High Life and beef jerky budget.

The overall economic thinking of someone in their 20s varies greatly from someone in their 30s or 40s, and should you obtain vast amounts of wealth at a young age there's a strong likelihood that you'll squander it all on materialistic things while indulging in alcohol, narcotics, gambling, and strippers without ever planning for your future or your old age.

Give this some serious thought; or you just may end up going from living on a tour bus to living on a bus bench one day.

If you aren't yet at the point where you can financially justify operating an LLC, you still have an additional option if you want to organize and run your band like a business, and this is to have a sole proprietorship or DBA (Doing Business As.)

A DBA can have several owners on file and can be amended each time a member joins, quits, or is fired.

Your internal agreement or operating agreement should be negotiated in the very beginning and each time a new band member joins the group while people are on friendly terms and can discuss this without being emotionally involved. Cutting up the pie during a nasty divorce is not an advisable course of action.

IS YOUR MUSIC BUSINESS REALLY ONLY A HOBBY?

If you are planning on designating your band, record label, management, or promotion company as a business entity (DBA, LLC, S Corp, C Corp, etc.) you will be filing tax returns every year.

Be advised that you cannot operate a business for several years running without turning a profit. The Internal Revenue Service will not allow you to continue to write off expenses.

Should your business remain in the red several consecutive years running, your accountant will furnish you with a warning letter and will refuse to continue to file losses on your behalf for the entity in question.

Below is information cited directly from the IRS that contains a section of eight primary questions that will help you determine if you are ready to turn your endeavor into a business or not:

The Internal Revenue Service reminds taxpayers to follow appropriate guidelines when determining whether an activity is engaged in for profit, such as a business or investment activity, or is engaged in as a hobby.

Internal Revenue Code Section 183 (Activities Not Engaged in for Profit) limits deductions that can be claimed when an activity is not engaged in for profit. IRC 183 is sometimes referred to as the "hobby loss rule."

Taxpayers may need a clearer understanding of what constitutes an activity engaged in for profit and the tax implications of incorrectly treating hobby activities as activities engaged in for profit. This educational fact sheet provides information for determining if an activity qualifies as an activity engaged in for profit and what limitations apply if the activity was not engaged in for profit.

Is your hobby really an activity engaged in for profit?

In general, taxpayers may deduct ordinary and necessary expenses for conducting a trade or business or for the production of income. Trade or business activities and activities engaged in for the production of income are activities engaged in for profit.

The following factors, although not all inclusive, may help you to determine whether your activity is an activity engaged in for profit or a hobby:

- *Does the time and effort put into the activity indicate an intention to make a profit?*
- *Do you depend on income from the activity?*

- *If there are losses, are they due to circumstances beyond your control or did they occur in the start-up phase of the business?*
- *Have you changed methods of operation to improve profitability?*
- *Do you have the knowledge needed to carry on the activity as a successful business?*
- *Have you made a profit in similar activities in the past?*
- *Does the activity make a profit in some years?*
- *Do you expect to make a profit in the future from the appreciation of assets used in the activity?*

An activity is presumed for profit if it makes a profit in at least three of the last five tax years, including the current year (or at least two of the last seven years for activities that consist primarily of breeding, showing, training or racing horses).

If an activity is not for profit, losses from that activity may not be used to offset other income. An activity produces a loss when related expenses exceed income. The limit on not-for-profit losses applies to individuals, partnerships, estates, trusts, and S corporations. It does not apply to corporations other than S corporations.

What are allowable hobby deductions under IRC 183?

If your activity is not carried on for profit, allowable deductions cannot exceed the gross receipts for the activity.

Deductions for hobby activities are claimed as itemized deductions on Schedule A, Form 1040. These deductions must be taken in the following order and only to the extent stated in each of three categories:

Deductions that a taxpayer may claim for certain personal expenses, such as home mortgage interest and taxes, may be taken in full.

Deductions that don't result in an adjustment to the basis of property, such as advertising, insurance premiums and wages, may be taken next, to the extent gross income for the activity is more than the deductions from the first category.

Deductions that reduce the basis of property, such as depreciation and amortization, are taken last, but only to the extent gross income for the activity is more than the deductions taken in the first two categories.

The music industry is far from a perfect place, but if you raise the bar for yourself and instill a sense of pride and a mantra of hard work and dedication you will move forward and climb higher at a much faster pace than those around you.

I am fully aware that what I am telling you contradicts the shenanigans that you see famous people do on a daily basis that gets them in entertainment news, but keep this in mind: while the media focuses on the negative things people do, not all of those people were originally like that in the first place anyway; they became like that.

Whether you obtain the gift of fame and fortune will depend on a number of things, but whether or not you become a fucking douchebag once you obtain fame and fortune will be entirely up to you.

CHAPTER FIVE

STAGE PRESENCE

There are many things that artists and musicians should take into consideration while performing live, because how your live show resonates with your audience can really make or break your career.

Many popular groups and artists have mastered the use of the stage as a branding platform for their individuality. Some of the bands that come to mind are Iron Maiden, GWAR, and unfortunately even the disgusting and repulsive live stage antics of the late G.G. Allin.

Whether or not I name a major pop act such as Lady Gaga, a highly visual alternative rock act such as Marilyn Manson, or even a more obscure band with an energetic stage show is irrelevant; what's important here is that you do something to make your live performance memorable.

Bruce Dickinson of Iron Maiden for example, is well known for his on-stage entanglements with "Eddie," the band's mascot, but what is more important is his understanding of crowd engagement.

It has been said that Dickinson performs for the person in the back of the crowd as much as he performs for the person in the front, and this is exemplified and expressed through his larger-than-life body gestures and his tendency to climb all over the stage furniture, props, and floor monitors.

It takes a certain amount of athleticism to keep up a high-energy live performance such as what I have just mentioned, and this is something that you need to develop and execute if you aren't doing it already. This is solely in your control. It doesn't take a budget to do this either; all it takes is passion. Well, passion and maybe a wireless system.

Before you take into consideration that some of these well-known artists have multi-million dollar stage sets constructed around their performance, you need to understand that it began with them exuding their personal energy under much more modest surroundings, where at one point in time the stage may have only been 6 inches higher than the floor.

It's what you are doing in these smaller clubs that will determine how big of a stage you will end up on later in your career.

Your time and tenure playing smaller venues will provide you with something that you and your audience will share that can't be replicated when you are on a massive stage that has barricades in front of it.

And that thing is intimacy.

Crowd going apeshit during a song chorus. Blood In Blood Out opening for Terror at Westport Community Center in Burns Harbor, Indiana 2007. Photo credit: Monica Zibutis

This intimacy and personal connection with your audience is what gets people talking about you and builds your draw.

When you play live, there is a certain energy that transmits back and forth in the room between the audience and the act. When the band plays hard, the audience is more engaged, responds louder, and gets more physical. The band digests this energy, gets more psyched, and then plays harder, which makes the audience get even wilder. This goes back and forth throughout the evening until a high point or climax is reached and then things level off or taper down from there.

These energy levels can become harder to maintain as you get older in life, however. I recently saw Ringworm, who was on tour in 2013 performing their entire *Birth Is Pain* (Victory 2001) album from front to back. After the show, I spoke to the band's frontman, *Human Furnace,* about the show and he told me that it gets tough to maintain the same kind of energy that he laid out on a CD that was released when he was 12 years younger, yet he manages to pull it off feverishly.

SIGNAGE

Most printing companies that make vinyl banners can make you a nice high resolution stage backdrop of your band logo that you can hang behind the drum riser.

Wretched performing at Mayhem Fest 2014. Photo credit: Eric Munnings (Victory Records)

Customizing your drummer's kick drum covers—and even the grill cloth on your amps—can help complete this diorama, or in the case of any rap artists that may be reading this, you also have the option of making a customized table cover made with your logo to throw over your DJ's table.

To add depth and dimension, you can also add a retractable banner on each side of the stage, or as in the previous photo, you can dress the whole stage as Victory Records did at Mayhem Fest.

If your signage is color-coordinated and artistically consistent, this can create quite an impressionable image—and possibly make you upstage the headlining act.

Emmure performing live. Photo credit: Eric Munnings (Victory Records)

As your act grows and you play on larger stages and arenas, the concept is the same, but the size and application of your signage can grow into whatever your imagination can conceive.

Iron Maiden's unforgettable stage show has developed over their entire career and includes stage props that represent every one of their albums.

FOG AND LIGHTING

Travesty of the band IDSFA. Photo Credit: Justin Koteff - Red Flame Photography

Fog and lighting, when combined, can create another dimension of atmosphere in your show that can bring it over the top.

I once saw the band *Integrity* at a Knights of Columbus Hall in Arlington Heights, IL and they actually had strobe lights behind the band and used heavy fog. During the performance, all you saw were the silhouettes of the band members playing. It was a very cool looking effect.

IT'S YOUR SHOW

As a live act, you have full control over the concert production during your time slot. Touring bands performing in large arenas have clauses in their performance agreements that clearly state this in detail and it may range from stage production, to sound, lighting, and more.

For emerging bands, most small clubs will let you do whatever you ask for within reason.

Keep this in mind if you ever get booked on a huge show. Don't be the band that says "Oh, we didn't know we could do that."

This is covered in the chapter on Performance Riders and Guarantees.

TECHNICAL DIFFICULTIES

There is a term called Murphy's Law, which states that anything bad that *can* happen, *will* happen.

There is no time or place that holds truer for this than when your act is on stage. Any number of things can happen here ranging from band members losing their place in the song or breaking a string to the problems listed in the chapter on Problems with Live Sound.

The important thing is that you recover from this as soon as possible.

I once played a show with a band whose bass player broke his E-string midway through the performance. Without missing a beat, he pulled the string off of the saddle and harmonized his bassline on another string for the rest of the set. This type of grace under pressure is what keeps a band from having a complete train-wreck on stage.

If this should happen, it is imperative that you come out of this in a professional manner. Getting combative with your bandmates while on stage is not a good idea.

If you are unable to get back on track within a few measures, then scrap the song and move on to the next one.

One thing that you should never do is repeat the phrase "we are having technical difficulties" to the audience. Hearing a band re-state the obvious several times in a row makes me cringe.

PERFORMING WHILE INTOXICATED

This is an all-around No-No and should be avoided at all costs. Now, I fully realize that many of you like to party, and that's understandable. But what I am talking about here is getting out and out wasted before your show.

I have seen rap artists who have gone on stage so intoxicated that they have forgotten their own lyrics and musicians that have forgotten to turn on the volume knob on their guitars, or even plug them in, for that matter.

These are all epic failures by any standards. So you should limit your pre-performance consumption of your preferred medication until after show time, because when you fuck up in public, you do it in front of a room full of people and in front of multiple video cameras and mobile devices that will be uploading everything onto the Internet anyway, including your most humiliating moments.

Exercise some preventative maintenance before your performances and you will be far less likely to need to implement damage control after them.

Some of you will wake up from a hangover one day and get an earful about how bad you fucked up the night before; this will be about the same time you remember this excerpt from this book.

But remember:

I told you so.

CHAPTER SIX

DEVELOPING YOUR BRAND

Las Vegas shock rock band I.D.S.F.A. fully recognizes the importance of individuality. Photo credit: Piero Giunti

Who are you? What defines you? What makes you stick out of a crowd? How can you be clearly identified amongst all the other artists in this industry?

Take a moment to think about this. You'll come to realize how important this is and how it will tie into both your marketing and advertising.

Brand development entails several things in this industry. If you're a solo artist, it can be as simple as your full name. Whether you're a solo artist, band, group, rap act, or solo rap artist, there are several things you'll need to do:

CHOOSE AN ORIGINAL NAME

Coming up with a cool name that fits your act is sometimes very simple or it can be very tough. I recommend that once you chose your name or an acronym for your name that you do a Google search, ReverbNation search, and even a MySpace search to see if this name is taken. Most bands I know do this. I have, however, noticed that some artists don't take the time to research this in advance and it can cause some very serious problems down the line. Identical names or different punctuations for the same word used as a name or different slang spinoffs of that word can confuse your fan base and even drive them to purchase music that isn't yours.

If your name is an acronym then make sure you do a Google search before you adopt this as your name. Whether you become known by a two-, three-, or four-letter acronym, you should know that a very distinct possibility exists that a company or corporation may already be using this as their name. This will also cause problems with your *ranking and indexing.* If somebody looks you up on a search engine and your name doesn't show up on the first page because it's buried under several pages of an established company's listings with the same name, you're screwed and people will give up before they find you.

MAKE SURE YOU DO A TRADEMARK SEARCH OF YOUR NAME

If a name is already trademarked, the owner has the exclusive rights to use it. You can create a lot of unnecessary grief for yourself if you don't look into this. I know a distributor who was aggregating music for a band when another band with the same name in a different country filed a trademark infringement complaint stating that the group using their name was interfering with their ability to sell their music in the volume they projected. This was a huge problem because both of those bands had their music on multiple retail sites such as iTunes, Amazon MP3, Deezer, Rhapsody, Big Pond, and several more including their licensees and subsidiary sites in other countries. Resolving this issue along with issuing a takedown order which can take up to 60 days was a headache that nobody wanted to deal with, yet could have had been easily avoided through due diligence and research.

Although this was inconvenient for the rightful owner of the trademark, imagine being the band that had to have its catalog removed from every online store across the globe. That pain runs deep, especially if you've developed a fan base and then find out that you don't even have the right to perform under that name.

If you find that the name you wanted is taken, don't get discouraged. You can still make good with your secondary choice. There is a story of a guitar player who once contacted a talent buyer and booked his newly formed band named Eric and the Dynamos at a concert hall. Upon arrival at the venue the night of their first show, the sign outside incorrectly read "Derek and the Dominos" and a young Eric Clapton was quoted as saying, "Well it's just as good a name as any." Needless to say, the name stuck.

Whatever name you eventually decide on, keep it and don't change it. Music recordings have a tendency to grow legs and walk around at different paces. Someone may find your album one day and become a fan but will not make the connection between your old name and your new name. That is a perfect example of how bands can undermine their own branding and the size of their fan base.

All the time you spend telling people about your group and promoting yourself online along with all the band profiles that you create will all be for nothing if you end up changing your name.

Doing this is branding and marketing suicide.

CHOOSE A LOGO AND STICK WITH IT

Some of the most famous bands out there have the most memorable logos. The Rolling Stones, Led Zeppelin, AC/DC, Van Halen, Iron Maiden, the Dead Kennedys, Black Flag, DRI, the Misfits, Blood For Blood, the Wu-Tang Clan, and several others have all taken the lettering of their name, artwork, and symbols—or a combination of all of these—and created a cult following behind them.

So why were these bands successful to the point that people are tattooing their logos into their skin?

Well, besides their musical capability, they created a logo that had the ability to catch people's attention. The one thing that every logo I mentioned above has in common is that you can recognize it from a distance and know exactly what it is if you are familiar with it. If you aren't familiar with it, you're at least intrigued by it and it's memorable enough for you to remember it when you see it again.

Keep this in mind when developing a logo and make it stand out. It doesn't need to be overly complex and it should be legible. To make it in a commercial market, people should be able to read your band name the first time they see it.

If you're in a metal band, your logo doesn't need to look like a flaming pile of deer antlers to be cool; nobody can read that shit anyway. Whether the design is complex or simplistic in nature, it needs to pop out at you.

BRAND CONSISTENCY AND CONTINUITY

The bands I mentioned above all consistently used the same respective logo over the course of several decades on all their albums, T-shirts, concert posters, and merchandise. This is their brand. It's no different than how any corporation advertises its product.

Having this consistency across all your marketing and advertising materials is what makes people know your unique brand. It is what sets you aside from everyone else. You should have great pride in it. It represents everything that you put into your writing and your recordings. It is the core part of your identity as a group.

It is imperative that you take heed to the information provided to you in this chapter. According to Jay Conrad Levinson in his book, *Guerrilla Marketing: Easy and Inexpensive Strategies for Making Big Profits from Your Small Business*, studies have shown that a person must view an image, brand name, or logo over 10 times before paying any attention to it.

Remember that consistency and repetition breed familiarity—which in turn breeds likeability—and likeability breeds fans and drives sales.

Once you do decide you have the name and the logo that you want to stick with, make sure you get a trademark if you plan on doing this professionally. This will not only protect you as an artist or band, but it will help protect you from anyone bootlegging your merchandise or products.

You can find all the information necessary on trademark information at the United States Patent and Trademark Office's website (http://www.uspto.gov/trademarks/index.jsp).

EXERCISE SOME INDIVIDUALITY

In the beginning of this chapter I asked you four very personal and distinct questions.

Who are you? What defines you? What makes you stick out of a crowd? How can you be clearly identified amongst all the other artists in this industry?

If you were not able to answer these questions the first or the second time around then you have a problem that many bands, artists, and even normal people are faced with—you have no identity.

One of the biggest pitfalls that musicians encounter is that they allow themselves to be influenced by trends. Being a part of what's happening now is not how you become iconic or timeless. Being a part of what's happening now means that you are a fucking sheep and that you ride people's coattails.

The fact of the matter is that nobody skyrockets to success by trying to be like someone else. This cookie-cutter-copycat-bullshit mentality will result in people starting a conversation about you with the phrase, "Well, he sounds like…" or "They sound like…" or "He's another _place artist name here_".

This is not good at all, and having this stigma shows lack of both individuality and creative artistry, as well as the fact that you are creatively driven by what's *around* you and not what's *inside* of you.

Frankly, if you are going to be that influenced by others then perhaps you should just be in a cover band.

The content of this particular chapter is very important, because you will start out on this path as a nobody from nowhere whose visibility is starting from absolutely nothing.

So before you concern yourself with widespread fame, understand that you need to first start figuring out how to create enough brand awareness just to get a few people to start talking about you, much less a few dozen.

I fully understand your need to make a name for yourself; trust me, I do.

But you need to fully understand that everything in life has a developmental phase. All things must grow from a stage of conception to infancy to adolescence and then eventually to full maturity. This universal law also applies to the visibility of your brand. This is something that's unavoidable, but by taking the information in this book and putting it to use, you'll speed up this whole process.

CHAPTER SEVEN

YOUR SUPPORT STRUCTURE

Do you know what the definition of a fan is?
Fan is short for "fanatic."
Merriam-Webster defines a fanatic as
"marked by excessive enthusiasm and often intense uncritical devotion."
In this case, that devotion is to a group (or artist) and its music.

The point I am going to make in this chapter is just as important as when I asked you what your personal work ethic was.

Let's get something perfectly clear—this is a fan-driven business. If you don't have fans and followers, you will not make it. There are no exceptions to this rule. Nobody cares how great you think your music is; if the people don't like it, they aren't going to buy it, they aren't going to see you perform live, and they aren't going to support you.

Fans are the one integral part of your career that will determine if you become successful or not.

It's often said that an act is only is a big as its network. This network usually starts with family and friends and spreads outwards from there.

Who is in your network? How big is your dedicated fan base? How do you communicate with them? How do you get the word to them about your performance dates and your music releases? Do they respond? What actions are you taking to grow your fan base? Is it comprised mostly of people you know? Or are you counting the random people that you never met who are following you on Twitter and Facebook?

How many people come and see you perform on a consistent basis? Are they spreading the word about you and bringing new people with them? Are there any people that volunteer to pass out your flyers and promote you online? If so, these are the people you need to get involved in your street team.

YOUR STREET TEAM

It's a good idea for you to know the people you choose for your team because they care about your success and you can depend on them.

If you're picking new people who want to get involved in your movement, I've learned that you get much better results with an open line of communication and with a team that understands that they're part of something much larger than simply handing out flyers for you. Giving these team members a glimpse of the big picture and an explanation of their role as part of a regional or national movement can be a huge motivational factor for them and may enhance their dedication to your cause. It will also help them understand the significance of meeting deadlines if they realize that there's a coordinated effort on many levels with multiple people in several locations.

Another thing that should be mentioned here is that many bands belong to *crews*. Crews are a little more involved than street teams. They are primarily a clique or fraternity of people involved in a genre of music that also help facilitate growth of the bands that belong to their group. Many of these crews make up a vast global network of support from city to city and country to country.

The hardcore music genre has many of these, and several bands belong to them. Crew members are essentially the bands' entourage from city to city and at times execute much of the promotional duties that a street team would provide.

Why is this worth mentioning? Because as I have stated before, if you make your street team feel that they are a part of something larger than just a promotional team comprised of fans, you will garnish the single most important thing that every emerging band needs for sustainability, which is loyalty.

Having this network within a network can keep the news of what you're up to flowing a lot better. Even though we live in a time where everyone seems to be connected via social media, creating a street team early on will help your buzz. Having people who are visibly taking the initiative to promote you makes a profound impact on people. They see that something is happening and they want to be a part of it.

TEAM VISIBILITY

One of the ways to maintain visibility and use it to your advantage is to get your team dressed up in your gear and work the crowd at one of your live events in an effort to get everyone's contact information. With a few pens and clipboards, you can have your team approach the audience and have them write down their email address in exchange for a free download, a sticker, or some other kind of incentive.

If you've already created a form on your website enabling people to submit their information online to join your mailing list, then you can have your team work the crowd with a tablet as well. This looks a little more modern and organized, but some venues have so much wi-fi interference due to the construction materials in the structure that this may not always work indoors. Whether or not your team is packing tablets or clipboards, keep in mind that it's always good to have a backup plan. I recommend that you take both.

Contacting your fan base through their email addresses is a little more personal than putting out a general post on Facebook or Twitter and is known as *direct marketing.* This is the best way to market yourself because it utilizes pre-existing contacts who want to receive your mail, and the best part of it is that it costs absolutely nothing.

Creating a street-level and online movement helps you gain access to potential fans that you yourself may not have had the chance to meet yourself if you are attending to the other things you will need to do, many of which are outlined in this book.

Once you have access to any number of fans, large or small, how do you intend to *engage* them? How will you keep them interested in you? What are you doing to keep people talking about you? Are you consistently doing something? Such as performing? Are you sending out updates of important developments in your career? *Do you even have any developments in your career?*

If you don't keep your *momentum,* you risk the possibility of losing part of your fan base. Remember Sir Isaac Newton's *First Law of Motion*; an object in motion has a tendency to stay in motion, and an object at rest has a tendency to stay at rest. You're either doing everything for your career or nothing for your career. What part of this statement defines you? Keep in mind that if your live show dates were booked by other groups and they asked you to get on the bill, you're relying on others and still doing nothing.

It's important not to look at a recent accomplishment or a recent string of accomplishments as something that you can rest your hat on. Keep moving, keep grinding, and chalk up one success after another, whether it's large or small. After all, your goal is not to just have the same people talking about you, but to have more people—and new people—talking about you.

Success is cumulative. It's not defined by one event. It's the culmination of many accomplishments that have advanced and supported one's upward mobility.

Another part of your network is the industry professionals you have developed a relationship with who support your endeavors. They may be radio personalities, bloggers, booking agents, or anyone else that can help create visibility for you. Keeping an open relationship, and more importantly, a friendship with these people can help get your music to their listeners and readers, which will help your cause immensely.

If you can maintain your presence and your visibility until you reach what's known as a *tipping point* then all your hard work will begin to work hard for you. This is effectively the instant where you become *viral,* a stage in your career where everyone starts talking about you, you begin *trending,* and your visibility is recognized by the masses.

No matter how fast your career is moving, even if you have a saddle strapped to a lightning bolt, don't ever forget to *interact* with your fans. By taking the time to create a solid foundation with the people who believe in you and admire you that will create foundation that cannot be knocked down.

Some bands with a solid following have such a close long-term relationship with their fan base that they never refer to them as fans; they address them as friends. If you apply this to your life, and if you are genuine about it, you will find that you have had help and support in places that you never even knew about. When people believe in you, great things can happen.

It's not uncommon for bands to crash at their friends' houses from city to city instead of staying at hotels. The people who really understand this industry understand the costs of being on the road and offer up their house on occasion to bands to offset their travel expenses. I've done it for bands and I've had it done for me. People like this are the glue that helps hold the independent music scenes together across the world.

Developing and maintaining a successfully functioning network like this will not happen overnight, and none of this can be achieved without an open line of communication between all parties involved.

Make yourself accessible and available to your fans at all times, because just writing a great song doesn't mean shit if you can't get anyone to listen to it. If you can't cultivate and harness ongoing fan support then what you do in the studio is absolutely meaningless.

CHAPTER EIGHT

A SOLID ONLINE PRESENCE

You'll need to have some things in place that will take time to develop, so it's a good idea that you do them right at the beginning of your solo career or the formation of your band.

These will include setting up your website and social media accounts.

YOUR WEBSITE

The first step in creating your official website is domain name registration. It will cost around $10 to register your domain name (the name of your site). You're going to want your website's domain name to be your band name or your performance name; this will make it easier on your fan base and anyone looking for you, not to mention the fact that it's just plain common sense.

This again drives home the point I made in the chapter on branding about doing a name search and choosing a completely original name.

The second step is choosing a host. Hosts can range anywhere from $60 to $100 per year depending on the amount of bandwidth, security options, and other bells and whistles that you choose to add to these hosting packages.

The third step is choosing a content management system, or CMS. Content management systems such as WordPress, Joomla, and Drupal are the most common free content mangers that you'll find and they are commonly embedded in your host server's control panel.

Content management systems create and manage HTML or *hypertext markup language.* This is one of the codes that programmers use to develop websites.

They also simplify Web design by offering you templates to choose from which are preprogrammed Web page designs that are pretty much ready to use even for someone with little or no Web design experience.

You can find tutorials for this—and almost everything else, for that matter—on YouTube and design the whole site yourself if you need to keep your out-of-pocket costs down. However, if you wish to get a more comprehensive step-by-step tutorial on how to use most software platforms, try out Lynda.com.

Content management systems also offer a lot of plugins that allow you to create additional functions for your website, and allow you to have a very competitive site online in a short amount of time.

As with anything, you'll gain experience over time and your websites will look better as your design techniques improve.

YOUR EMAIL ADDRESS

Your hosting company should be providing you with multiple email accounts and it's not uncommon to be allowed up to 35 email addresses for each primary domain that you host.

Once you have your own website, your email should come from that website address. For instance, if your band name is The Spoilers, your website should be "thespoilers.com" and your email address should be "you@thespoilers.com". It looks unprofessional to send an email from "you_of_The_Spoilers@yahoo.com" or something to that effect if you have your own website.

Keep in mind that everything you do is branding, so even when you give people your email address, it is a part of your brand.

SETTING UP YOUR WEBSTORE

This is the critical part of your website and the main reason that all of your Web pages, profiles, and social media accounts need to redirect back to your website.

Your webstore is your point of purchase; it is the end of the funnel that you have created online. This is where you convert all of your marketing and branding into sales.

E-COMMERCE

As stated earlier, your website allows you to install plugins that will enable it to perform different functions, such as e-commerce.

Should you want a full catalog available on your webstore, you can get free plugins from companies such as WooCommerce that will allow you to set up an in-depth online storefront in a short and reasonable amount of time. This site will not only accept automated payments and process orders, but it will keep track of your inventory as well.

PAYPAL

An older method of online payments is PayPal. This is still a very viable platform and ideal for you if you have limited merchandise.

After setting up an account with PayPal you can go into the Merchant Services section of their site and create buttons to use on your site.

You can program the buttons that you want to use to sell items with different options, such as shirt sizes or colors, and the quantity that you want to purchase. There is also an Add to Cart function, which allows people to purchase multiple items on the same order.

You can even program the buttons to display a success message or "thank you for your purchase" message and redirect to a different page on your site once the order is completed, if you wish.

Once you successfully program your buttons, PayPal will generate an HTML code for you to copy and paste onto the desired page of your website. Once you embed this code on your Web page and update your changes you will be immediately ready to take orders and payments for online sales.

SHIPPING

One thing that I absolutely love about PayPal is their shipping label function.

After the release of the first edition of this book I used to package my orders and go wait in long post office lines. These slow-moving, blood pressure-elevating extended wait times were due solely to the lazy and ignorant fucking pieces of shit complicating the mail process with their utter inefficiency and lack of respect for their customers.

PayPal has eliminated this headache for me because they have teamed up with the United States Postal Service to allow you to print shipping labels right from your printer. The USPS deducts the charges directly from your PayPal account and then generates your shipping label and tracking number on the spot.

The postage fees are determined by the type of package you are sending and the class in which you ship (first class, priority, priority express, etc…).

FLAT RATE SHIPPING

To make this whole process even easier for you, the USPS allows you to register a free account on their website (*www.usps.com*) and lets you order free shipping supplies which your mailman will drop off at your home or office.

Flat Rate shipping envelopes and boxes have a set rate and operate under a "if it fits it ships" rule. Basically, if you can fit the item in the Flat Rate shipping package—and it weighs less than 70 pounds—they will ship it for a flat fee regardless of the weight of the contents.

Now I process all of my orders and print all of my shipping labels from my office and just drop the packages in the mailbox.

If I absolutely do need to stop in the post office, I can just walk in and leave everything on the counter or in the mail drop because I paid all of my postage ahead of time and therefore don't need to wait in line.

Depending on the amount of volume you are sending out, your mailman will even pick up your outgoing mail from your location. This is a massive perk, because every time you leave to run an errand, you are sacrificing valuable time that could be used elsewhere for something productive.

DECREASE LOAD TIME AND OPTIMIZE PERFORMANCE

Getting people to visit your website is a skill in itself and challenging enough. Once they are there, especially if you have multiple visitors at once, you don't want to piss them off because it runs like shit— and run like shit it will if it's not optimized.

If you have already built a website before reading this book and are experiencing slow pageload time, there are a few things that you can do to throttle up your pageload speed. After all, if your website is loading slowly for you, then it is loading slowly for everyone else as well.

One of the most common reasons for this is the file size of the photo images that you are placing on your website.

PHOTO FORMAT AND RESOLUTION

Digital photographs are generally placed in two categories: those for use in print and those for use on the Web.

PRINT-QUALITY PHOTOS

Print-quality photos are of a higher pixel resolution, usually 300 dots per inch or *dpi*. This results in the image having a larger file size in bytes, which will result in the page taking longer to load.

These photos are also formatted in a four-color process known as CMYK (cyan, magenta, yellow, and key (black)). Uploading an image in CMYK format to your website will result in its failure to display regardless of its file size because it is not the correct format.

WEB-QUALITY PHOTOS

Web-quality photos are much smaller than those formatted for printing. These photos are usually 72 dpi resolution and are formatted in a three-color process called RGB (red, green, and blue) which is the format read by all computer monitors and electronic devices.

Even though the pixelation is much less condensed than that of a print-quality photo, it will still appear as a high resolution photo online.

Be cautious when using raw camera footage taken by a cell phone camera. You will see that even though these files are 72 dpi, the dimensions are often quite large and will take up a lot of space.

FILE FORMAT

File format—as opposed to *color format* as described above—is the format in which you save your image when working in such programs as Adobe Photoshop or Illustrator. Ideally you should save your image files as a JPEG, GIF, or PNG when preparing them for online usage.

So taking into consideration everything that we have discussed, let's say you have a picture of your band that is a full color RGB JPEG saved at 72 dpi resolution with dimensions reflective of where you want this image placed on your site.

As an example, we will say that the file size for your image is somewhere between 500 KB (kilobytes) and 3 MB (megabytes) which makes the page load somewhat slow. Then after uploading a few more pictures to this page you notice that it is running much slower than desired.

Ideally, you don't want any of your images of any size dimensions to exceed 100 KB. I use this number as a rule and have noticed an immediate difference in pageload time when I reduce the size of all of the image files on my website to reflect this. These image files affect the amount of bandwidth that is used when loading a page, and when you have several people visiting your site at once it increases the bandwidth traffic which in turn slows your pageload time down.

If you use Adobe Photoshop, the easiest way to scale down these image files is to save them as a JPEG and use the sliding scale to reduce the size when saving the file.

Keep in mind when you are choosing your image file sizes that 1 gigabyte is equal to 1000 megabytes and 1 megabyte is equal to 1000 kilobytes.

CLEANING YOUR MEDIA LIBRARY

To help keep your site working at optimal performance you should also remove unused image files from your media library. This help reduce the amount of resources your database uses and allows the extra RAM (Random Access Memory) to be allocated for other things on your site's server.

REDUCING THE AMOUNT OF PLUGINS ON YOUR SITE

If you are using a content management system such as *WordPress*, you have access to a lot of free plugins that are tempting to download and activate on your site. However, these plugins all attach scripts or code to your site and will always be running in the background. If you are not using the plugins that you have installed, you should deactivate and uninstall them. This type of ongoing management will keep your website running smoothly at all times.

REDUCING THE AMOUNT OF HTML ON YOUR SITE

As I just mentioned, running any types of script or code on your site will slow down its overall performance. This rule also applies to HTML, which is the code you are using to embed your YouTube videos onto the site, among other things.

If possible, try to eliminate excessive, unnecessary, or out-of-date HTML scripts or posts so you can optimize your site performance.

INDEXING, RANKING, AND SEARCH ENGINE OPTIMIZATION

Continually updating your pages along with consistent networking will improve your *indexing and ranking*, which determines how you are found on search engines.

Your own website should be utilizing *metadata* that makes your site visible in searches pertaining to categories regarding your act, your genre, your region, your album, and your titles. This is known as *search engine optimization,* which utilizes specific high-traffic keywords that will actually help bring traffic to your site. Most host servers have content management systems have plugins that can help you achieve this.

Keywords will cross-reference information on your site for the person who is looking for it. For instance, say someone doesn't remember your band name, but they know your guitar player's name and search for him online. Now because you have used his name as a keyword when you programmed your *SEO*, your band's website will automatically populate the search results that come up from your guitar player's name search.

You can use your band name, members' names, album names, song titles, genre classification, and more. There really is no limit on what you can use for your keywords and these sites will allow you to program a lot of keywords into them.

To ensure that your group itself indexes and ranks well, make sure that you name each of the webpages or social media platforms that you are on with your *group's name only*. Little or no variation of this should be used.

The number one driver of traffic to content websites is the individual search, so if people don't yet know about you, how can they search for you? Getting people to talk about you is critical to your success, and getting them to talk about you on social media can create trending, but at the end of the day, the individual search beats social media by more than 300 percent when directing traffic to your site.

ARTIST PROFILES ON OTHER WEBSITES

So now let's move on to other platforms such as websites that host band profiles and social media. Later in this chapter I will also provide you with a few lists of platforms to help get you started.

Make sure you dedicate a page on each of these platforms as your "official" page. This page should have the most presentable photos that you have available, both live shots and group photos. This is not where you post one of your "selfie" pics that you took with your cell phone in the bathroom mirror. This is where you have professional photos that have been enhanced in Photoshop and have your logo embedded on them etc..., because this will be where you do most of your promoting from and it should exude as much professionalism as you can afford to give it. It will also be the link that you give out the most. You don't want your followers scattered all over the place. Have all your traffic stemming from the same dedicated page on each platform. *ReverbNation.com* has become the largest Internet hub for musicians and helps you integrate all of these together on your dashboard so you can see your totals in one place. You'll eventually be asked how many online followers you have, and if you can provide evidence of this number with only a few links it will help corroborate any research that someone is doing on you.

SOCIAL MEDIA

Also be sure to take advantage of all the different social media platforms. New ones are springing up at a rapid rate and each one of them has a certain intrinsic value that separates it from the others, creating visibility for you that the others will not.

To help you get the most out of these social media platforms, I've provided a list of the top 15 most popular social networking sites as of September 2015 along with the estimated amount of monthly users as provided by eBizMBA.com:

1. Facebook 900,000,000 estimated unique monthly visitors.
2. Twitter 310,000,000 estimated unique monthly visitors.
3. LinkedIn 255,000,000 estimated unique monthly visitors.
4. Pinterest 250,000,000 estimated unique monthly visitors.
5. Google+ 120,000,000 estimated unique monthly visitors.
6. Tumblr 110,000,000 estimated unique monthly visitors.
7. Instagram 100,000,000 estimated unique monthly visitors.
8. VK 80,000,000 estimated unique monthly visitors.
9. Flickr 65,000,000 estimated unique monthly visitors.
10. Vine 42,000,000 estimated unique monthly visitors.
11. Meetup 40,000,000 estimated unique monthly visitors.
12. Tagged 38,000,000 estimated unique monthly visitors.
13. Ask.fm 37,000,000 estimated unique monthly visitors.
14. MeetMe 15,500,000 estimated unique monthly visitors.
15. ClassMates 15,000,000 estimated unique monthly visitors.

DECEPTIVE DIGITAL METRICS

A word to the wise: since the days of band promotion on MySpace, artists and bands have found ways to manipulate song play totals through the use of hackers who present themselves as promotional companies and charge a small fee for these false increases of numbers. Now you can pay for Twitter followers, Facebook likes, YouTube plays, and downloads of your music on sites like DatPiff. This is completely asinine.

I have had artists lie to me about the amount of music they have sold time and time again. I have also seen artists that pay to have their plays, views, likes, and download numbers boosted by the tens of thousands in an attempt to make it look as if they actually were doing something with their careers.

This has resulted in the creation of hundreds of bullshit promotional companies popping up on Twitter and other social media sites that are doing nothing more for this industry than perpetuating false hope and deception.

The labels and the entire industry are aware of this practice. If you give people money to do this, you are spending it in the wrong places. Having 20,000 bought and paid-for followers will do nothing for you. You're better off having 50 followers who are concerned with what you're doing and will buy your records than having tens of thousands of imaginary friends.

If you aren't getting organic followers one at a time who find you on their own, listen to your music, read about you, and become interested in you then they aren't legitimate followers.

Whatever these promotional companies offer you, it's not legitimate so don't bother spending your money on it. Get your fans the old-fashioned way: earn them. Those are the fans that will support your career. The ones you paid for won't, and this is definitely not what I was referring to when I said "solid" online presence.

If you think this is helping you, you are sadly mistaken. All you are doing is attempting to circumvent the work process that you will eventually need to endure anyway, so it's best to stop trying to find a way around the work and just roll up your sleeves and get it done in the first place instead of wasting your valuable time.

If given an option, a better way to effectively promote yourself on these sites is to pay the actual website itself. Facebook has a program that will promote your posts, *TwitterAds* is an effective tool for promoting tweets beyond the reach of your followers, and ReverbNation has an option for promoting yourself within that site and has expanded its reach beyond its own bandwidth. These all offer analytics so you can gauge the performance of your efforts against your total dollars spent—a much better idea than the hocus pocus I mentioned earlier.

OTHER SITES FOR MUSICIANS

Moving along now that we covered social media and ReverbNation, you should be aware that there are many other websites that host artist pages, and you need to be on as many of them as is viable for an artist in your genre. Find a way to promote and network on these sites to maximize your visibility.

In an effort to help you achieve some widespread visibility, here's a list of 41 websites dedicated to recording artists and musicians that you can use immediately:

1. Aampp.net
2. Bandmix.com
3. Bandzoogle.com
4. Broadjam.com
5. Copromote.com
6. Getsigned.com
7. Gigmasters.com
8. Grooveshark.com
9. Harmonycentral.com
10. imusicfx.com
11. indiecharts.com
12. indie-music.com
13. Jango.com
14. Jembler.com
15. Jpfolks.com
16. Jukeboxalive.com
17. Last.fm
18. lastminutemusicians.com
19. Liveunsigned.com
20. mohawkradio.com
21. Mp3.com
22. Musicgorilla.com
23. Musiclivesbeyond.com
24. Musicxray.com
25. MyDiveo.com
26. Numboronomuoio.oom
27. Numubu.com
28. Ooizit.com
29. Onlinerock.com
30. Openkanvas.com

31. Ourstage.com
32. Pitchmystuff.com
33. Songdew.com
34. Soundswift.com
35. Soundclick.com
36. Soundcloud.com

37. Stereokiller.com
38. Talentwatch.net
39. Tweewoo.com
40. Unsigned.com
41. Unsignedbandweb.com

Some of these will be more resourceful for you than others, so feel free to pick and choose which sites you want to register on. If you do some additional research you'll find many more sites like these.

Registration on any website usually only takes a few minutes and is only a minor pain in the ass, but as I said before, *you have to do the damn work.*

It is very important for you to remember to backlink each of these artist profiles to your official website and to any e-commerce websites where people can purchase your merch and music.

USING GROUPS TO PROMOTE YOURSELF

Another way to maximize your visibility on these websites is to join groups or communities that are specific to your genre of music. Each of these groups may potentially have thousands of members. Posting a link to video or to a place where your music can be streamed and purchased in each of these groups will make it visible to all of the group's members, potentially giving you exposure to thousands and even tens of thousands of people in a relatively short period of time.

You can search for groups on most of these sites and joining them is usually just a matter of clicking a button. Oftentimes you can start posting immediately thereafter.

This is an aspect of networking on social media that you need to be using to your advantage if you aren't already. This is how you create awareness in front of people who don't know who you are yet. Posting on your timeline in front of your existing network merely sends your message to people who already know you.

Although keeping your existing network and fanbase abreast of your new developments is imperative, your objective in creating brand awareness and visibility is to expose yourself to people who don't know you or haven't yet heard of you or heard your music.

I am a member of many of these groups on these websites, and when I post something, I post on each and every one of them.

I'm not going to lie to you; it's a task. *And you have to want to do it* in order to get it done. This procedure is monotonous and time consuming; so put on some jams, crack open a six pack, and sit down—because you're going to be busy for a little while.

Be thorough and always complete what you set out to do, even if it has to be done in installments. Just make sure it gets done.

FORUMS AND MESSAGE BOARDS

Becoming a member of an online community-based forum is also a time-proven method of communicating directly with other people that share your interests. These message boards usually focus on specific music genres, so if you can find some of these within your genre, start becoming active. You don't want to pop up out of nowhere and start promoting your new release. Shameless self-promotion on these boards will backfire on you, and they will flame your threads. I've seen this happen before, and it gets as ugly for the person defending himself as it gets humorous for the people in the public forum to read. If you manage to get in an online battle with someone, that person is most likely only pushing your buttons because you showed him that he can. That person is probably stoned and is also probably 14 years old, so quit being so sensitive and stop being a keyboard warrior; be the bigger person and walk away before you embarrass yourself.

Many of these forums have rules or posting guidelines to ensure "proper forum etiquette." Take the time to read over their policies before you piss off the moderator and need to have all of your posts approved by him or get your account permanently suspended for spamming.

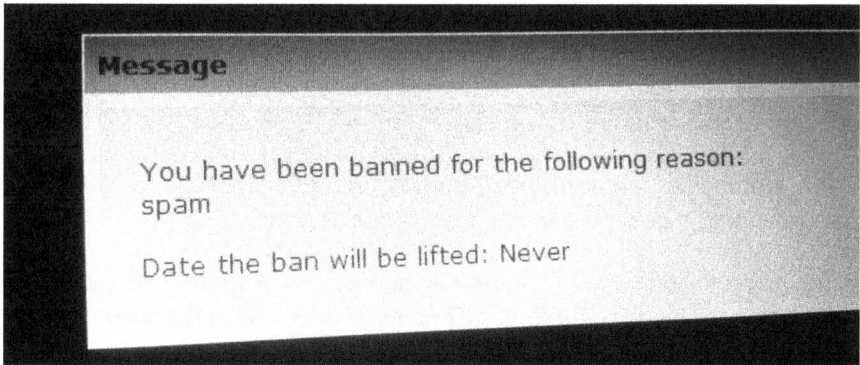

Message

You have been banned for the following reason:
spam

Date the ban will be lifted: Never

Take a wild guess who this happened to.

Here is a list of 24 message boards that you can register on for posting and networking. Some of these forums are specific to one genre or discipline, so once again, utilize the message boards that fit you best.

1. Absolutepunk.net/forum.php
2. Australianmusic.info/forums
3. Bristolmusic.myfreeforum.org
4. Futureproducers.com
5. Gearslutz.com
6. Forums.digitalspy.co.uk
7. Homerecording.com/bbs
8. illmuzik.com
9. Leedsmusicforum.co.uk
10. Forum.mp3unsigned.com
11. Mpg.org.uk/forums
12. Musicradar.com
13. Musicboards.com
14. Musicbanter.com
15. Music-discussion.com
16. Prorecordingworkshop.lefora.com
17. Forums.stevehoffman.tv
18. Forums.songstuff.com
19. Recording.org
20. Songramp.netforum
21. Soundonsound.com
22. Sputnikmusic.com/forums
23. Thewombforums.com
24. Unsignedbandweb.com/forums.html

THE BIG PICTURE

Within the World Wide Web, you need to create a little net of your own. My personal philosophy is that you should try to be everywhere you have access to all at once, and this is actually the goal which you will be working towards during your marketing campaign, which we will cover later.

Even though you'll never be *EVERYWHERE,* I set myself up mentally to pursue that goal when I'm looking for places to achieve visibility. I purposely set the bar very high for myself. When I get to the point that I've done every single thing that I possibly could have, I then go over my work and try to figure out what I missed. There is a certain element of investigative research that goes into this; it's tedious and you need to be focused enough to keep peeling the layers of the onion back until you find what you're looking for. This will involve alternate keyword searches, following recommended links, asking other bands what sites they're using, and any other research you can dedicate your time to do.

SETTING THE STAGE

As for now, consider this the *staging* part of your marketing campaign. Start building up a presence on all of these different websites and social media platforms to give you multiple springboards off of which to launch when you start your marketing campaign.

You'll need to do this if you want to maximize your results. How else do you expect to be found or discovered? As of September 20th 2015, Worldwidewebsize.com estimates that the indexed Web contains at least 4.77 billion Web pages. How are you going to stand out in that large of an online community?

I'll tell you how.

You're going to start registering pages on these music sites and dedicating at least an hour a day towards networking on them and ensuring that they're updated.

Is that going to take too much time out of your day?

No, it won't. You just need to log yourself out of Facebook because chances are you're spending way too much time on there anyway.

The networking aspect will be a critical part of your online activity, because if you aren't reaching out to people from these pages and creating awareness for these pages and for yourself, then it will be difficult for people to just find you.

Yes, it does happen, and it's one of the reasons you should use sites like Stumbleupon—which is a discovery engine that finds and recommends Web content to its users based on their tastes—but no matter what site you're on, you need to network, because on many of these sites, most of the people that will find your page—such as on Facebook—are friends of friends so they're already in your *extended* network.

Moving on, I still feel the need to mention MySpace even though everyone had pretty much migrated away from it after News Corp. (the parent company of FOX) purchased the company in 2005. Prior to the suicidal redesign of the site, which made advertisers and users flock to Facebook, it was an incredible place for bands to network with each other and expose their music to new people. It has changed hands once again and is now owned by a small group of investors including Justin Timberlake who abandoned the Classic MySpace platform, redesigned it as a music site, and launched MySpace Radio as a streaming platform.

It is sporadic at best that people actually do check their profiles, but when they do go on there, they're often checking out music. I still recommend you establish a profile on this platform for your act because now you get paid streaming royalties every time your music plays on MySpace Radio if your distributor delivers titles to MySpace.

With massive losses exceeding $40 million in 2012, MySpace may never have the opportunity to return to its former glory, so in regards to social media my recommendation to you is to find out where the kids are currently going and make sure you have a presence there.

You can also develop your own artist page and profile on some Internet radio stations. These are also self-contained music communities and you get some networking done on these as well. IMradio.com is a perfect example of this.

You can type up a list of all of these sites and their login information and share them with the band. This way you can all share the responsibility of networking on them and maintaining them. If you are a solo artist, well, here's your chance to prove to yourself that you can do more than your competition and your peers.

You can get a lot done on a majority of these sites and it will not cost you a dime. Developing a Web presence using several different methods is critical to the online part of your *MULTI-PRONGED MARKETING CAMPAIGN STRATEGY.*

The most important thing to understand about your online presence is that when you develop these sites, don't abandon them. Keep them current. Update them as soon as you have new information. You never know when a booking agent or staff writer for a magazine will come across one of these profiles.

As important as it is to keep these sites and pages current and maintained, please do not forget how important it is to keep up your personal *physical* appearances. You need to keep an active performance calendar in order to direct traffic to these sites as well. If people don't know who you are then they won't be looking for you now, will they?

NEW WEBSITES AND NEW SOCIAL MEDIA PLATFORMS

One thing for certain is that there will always be new websites and social media platforms springing up. What may look like a dead site at first glance may be something viable that has not yet reached its growth spurt or tipping point. Getting in and growing with this website from the early days could be extremely beneficial to your career.

For those of you old enough to remember Tila Tequila and MySpace, she was all over this platform since very early on and friended everyone. She became famous by exploiting herself on MySpace, and this website pretty much launched her career to the point where she became a household name. She pimped that site hard and it did for her exactly what it was designed to do.

Facebook then became the replacement for MySpace and the Facebook music industry groups were actually very small when they were first created. I remember when finding a group with more than 10,000 members was a big deal. Now finding a group with 75,000 members or more is not uncommon.

Google+ is the next example of a community-based social media platform that has undergone some substantial growth. At the time that I wrote the first edition of this book, there were only a few music industry-related Google+ communities (less than 10) and they had a very limited amount of members. Now, that platform's amount of music-based communities has expanded exponentially.

There is some tech buzz that Google may shut this platform down in the future to make way for other products, but at the time of this book's release, I am still getting traffic to my website from the Google+ communities that I am a member of.

Whether or not this site will be shut down in the future remains to be seen, but in the meantime, keep in mind that your goal is to obtain exposure and reach, and I recommend that you utilize all the options that are available to you.

CHAPTER NINE

MERCHANDISING

Merchandising area at Cobra Lounge Chicago, June 2014.

I was no more than 11 years old when I first walked into Kroozin' Music at 4069 S. Archer on Chicago's south side.

The east room of this double storefront smelled like incense and had racks of full color double-sided official tour T-shirts from all the bands I was listening to at the time, including buttons, posters, backpatches, and much more. I soon had my jean jacket covered with memorabilia from every band that I was listening to that had cool enough artwork worthy of obtaining some real estate on my sleeve.

A few short years later, I was attending my first concert. Suicidal Tendencies performed at Medusas located at 3557 N. Sheffield on Chicago's north side. For the first time in my life, I saw a touring band's merch table. LPs, T-shirts, posters, stickers, and buttons were all available, not only from the touring band, but from the local acts as well. This tied in directly to what I was used to seeing at my local record store.

Since that time, I've been blessed with the opportunity of taking a peek into several independent music scenes, in several locations, and in several genres.

I can't for the life of me understand why artists across the board are not merchandising from their first show forward.

Providing your family, friends, and any fans you may win over the opportunity to take home a keepsake of the evening such as a T-shirt or bumper sticker to support your band will help you finance your group and will also help increase your visibility.

If you have fan support, and you're merchandising, *you're actually not doing all the promotional work yourself.*

For every T-shirt and every bumper sticker that you sell, you are creating a walking or driving billboard for your band.

This grassroots branding is some of the most valuable visibility you'll have. Because if somebody sees another person wearing your shirt, he'll immediately see that you have support and may want to look further into your band. As your fan base grows, so will your visibility. Your fans may be wearing your shirts at other concerts and your friends in other bands may even be wearing your shirt when they're performing.

Maybe in order to make this cross-promotion between bands happen, you'll need to rock another band's shirt while you're on stage. Take the first step and set a precedent of support for the other bands in your scene and show that you stand united.

Merchandising legitimizes your existence as a band. It separates you from those that talk about it and those that are actually doing it.

Now I've already stated that merchandising will help you finance your group; what I'll stress now is that you must have merch while you're on tour or traveling anywhere on the road.

You have a van that needs to be fueled and it's full of people that need to be fed. Guarantees sometimes fall apart and attendance isn't always as good as projected, especially if you have been stuck with a worthless promoter in one of these cities. Not having merchandise to sell to help offset your travel expenses can potentially put you in a bad place financially.

MERCH TABLE OVERVIEW

Let's look at the display layout of what is on a band's merch table and then discuss the costs associated with manufacturing these items as well as what your potential profit margin is.

THE TABLE – A 6- or 8-foot long banquet table is usually the standard table size for this. Many venues supply them, but some don't. You can also have a tablecloth custom screened with your band logo and artwork which will make your merchandising area stand out by being more visually appealing. These table covers come in fitted sizes for 6- and 8-foot tables and have multiple sides.

My table at the Global G-Mixx summit 2014 - Chicago

T-SHIRTS – Single-screen, one-color shirts are the staple of every emerging band's merch table. These shirts are primarily cheap to make and can become profitable enough for you to purchase double-sided shirts the next time around or invest in another run of single-sided garments and additional merchandise.

The best way to display your shirts is to hang them behind your merch table. I have tapped a few finish nails into the wall behind me to hang the shirts from and even duct taped the hangers to the wall in my early days as well.

A far better way to do this is to bring a wire frame divider that you can position behind you or suspend from the wall itself.

Folding your shirts around a rectangular-shaped piece of sturdy cardboard (the kind from a shipping box) so only the shirt's graphics are displayed and using thumbtacks or duct tape to secure them will create an actual canvas of your shirt artwork that you can display in full view by affixing these to the wire frame behind you.

Your shirts are usually your big ticket item as far as cost is concerned and are also a popular sales item, so placing them behind you is a good way to keep the grubby hands of thieving drunks off of your stock.

It's important for you to display each shirt design you have available including the backs of any double sided T-shirts that you have in stock.

You can affix a price tag to the actual shirts by simply taping a white 3 X 5 index card to the shirt after writing the price on the card with a permanent marker. I've seen this done with a piece of cardboard, or even a paper plate in some instances.

Since many clubs are dark, and a well-lit area is not always an option, many bands have implemented a little of their own scumbag ingenuity to illuminate their displays. I have seen rope lighting surrounding some of these displays and this works well as long as an outlet is available.

A nice durable Rubbermaid tote is sturdy enough to store your shirts in and fits conveniently under your merch table as well. If you are on the road this is a good option as it can be sealed and won't be subject to spilled drinks, humidity, cigarette smoke, or any other funk that you create in your van while on the road.

Although there is no right or wrong way to lay out your merch table, there are a few things that people do that stick out in my opinion.

LPs, EPs, and CDs – Your music is obviously the item that you want displayed and that you want to move units of. With a rekindling interest in vinyl overall, having this format available and for sale is a good idea. Since many breaking bands are on a budget, they usually opt to have a limited pressing of their release. Oftentimes, a portion of these limited pressings are released on colored or marbled vinyl. These limited pressings are usually picked up by collectors and prove to increase in value over time.

Using a display stand for 12-inch LPs in the back of the table while the smaller items are placed flat on the table in front of it creates an additional dimension that can be seen from a distance and may help direct traffic towards you.

Seven-inch EPs in plastic covers and CDs can be laid flat on the table and actually taped down to help prevent theft.

POSTERS – These are large enough to place on the wall behind you, lay flat on the table, or tape to the front of the table, allowing for it to drape over.

Smaller items such as stickers of various sizes, buttons, patches, guitar picks, customized lighters, shot glasses, coffee mugs, download cards, and other items can be organized in front of the larger items to create a very visual spread that will give your friends and fans a lot of options to pick and choose from.

ACCEPTING CREDIT CARDS

Today a lot of people favor carrying plastic as opposed to cash. Many tech-savvy bands have embraced this and now accommodate these payment methods at their merch table.

Mobile payment companies such as the ones I have listed below and others allow you to take credit card payments for merch sales on your mobile device by swiping a card or by tapping NFC-enabled credit cards to NFC-enabled mobile devices.

- Apple Pay
- Flint Mobile
- Square
- GoPayment
- ROAMpay
- PayPal Here
- Dwolla
- Google Wallet
- LevelUp

There are fees associated with many of these services, so you may only want to consider using these if you are on tour or have enough local show dates booked to justify the expenses you will incur for utilizing these platforms.

KEEP YOUR TABLE STAFFED AT ALL TIMES

Walking away from your table is walking away from sales. It also invites the possibility of theft. Keep your table staffed at all times. Make sure you relieve your merch person every so often so they can use the bathroom, get something to eat or drink and maybe socialize and watch a band or two when you are not on stage.

Many bands bring a merch person with them when on tour; if you do, be sure to pick someone who is reliable and trustworthy.

ALWAYS HAVE YOUR WEBSTORE INFORMATION AVAILABLE

It's quite common for bands to run low on stock while on tour or even at a good local show. People will want shirts that you don't have sizes for or other items you are out of and will want to purchase them if they like you.

If you sell these items on your webstore then someone can make a purchase via credit card or PayPal while at the show and let you ship it the next day.

Also, you may have someone who just blew all of his cash at the bar but wants to buy something. If they are able to purchase something from your site by using PayPal, you can give them the merchandise as soon as you receive an email notification of payment. I have done this in the past and I just give the person a cash reimbursement for the shipping costs (usually between $5 and $6). This is a win-win for everyone and it also gives your fan a few bucks so he can get himself another beer.

REPLENISHING STOCK WHILE ON THE ROAD

T-shirts are probably the number one item that sells out first if not managed correctly and not ordered in sufficient amounts. I'm a big guy and by the time most of the bands I listen to get to the Midwest, they don't have any plus-size shirts either.

So what do you do when you run out of stock?

Well, the answer is simple. Take some of the money out of your lockbox, deposit it in a bank account, and place an order with your screen-printer. Find out how fast he can get an order into production and then the amount of days it will take to ship.

Choose a mailing address of a hotel or friend's house in a city that is ahead of where you are on your tour schedule, but that is one or two days behind the estimated date of arrival. This will ensure that the merch order arrives before you do. It's better to have the package waiting for you than to be waiting for a package when you are on a tight schedule.

I pick up boxes of promotional stuff from the front desk of my hotel all the time when I show up for music conferences; from the stories I have been told, this is a much safer option and a better idea than having it shipped to the venue where you are performing.

MERCHANDISE MANAGEMENT & THE LEDGER

Learning basic accounting is very important to a band that invests in itself. Understanding the need to break even, make a profit, or even reallocate funds towards things like gasoline is critical to a band's success.

A ledger is a hardcover book where the pages are divided into rows and columns. You can keep track of your inventory, income, and expenses in this or you can even use a notebook, for that matter. For the band on the road with a laptop (which should be everyone at this point), you can create an Excel spreadsheet and keep your records on your computer.

You need to manage your band as a business and learn how to do this from the beginning; the ability to balance a ledger and to be your own accountant is a very basic necessity—not only to your band's growth and development, but to your daily life. After all, if you can't successfully manage the revenue from a few T-shirts and CDs, what makes you think you will eventually be able to successfully pay your rent, utilities and grocery bills, credit cards, children's tuition, etc.?

Even if you spent money on alcohol and drugs, you may want to write it down as a "recreational" expense. Only then will you truly know what you're making and exactly where it's being spent.

If you can carry out these tasks when you're managing a few hundred dollars at a time, then you'll be more prepared to manage your money when it's a few thousand dollars at a time—or even a few hundred thousand dollars at a time.

Low manufacturing costs and the benefits of the visibility you'll receive from merchandising make this a no-brainer. You must do this, and you must do it at every show; set a precedent and stay consistent.

If the bands you're performing with aren't doing this, it's okay to continue to do shows with them and stay loyal to your grassroots fan base, but start getting booked on shows with the bands that have their shit together, because it appears that you may be outgrowing your surroundings.

It's time for you to climb into the next area.

CHAPTER TEN

ALBUM ARTWORK

What is it about the combination of art and music that is important?
Simply put, the ability to appeal to multiple senses at once.

During the wax era of music, a 12-inch LP was loaded with artwork and the first time I would listen to the album I would look at its cover art. Did it have hidden meaning? What was its purpose? What are the liner notes? Where was it recorded? Most people I know would dwell over the album's artwork and its inserts, which usually had the lyrics to the songs on them.

Although the format in which we embody music changed to compact disc quite some time ago, the artwork is still just as important as ever. Album artwork is how we quickly identify the record we are looking for or how we find the next band's music on our playlist, but it goes much deeper than that. Beyond the music, it's how the artist identifies with his fan base and the subculture he's involved in. Well thought-out album covers have become iconic parts of pop culture history for decades. At times the music genre itself can be determined by the album cover artwork.

If you've put a lot of thought into the composition of your album, you should put a lot of thought in your cover art, especially if you have a concept or anthology album.

If you need to get someone to do the artwork for you, look at their work to the minutest detail. This after all, is going to be how you package your music and it very well might be the first impression the world gets of your product.

One of the most historically important album cover artists of the last 30 years is *Pushead* (a.k.a. Brian Schroeder), whose attention to detail and distinctive skull-themed artwork is now recognized by the masses in a fraction of a second.

Pushead's first contribution to album cover artwork was on The Better Youth Organization's 1982 compilation *Someone Got Their Head Kicked In,* which depicted a violent blood-filled mosh pit between skinheads and punk rockers. More artwork came quickly thereafter for a myriad of punk, hardcore, and thrash bands including his own band Septic Death. Most of the latter artwork incorporated his detailed use of skulls.

His portfolio quickly grew to include The Misfits, Prong, Metallica, and even the official *Chronic* album T-shirt design for Dr. Dre.

Already an icon in the underground music and skateboard community, once Metallica commissioned him for several albums his place in mainstream rock art history was set.

It almost became a mandatory practice while visiting a record store to pick up an album embodying his artwork and mill over the details in an effort to analyze the piece overall.

Album cover artwork can clearly create interest in a band you never heard of and it can also be a determining factor in which album you decide to purchase.

I once had two albums strongly recommended to me at the same time, the Cro-Mags' *Age of Quarrel* (Profile 1986) and Agnostic Front's *Cause for Alarm* (Relativity/Combat Core 1986).

I found myself at the record store and only had the money to purchase one of the two albums. It took some contemplating to make a decision on which to buy. I had never heard either band before, so all I was left with were the two shrink-wrapped 12-inch LPs I was holding in my hand.

The Cro-Mags album had a polished layout with a huge color photo of an atomic explosion and mushroom cloud on the cover along with a mean lineup photo of the band in full color on the back. The layout was cleaner and more pristine looking and it just had that overall polished look to it. The track listing and the names of the songs interested me as well as the fact that the band landed a deal with Profile.

In my other hand was Agnostic Front's hand-drawn album cover by Sean Taggart, which had some controversial artwork on it. There was a demonic skinhead, a heroin addict shooting up, a punk rocker being robbed at gunpoint, and a fat business man shoveling people into his mouth with a fork. All of this was done with the earth cracking apart beneath their feet and a huge American flag in the background. The band lineup photo on the back of the album was black and white, grainy and of bad quality.

Agnostic Front's Cause For Alarm album cover artwork furnished by Sean Taggart www.seantaggart.com

After examining the tracklist and liner notes for each album and giving it some thought, I put back the more polished looking Cro-Mags album and bought the Agnostic Front album because the cover artwork intrigued me.

Both bands came highly recommended, it was before the Internet existed, and I had heard neither group before. My purchase that day was based solely on the album cover artwork.

As it would turn out, both of these bands were two of the most important bands of their genre.

On July 9, 2013 the *Village Voice* listed the "Top 20 New York Hardcore and Metal Albums of All Time." Agnostic Front's *Cause For Alarm* came in at number 8 and The Cro-Mags' *Age of Quarrel* came in at number 2, being a runner-up only to Anthrax's *Among The Living* in the number 1 spot.

Although times have changed drastically over the last 27 years since these albums were released, dedicated collectors still go after rare 12-inch pressings and collectors represent a small but important part of the industry. These collections are an art gallery of historic media. This holds true on a smaller scale with CD collectors as well, but whether music is released in the form of an LP, 7-inch, CD, or solely in digital format where the album cover only exists as a digital image, please keep in mind the importance of your album cover artwork. It's a huge part of your product and should be well thought-out. It may, after all, become a part of pop culture history.

For all of you bands out there who are considering packaging your upcoming release, you should be advised that the vinyl LP has been making a quiet but deliberate comeback since 2007 and is a nice option to have on your merch table or webstore.

Most importantly, you should keep this in mind:

If a group was trying to sell you a packaged item, and the packaging looked like shit with rudimentary graphics that looked like a child was experimenting with Photoshop for the first time, would you buy this product from them? If it was a CD and the cover looked like a low quality job, what would you assume the recording would sound like?

Your album cover artwork is the first impression your packaged music will make.

Make it count.

CHAPTER ELEVEN

YOUR FIRST RELEASE

You get so caught up in the whirlwind of activities that lead you up to the point in your life where you're ready to record your first album or demo that you never really take the time to look in retrospect into how much development you actually underwent that has taken you to the front door of a recording studio.

Going from a kid who was playing air guitar or lip syncing in front of a mirror to having your first music lesson to the point where you've assembled a band that has written, developed, and rehearsed a handful of original songs that you're ready to commit to a recording proves that you've come a long way.

The overall feeling of excitement about recording your first release has everyone putting forth their best effort and at least for now the band is working together as a single unit.

Now comes the quality control part of the operation.

If you're recording in a professional studio, you're on the clock; and you'll be billed by the hour. Prices in today's market are averaging $30 to $250 an hour depending on the caliber of the studio.

Your entire tracklist along with the vocal performances should be rehearsed day in and day out before you go into a studio. You want to record the best performances you can in the least amount of attempts possible to keep your overall costs down.

A vocalist leafing through the pages in a notebook while recording a performance creates a noise that can't be filtered out of a track if he happens to flip the page at the same time he's annunciating a word. This leads to multiple takes and more billable hours because he wasn't prepared.

A lot of artists insist that they need to be high before they track their performance and nine times out of 10 it ends up sounding like shit.

Writing your music while high is one thing, recording it while high is another, and being intoxicated in general will impair your judgment. This is an undeniable fact.

I have had a rap artist in my vocal booth with a 40-ounce in hand, fucking up every vocal track he tried recording. After hearing "one more time" more than 10 times, I just shut the studio down for the night

Even though you may be paying the sound engineer by the hour, it's frustrating to continually record take after take of the same performance because you showed up to the studio drunk and nobody in any field wants to do double the work.

Furthermore, the recording studio is a professional work environment, not a bar. Many of them have signs telling you there is no smoking and no drinking inside. Smoke gets into equipment and acoustical tiles and it doesn't come out.

The cost of a high quality digital/analog console starts around $66,000 and the engineer doesn't want you resting or knocking your beer over on it.

You also need to keep in mind that what you're doing in the studio is permanent. This recording will outlive the life of your band. You owe it to yourself to set out to accomplish this recording with no fucking around.

In other words, it doesn't take the assistance of 20 of your friends to make a recording.

Unnecessary distractions should be left outside of the door and you should focus on what your individual part is. This is the one time where it's critical that you muster up all of your best qualities and put forth your best effort.

You will first need to record a scratch track. This is primarily a live recording where you're all playing together. Its purpose is really only to catch the timing, the feeling, and the vibe that you have when you're all playing together. This is done sometimes with or without a click track or *metronome* (a device that clicks repetitively at a certain BPM or *beats per minute* and is used to keep all the musicians in time with each other), depending on the skill level of the musicians.

Once your scratch track is done, you may be going to the studio yourself to lay your instrument tracks one at a time for each song until you get them right. You'll hear everyone else on the playback except yourself. This eliminates the *bleed* (unintended noise from other instruments not intended to be picked up by a particular microphone, i.e., picking up the guitar in the kick drum microphone) from the live recording.

After you're done with your takes, it's likely that the engineer will work with you to get the optimal tone that you desire. Once your performance tracks are mixed down, it's on to the next musician.

Once everything is recorded, it's time to mix the songs down.

Appoint a designated person in the band who you trust to attend the final mixdown sessions.

The engineer can't do his job if there are four different opinions on how something should sound. If you have a snare that's cutting through the mix and is way too hot and everyone knows it, you won't get that volume fader turned down if the drummer's in the room. Trust me, I've been there.

These sessions should be done in four-hour blocks or less. Your audio perception becomes diminished over an extended period of time and it's recommended that you not work with audio for longer than this amount of time.

After a long mixdown session, try sleeping with earplugs in and then listen to your mix the next day; you'll be surprised at all the things you didn't hear when your ears were fatigued.

THE DEMO VS. THE PROFESSIONAL RECORDING

Today you have the ability to set up a budget recording studio at home and record yourself there. If you take a few steps to acoustically treat the room you're recording in and purchase good microphones and monitors, you'll have the ability to get a decent demo recording if you follow the steps outlined above.

With the readily available amount of recording software available, it seems that everyone is now recording music, and they're all giving shit away.

That's what they're doing—giving SHIT away.

Going to a good studio with analog outboard gear will make all the difference in your sound quality. Your mixing engineer will be able to take this as far as his set of ears will allow him.

Many mixing engineers have the ability to deliver you a great-sounding finished product, but this isn't the route that the professionals take. They prefer to take the engineer's final mix and take it to an established mastering house to complete the process.

You should require that your mixing engineer finds the songs' "sweet spot" and that he leaves some headroom for the mastering engineer to do his work.

The mastering engineer offers another set of ears to go over the mix, enhance it, correct sonic defects, and ensure overall continuity and commercial quality. Prices on mastering run about $75 to $125 dollars per song, which will ensure you the commercial quality that will put your recording in competition with what record labels are putting out.

A good mastering house will give you two or three versions to choose from and it's a good idea that you take this audio and listen to it in several different environments, such as your car, your home stereo, through your ear buds, and on a P.A. system so you can get an overall idea of how the finished product will sound in each of these different scenarios. I once went to an electronics store and listened to my recording on several different home and car systems in a short period of time because all I had to do was walk from aisle to aisle.

Upon completion—and upon payment—your mastering engineer will provide you with a *Red Book Master* or a high quality CD that a manufacturing plant can make a suitable glass master from.

A high quality recording of a great song has unlimited possibilities. A mediocre or substandard version of the same song has extremely limited possibilities. Take this into consideration when recording and mastering your music, because as I said before, making shortcuts only means that you are cutting yourself short.

It comes into question now if a demo is even a viable option in today's industry. Historically, bands would record demos and rap artists would record mixtapes in an effort to create interest among a potential fan base and to shop to labels.

This is pretty much becoming a by-gone era due to the fact that such a massive volume of music is being created on a daily basis. Many people that I have spoken to in the industry do not want to hear a demo; they want to have a mastered recording of the highest sound quality submitted to them before they will take a group or an artist seriously.

However, once your product is finished, it's time for the next step, which is securing your rights.

CHAPTER TWELVE

COPYRIGHT INFORMATION

American law provides contingencies within its legislation that allow an author of a work the ability to benefit from his or her intellectual creativity for a general effective term of life plus 70 years.

The United States Copyright Office provides a place where claims to copyrights are officially registered under the requirements of copyright law along with providing an official public record of these registered copyrights. It also plays an essential role in the dissemination of these works on an international basis.

Circular 1 from the U.S. Copyright Office states that:

"Copyright is a form of protection provided by the laws of the United States to the authors of "original works of authorship," including literary, dramatic, musical, artistic, and certain other intellectual works. This protection is available to both published and unpublished works.

Section 106 of the 1976 Copyright Act generally gives the owner of copyright the exclusive right to do and to authorize others to do the following:

reproduce the work in copies or phonorecords,

prepare derivative works based upon the original work,

distribute copies or phonorecords of the work to the public by sale or other transfer of ownership, or by rental, lease, or lending

perform the work publicly, in the case of literary, musical, dramatic, and choreographic works, pantomimes, and motion pictures and other audio-visual works, display the work publicly, in the case of literary, musical, dramatic, and choreographic works, pantomimes, and pictorial, graphic, or sculptural works, including the individual images of a motion picture or other audio visual work perform the work publicly (in the case of sound recordings*) by means of a digital audio transmission."

Copyright protection is available to original works the moment they're created in a fixed or tangible form for the author who created the work. If multiple authors have contributed to the creation of a sound recording it's up to the authors to determine who the copyright owner is, be it one author or many and if anyone is deemed a "work for hire."

These questions are all asked in a step-by-step basis during online copyright registration.

Registering your original work is important for several reasons, which are also explained in Circular 1:

> "Registration establishes a public record of the copyright claim.
>
> Before an infringement suit may be filed in court, registration is necessary for works of U.S. origin.
>
> If made before or within five years of publication, registration will establish prima facie evidence in court of the validity of the copyright and of the facts stated in the certificate.
>
> If registration is made within three months after publication of the work or prior to an infringement of the work, statutory damages and attorney's fees will be available to the copyright owner in court actions. Otherwise, only an award of actual damages and profits is available to the copyright owner.
>
> Registration allows the owner of the copyright to record the registration with the U. S. Customs Service for protection against the importation of infringing copies."

Some myths about copyrights need to be debunked as well:

When I was young, back in the dark ages before the Internet when phones were connected to a wall, bands would record their demos on a Tascam 4-track recorder and wanted to make sure that their intellectual property was protected, even if it was recorded in the basement or the garage.

Many of them relied on a "poor man's copyright," which consisted of sealing the finished recording in a tamper-resistant package and mailing it to themselves through the United States Postal Service.

The belief behind this was that the dated postmark is an official time stamp of the first registered record of this recording, and that since the music was sent through the post office—which is a federal agency—and tampering with the mail is a federal crime, that technically your contents are protected under federal law.

Sounds pretty legit, huh? Well think again, buddy.

There's nothing that proves that the contents of your envelope are original compositions or have even been created by you. It's also possible to circumvent the actual postmark time stamp by sending yourself pre-paid envelopes. Therefore, this whole concept and practice isn't what your lawyer wants to have presented to him as evidence if you're trying to sue a major label for using your song.

In regards to the "poor man's copyright," the United States Copyright Office spells its policy out clearly on its website and in its circulars:

There is no provision in the copyright law regarding any such type of protection, and it is not a substitute for registration.

In actuality the actual registration process isn't too daunting, and after your first registration it's actually quite easy.

REGISTERING A COPYRIGHT FOR YOUR MUSIC

For a fee of $55, you can register one song or your whole CD; the registration fee will remain the same per each *work* that you register. A single and a full-length album are both considered a single *work* to be registered. Two separate full-length albums are considered two separate works and therefore require two different registrations and two separate fees.

You want to protect your intellectual property at all times because if you manage to write a hit song, whether it be a musical composition or a full song and you don't have your rights intact, someone can take that material, release it on their own, get rich, and you'll never see a dime.

In the section that follows, you will be provided a step-by-step guide on how to fill out an online copyright registration form. If you need further information on each section, the Copyright Office website will provide you full explanations for each section along with legal statute definitions.

I will only cite extended parts of copyright definitions in this section where I deem it absolutely necessary for you to learn enough about this form to get through a registration on your own and without the assistance of another person.

REGISTRATION

You can register and submit your works online at the *Electronic Copyright Office* website (https://eco.copyright.gov/), where you'll be asked to register as a new user.

A STEP-BY-STEP GUIDE ON HOW TO FILL OUT THE COPYRIGHT FORM

Once registered you will then need to disable your pop-up blocker.

In the left column of the site you will see a category named "COPYRIGHT REGISTRATION." Under this category, click on the link that says:

REGISTER A NEW CLAIM.

You will be asked the following three questions.

1. Are you registering one work?
2. Are you the only author and owner of the work?
3. Does the work you are sending in contain work created only by this author?

These questions will appear as checkboxes on the website; please refer to the following image for an example.

After answering these questions, click on the button below that says "[Start Registration]."

You will be redirected to a page that will require you to follow a simple step-by-step process as you fill out the form.

CHOOSING THE CORRECT FORM

The copyright form that you need to submit is the SR FORM or Sound Recording form.

> *This is used for registration of published or unpublished sound recordings. Form SR should be used when the copyright claim is limited to the sound recording itself, and it may also be used where the same copyright claimant is seeking simultaneous registration of the underlying musical, dramatic, or literary work embodied in the phonorecord.*

> *With one exception, "sound recordings" are works that result from the fixation of a series of musical, spoken, or other sounds. The exception*

is for the audio portions of audiovisual works, such as a motion picture soundtrack or an audio cassette accompanying a filmstrip. These are considered a part of the audiovisual work as a whole.

Please refer to the dropdown menu at the "**Type of Work**" field to access the SR form.

Once you choose the type of work you will be filing, there is also a checkbox at the bottom that will ask you to confirm that you have chosen the correct form.

Once completed with this section, hit the "[Continue]" button on the top of the form to access the next page. Do this for all sections on the form.

You should also take note of the red arrow on the left-hand side that is used as a place marker. This will help you keep track of your progress as you complete the various sections of your copyright registration.

Also, you can access any page of this form quickly by clicking any of the page links in the left column.

TITLES

On the next page of your registration you will enter the official title of your work. Click the "[New]" button for each new title you will be registering.

You will also be asked what type of title you will be registering. There is a link provided on the site to help you make the correct decision. The following image shows you what your options are when choosing a title.

Determining the Title Type

Common Situations

Sample Situations	Select this "Title Type"
Work has only one title	"Title of Work Being Registered"
Song on a CD or album	"Title of Work Being Registered'
Album title if you're not registering the entire album	"Title of Larger Work"
Album title if you are registering the entire album	"Title of Work Being Registered"
Track title on a CD if you are registering the entire CD	"Contents Titles"
Episode of a TV series	"Title of Work Being Registered"
TV series	"Series Title"
One article from a magazine	"Title of Work Being Registered"
Magazine title if you're not registering the entire magazine	"Title of Larger Work"
One book in a series	"Title of Work Being Registered"
Book series if you're not registering the entire series	"Series Title"
Previous or alternative title	"Previous or Alternative Title"

PUBLICATION

The publication page will ask you if the work has already been published and if you have already distributed copies of this work or made it available for public display, such as on Bandcamp, ReverbNation, or YouTube.

Enter your answer using the dropdown menu in the "**Has this work been published?**" field.

PUBLICATION / COMPLETION

On the Publication/Completion page of the form you will be asked to provide the year the work was created and completed. You will only need to provide the four-digit calendar year in this field.

You will then be asked if you have a preregistration number.

You are not required to have a preregistration number to fill out this form and you can leave this field blank if you do not have one.

AUTHORS

This is the area where you list the authors of the music, be it the songwriter, composer of musical arrangements, production engineer, etc. This section will show who is actually involved in the creation of the content that is being registered.

On the first page of this section you will be able to add a new author or you can add your personal registered user information by clicking either the "[New*]" or "[Add Me]" buttons.

If you clicked the "[Add Me]" button, the fields in the following page will be populated with your personal registered user information. As you fill out this form you will begin to see that many of the sections require the same information. Using the "[Add Me]" button will save you some time.

If you clicked on the "[New*]" button, these fields will be blank and you will need to enter the author's information manually.

You will need to enter data for the following fields:

Your full name as an individual or as an organization/band or business (but not both).

You will need to fill out information on the citizenship of each author and the country of domicile (residence) as well.

The year of birth and year of death also is attached to this form.

WORK MADE FOR HIRE

You will also be asked on this page if the author's contribution was a work made for hire.

Whether he was a fill-in musician, provided the beat for the song, was a featured artist, or did the final mix, he can be designated as a work made for hire. The copyright office gives this explanation on its circulars:

> If a work is made for hire, an employer is considered the author even if an employee actually created the work. The employer can be a firm, an organization, or an individual.

In the case of sound recordings, the employer is often the record label.

Be advised though, it is not uncommon at all for the label to own your sound recordings. After all, in most cases they are paying for the studio time and recording expenses along with eating an advance against your sales. But just because a record label owns the copyright to this particular recording does not necessarily mean that they own the copyright to your songwriting or musical compositions; that is a different copyright altogether.

PSEUDONYMS OR ARTIST NAMES

Oftentimes artists, writers, and musicians prefer to have some level of privacy outside of the public eye and adopt an alias, a pen name, or an artist name.

There is a field for this information on the form that will allow you to remain anonymous or pseudonymous to the public and can be submitted in lieu of the actual author information if this is not a work made for hire.

The copyright office explains this in detail as follows:

An author of a copyrighted work can use a pseudonym or pen name. A work is pseudonymous if the author is identified on copies or phonorecords of the work by a fictitious name. Nicknames and other diminutive forms of legal names are not considered fictitious. Copyright does not protect pseudonyms or other names.

If you write under a pseudonym but want to be identified by your legal name in the Copyright Office's records, give your legal name and your pseudonym on your application for copyright registration. Check "pseudonymous" on the application if the author is identified on copies of the work only under a fictitious name and if the work is not made for hire. Give the pseudonym where indicated.

If you write under a pseudonym and do not want to have your identity revealed in the Copyright Office's records, give your pseudonym and identify it as such on your application. You can leave blank the space for the name of the author. If an author's name is given, it will become part of the Office's online public records, which are accessible by Internet. The information cannot later be removed from the public records. You must identify your citizenship or domicile.

In no case should you omit the name of the copyright claimant. You can use a pseudonym for the claimant name. But be aware that if a copyright is held under a fictitious name, business dealings involving the copyrighted property may raise questions about its ownership. Consult an attorney for legal advice on this matter.

Works distributed under a pseudonym enjoy a term of copyright protection that is the earlier of 95 years from publication of the work or 120 years from its creation. However, if the author's identity is revealed in the registration records of the Copyright Office, including in any other registrations made before that term has expired, the term then becomes the author's life plus 70 years.

Once you fill out this form and save it, you will be redirected to another page that will ask you what the author created.

As stated earlier, the author may have created any number of things on the recording, and you can check the box or fill out the "**Other**" field to specify what the author created.

Once you save the author's information and his contribution to the sound recording you can then hit the "[Save]" button and enter data for as many authors as necessary.

CLAIMANTS

The author is the original copyright claimant. However if the work has been transferred to another party such as the band as a business or to a record label, then the record label or entity that will be designated as the owner of the sound recording will be the claimant.

If you are the claimant—or if there is another claimant on your copyright filing—then you will need to either click the "[Add Me]" or the "[New*]" button on the claimant page of the registration form.

The page you will be redirected to will allow you to fill out the claimant information. This is similar to the form you filled out for each one of the authors with the exception of the "**Transfer Statement**" section on the bottom of the page.

Copyright
United States Copyright Office

Form	Pay	Submit Work

Case #: 1-2185030469
Application Format: Standard

Type of Case: Sound Recording

Claimants

‖Save‖ ‖Cancel‖

Claimant's Name Give either an individual name OR an organization name, but not both.

Individual Claimant: OR Organization:

* First Name:
Middle Name: Help
* Last Name:

* Address 1:   State: -Select-
Address 2:   Postal Code:
* City: Country: -Select-

* Organization Name:

If any claimant is not an author, you must include a transfer statement showing how the claimant obtained the copyright.

Transfer Statement: -Select-
Transfer Statement Other:

TRANSFER STATEMENT

Claimants are named only through a legal transfer of ownership and must have ALL of the copyrights assigned to them by written agreement or other form of legal transfer. This is a provision that is usually covered in any standard recording agreement or record contract. Below is a section from the Copyright Office explaining transfer statements:

Transfer Statement

Transfer information is required if this claimant is not an author. Please indicate how copyright ownership was acquired by this claimant. "By written agreement" includes "by assignment" or "by contract." "By inheritance" (which may be "by will" or "by intestate succession") applies only if the person from whom copyright was transferred is deceased. If necessary, select "Other" and give a brief statement explaining how copyright was transferred. If the transfer is by operation of law other than by inheritance, select "Other" and state the means, for example, "by operation of state community property law".

Transfer Statement for Single Serial Issue

Five transfer statements are offered from which you should pick the one appropriate to your situation, if applicable.

- *By written agreement(s) with author(s) named on the application/certificate*

- *By written agreement(s) with individual contributors not named on the application/certificate*
- *By written agreement(s) with authors named and contributors not named on the application/certificate*
- *By written agreement*
- *Other*

If you elect to name all of the individual contributors to the collective work as authors on the application, and the rights to those contributions were transferred to the claimant, you would pick the first option.

If you elect not to name individual contributors as authors but still wish to claim contributions wherein the rights were transferred to the claimant, you would pick the second option. If you elect to name some but not all of the individual contributors to the collective work as authors, and the rights to those contributions were transferred to the claimant, you would pick the third option.

NOTE: If both compilation and contributions are being registered and the rights to both were transferred to a non-author as claimant, you would pick the first or third option.

If none of these options apply, you may select "other" and provide the specifics in the space provided. Please note, a transfer statement must include the manner in which rights were transferred (e.g. by assignment, by contract, etc.).

LIMITATION OF CLAIM

If a song on your album was previously released as a single, is previously registered, or is part of the public domain or creative commons, you may need to limit your claim.

This will make the distinction between the previously registered material and the new material that you need to copyright on your sound recording.

If you do not have any preregistered or preexisting material on your song or album release you can simply hit the "[Continue]" button and skip this step.

Copyright United States Copyright Office

Form	Pay	Submit Work

Case #: 1-2185939469
Application Format: Standard

Type of C

eCO Navigation Tips

Limitation of Claim

(<< Back) (|| Continue >>)   (|| Save For Later ||)

Links	Completed
Type of Work	✓
Titles	✓
Publication/Completion	✓
Authors	✓
Claimants	✓
> Limitation of Claim	
Rights & Permissions	
Correspondent	
Mail Certificate	
Special Handling	
Certification	
Review Submission	

Complete this screen to limit your claim if this work contains or is based on previously registered material, previously published material, material in the public domain or material not owned by this claimant. The purpose of this section is to exclude such material from the claim and identify the new material upon which the present claim is based.

If your work does not contain any preexisting material, click "Continue" to proceed to the Rights and Permissions screen.

Material Excluded: Previous Registration: New Material Included:

☐ Sound Recording   1st Prev. Reg. #: [   ]   ☐ Sound Recording

Other: [   ]   Year: [   ]   Other: [   ]

2nd Prev. Reg. #: [   ]

Year: [   ]

RIGHTS AND PERMISSIONS INFORMATION

You can add contact information for people seeking permission to cover your work or use it for other purposes.

You can fill this out as an individual or as a business just like the other forms you have seen during this process.

This information will be shared publicly, but you are not required to fill out this section.

Copyright United States Copyright Office

Form	Pay	Submit Work

Case #: 1-2185939469
Application Format: Standard

Type of Case: Sound Recording

eCO Navigation Tips

Rights & Permissions Information (Optional)

(<< Back) (|| Continue >>)   (|| Add Me ||) (|| Save For Later ||)

Links	Completed
Type of Work	✓
Titles	✓
Publication/Completion	✓
Authors	✓
Claimants	✓
Limitation of Claim	✓
> Rights & Permissions	
Correspondent	
Mail Certificate	
Special Handling	
Certification	
Review Submission	

You may provide contact information for a person and/or organization to be contacted regarding copyright management information or permission to use this work.

Important: If you prefer not to provide personally identifying information, you may list a third party agent or a post office box.

Individual: Organization:

First Name: [   ]   Organization Name: [   ]

Middle Name: [   ]

Last Name: [   ]

Email: [   ]   Address 1: [   ]

Phone: [   ]   Address 2: [   ]

Alternate Phone: [   ]   City: [   ]

State: [-Select- ▼]

Postal Code: [   ]

Country: [-Select- ▼]

140

CORRESPONDENT

This section of the form is mandatory and is used by the Copyright Office if they need to contact you for any reason regarding your submission.

MAIL CERTIFICATE

In the mail certificate section of the form you will be filling out the same fields as you have in many of the other sections, but this section dictates who the actual copyright certificate will be mailed to.

Once mailed, this will be your official copy. It will take some time to arrive so don't anticipate getting it soon. However, when you do receive it, it is time stamped with the actual time you delivered it to the Copyright Office—or in this case, the time that you actually uploaded it.

SPECIAL HANDLING

Special handling of your copyright registration is available for an additional fee if you have extenuating circumstances and fit the criteria required allowing you to file for special handling.

These criteria are usually used in the event of pending litigation or pending release deadlines that must be met.

CERTIFICATION

This is the section where you certify that you are legally authorized to register this copyright under your name or under your company's name, by authorship or ownership of exclusive rights.

REVIEW YOUR SUBMISSION

Once you complete the certification section, you will be allowed to review a summary of the entire copyright registration form as a whole.

This will allow you to look over your data and ensure that everything is filled out as you had intended prior to making your submission.

If any changes need to be made, you must make them prior to submitting this form. Once this form is submitted you will not be able to make changes or corrections.

If you are unable to make your corrections immediately, you are allowed to save this as an open case and log in at a later time to complete your registration.

Once you deem that everything is filled out correctly and completed to your satisfaction, hit the "[Add to cart]" button on the top of the Review Submission page.

CHECKOUT

As with any e-commerce website, once your product is in the cart you proceed to the checkout area of your online purchase by clicking the "[Checkout]" button.

If you are filing multiple copyrights at once, please be sure that you have the right case in your cart prior to moving forward.

CHOOSE PAYMENT METHOD

After moving to the checkout area of your cart you will be asked if you want to change your order or to choose your payment method.

Your payment options will be to pay from either a deposit account or from a credit card/ACH. Select your choice by clicking on the appropriate button.

REDIRECT TO PAYMENT SITE

Once you choose your payment method you will be redirected to a page that will inform you that you are going to leave the electronic Copyright Office website and enter the U.S. Treasury site (pay.gov) where you will be submitting your payment. *Please refer to the image on the following page.*

After making your payment you will be redirected back to the copyright website where you will be able to upload your deposit.

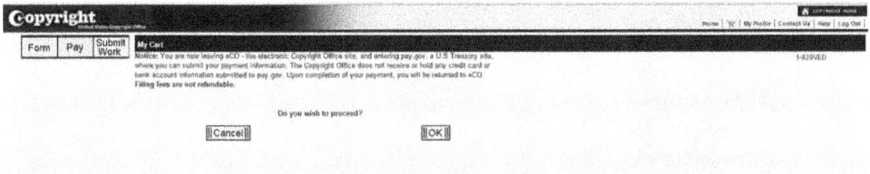

SUBMITTING PAYMENT

In the event that you are paying with a credit card, Pay.gov will ask you to fill out a credit card payment form.

This is a standard online payment form that has two sections. You are only required to fill out one of them.

ACH

On the top of this form is the ACH form, which basically allows you to pay by electronic check. You will need to give an actual valid check number from your checkbook if you choose this method. Once you make a payment using ACH, you need to write "VOID" on the actual paper check in your checkbook to avoid using it a second time by mistake (your bank will stop this anyway).

CREDIT CARD

The bottom half of this form is for credit and debit card processing.

System Message

- The system has populated the Payment Date with the next available payment date.

Online Payment Return to your originating application

Step 1: Enter Payment Information 1 | 2

Pay Via Bank Account (ACH) About ACH Debit

Required fields are indicated with a red asterisk *

Account Holder Name:	_____ *
Payment Amount:	$55.00
Account Type:	_____ ▼ *
Routing Number:	_____ *
Account Number:	_____ *
Confirm Account Number:	_____ *
Check Number:	_____

Routing Number   Account Number   Check Number

⑆0 26 946 7 8 3⑆: ⑈9 24 3 76 7 3 90⑈ 1 2 3 4

Payment Date: 03/03/2015

Filing Fees are NON-refundable.:

Select the "Continue with ACH Payment" button to continue to the next step in the ACH Debit Payment Process.

[Continue with ACH Payment] [Cancel]

Pay Via Plastic Card (PC) (ex: American Express, Discover, Mastercard, VISA)

Required fields are indicated with a red asterisk *

Account Holder Name:	_____ *
Payment Amount:	$55.00
Billing Address:	_____ *
Billing Address 2:	_____
City:	_____
State / Province:	—— ▼
Zip / Postal Code:	_____
Country:	United States ▼

VISA MasterCard AMEX DISCOVER

Card Type:	_____ ▼ *
Card Number:	_____ * *(Card number value should not contain spaces or dashes)*
Security Code:	_____ * Help finding your security code
Expiration Date:	▼ * / ▼ *

Filing Fees are NON-refundable.:

Select the "Continue with Plastic Card Payment" button to continue to the next step in the Plastic Card Payment Process.

[Continue with Plastic Card Payment] [Cancel]

Note: Please avoid navigating the site using your browser's Back Button - this may lead to incomplete data being transmitted and pages being loaded incorrectly. Please use the links provided whenever possible.

It is important that you do not hit the "[Back]" button while making a payment. If you interrupt this process because of a slow connection or lack of patience you may break the data chain, which will result in you paying a fee and getting nothing accomplished.

UPLOADING YOUR DEPOSIT

After you make payment you will be directed back to the copyright website to a page where you can upload your music one track at a time.

You will be asked to provide the name as it appears on the album and then to browse for the actual file on your computer.

You will do this for each track on the album and also for the album cover artwork—yes, that can be copyrighted on this form as well.

Once you have all of this data in queue you can then upload it.

Double and triple check everything you do in this process so you don't submit any errors.

Once your deposit is made it is final.

The information listed above should be enough to get you started with the process of protecting your work the correct way. You're also allowed to send a physical copy of your work to the Copyright Office, but their mail service is severely disrupted due to the off-site mail screening that is done for all parcels sent to Capitol Hill; this will create an additional three- to five-day delay in the delivery of your works and registration. There is a larger fee of for this method of registration, and your registration date will be effective on the date and time that it's stamped as received by the Copyright Office.

YOU ARE YOUR OWN WORST ENEMY

In closing this chapter I feel a strong need to address the artists reading this book who are eager to get their music heard.

Your rights can't protect you from yourself if you start emailing your new release to everyone that you come in contact with. Should you become popular, the digital files that you were once so eager to send out in the beginning will eventually bite you in the ass and undermine your sales because they most likely will be found on file sharing sites, and once your best songs are available for free you'll hardly be able to sell a fucking thing.

COPYRIGHT TROLLS

Once you file a copyright, your music becomes a matter of public record. Before you ever receive your certified copy of your copyright you will be getting mail from record labels on Hollywood and Vine.

Don't get too excited; this doesn't mean that you are getting your big break.

This is a standard fishing expedition from a very limited amount of companies that cast lines out as far as they have access to in order to see if they can find something valuable to suit their own needs.

The language on the letter you will receive will say something on it to the effect of "we are not interested in signing you, but we may be interested in your music or songwriting."

ONLINE PIRACY REMEDIES

Once anything is placed online, there is a potential threat of piracy. In most cases you can find out if your content is being downloaded illegally and without your authorization by simply doing an online search of your band or artist name and song title.

Should you find out that your rights are being infringed upon, you can initiate a takedown process somewhat quickly.

THE INTERNET COMPLAINT CENTER

The IC3 or *Internet Crime Complaint Center* is co-sponsored by the Federal Bureau of Investigation (FBI) and the National White Collar Crime Center (NW3C). Complaints filed via this website are processed and may be referred to federal, state, local, or international law enforcement or regulatory agencies for possible investigation.

The IC3 has a complaint form you can fill out on their website (http://www.ic3.gov/). This is an intake form for various types of online crimes, but should the nature of your complaint be related to online piracy, the information you provide in this form will initiate what is known as a DMCA *(Digital Millennium Copy Right Act)* Takedown Notice.

I have personally seen results effectuated within 24 hours of registering a complaint resulting in entire websites being shut down and permanently removed.

However, this action itself still doesn't address the copyright violations that actually occurred as a result of the piracy.

Although the Feds can take down content, remove the sites hosting it, and initiate criminal prosecution in these matters, you will still need to pursue a civil action if you intend to seek remedy for your monetary losses.

In each instance of copyright infringement, the court can actually award statutory damages ranging from no less than $200 to no more than $150,000 per violation. If these statutory damages apply, your reward will actually far exceed the original damages you have incurred.

To fully understand the scope of where a situation like this can go, whether you are the offender or the victim, please read this excerpt from Section 504 of the *Copyright Law of the United States of America and Related Laws Contained in Title 17 of the United States Code.*

Section 504 of the Copyright Law of the United States of America

§ 504. Remedies for infringement: Damages and profits

(a) In General. — Except as otherwise provided by this title, an infringer of copyright is liable for either —

(1) the copyright owner's actual damages and any additional profits of the infringer, as provided by subsection (b); or

(2) statutory damages, as provided by subsection (c).

(b) Actual Damages and Profits. — The copyright owner is entitled to recover the actual damages suffered by him or her as a result of the infringement, and any profits of the infringer that are attributable to the infringement and are not

taken into account in computing the actual damages. In establishing the infringer's profits, the copyright owner is required to present proof only of the infringer's gross revenue, and the infringer is required to prove his or her deductible expenses and the elements of profit attributable to factors other than the copyrighted work.

(c) Statutory Damages. —

(1) Except as provided by clause (2) of this subsection, the copyright owner may elect, at any time before final judgment is rendered, to recover, instead of actual damages and, an award of statutory damages for all infringements involved in the action, with respect to any one work, for which any one infringer is liable individually, or for which any two or more infringers are liable jointly and severally, in a sum of not less than $750 or more than $30,000 as the court considers just. For the purposes of this subsection, all the parts of a compilation or derivative work constitute one work.

(2) In a case where the copyright owner sustains the burden of proving, and the court finds, that infringement was committed willfully, the court in its discretion may increase the award of statutory damages to a sum of not more than $150,000. In a case where the infringer sustains the burden of proving, and the court finds, that such infringer was not aware and had no reason to believe that his or her acts constituted an infringement of copyright, the court in its discretion may reduce the award of statutory damages to a sum of not less than $200. The court shall remit statutory damages in any case where an infringer believed and had reasonable grounds for believing that his or her use of the copyrighted work was a fair use under section 107, if the infringer was: (i) an employee or agent of a nonprofit educational institution, library, or archives acting within the scope of his or her employment who, or such institution, library, or archives itself, which infringed by reproducing the work in copies or phonorecords; or (ii) a public broadcasting entity which or a person who, as a regular part of the nonprofit activities of a public broadcasting entity (as defined in section 118(f)) infringed by performing a published nondramatic literary work or by reproducing a transmission program embodying a performance of such a work.

(3) (A) In a case of infringement, it shall be a rebuttable presumption that the infringement was committed willfully for purposes of determining relief if the violator, or a person acting in concert with the violator, knowingly provided or knowingly caused to be provided materially false contact information to a domain name registrar, domain name registry, or other domain name registration authority in registering, maintaining, or renewing a domain name used in connection with the infringement.

(B) Nothing in this paragraph limits what may be considered willful infringement under this subsection.

(C) For purposes of this paragraph, the term "domain name" has the meaning given that term in section 45 of the Act entitled "An Act to provide for the registration and protection of trademarks used in commerce, to carry out the provisions of certain international conventions, and for other purposes" approved July 5, 1946 (commonly referred to as the "Trademark Act of 1946"; 15 U.S.C. 1127).

(d) Additional Damages in Certain Cases. — In any case in which the court finds that a defendant proprietor of an establishment who claims as a defense that its activities were exempt under section 110(5) did not have reasonable grounds to believe that its use of a copyrighted work was exempt under such section, the plaintiff shall be entitled to, in addition to any award of damages under this section, an additional award of two times the amount of the license fee that the proprietor of the establishment concerned should have paid the plaintiff for such use during the preceding period of up to 3 years.

Rap artists that I worked with in the past did not understand at first why I was so adamant about only using original music and were curious as to why I avoided mixtapes like the plague. The fact of the matter is that as a rule of law, using uncleared samples of music should be avoided at all costs. In reality, a website like DatPiff is ripe for the possibility of getting itself shut down, and although many artists may be working under the misconception that no violation occurred since it was a free download, I can assure you, my friends, that this is not the case. But this is a subject that I will cover later in the book in the chapter on Rap and Mixtapes.

CHAPTER THIRTEEN

PUBLISHING, PERFORMANCE RIGHTS
AND ROYALTY COLLECTION AGENCIES.

In the preceding chapter, we covered the importance of *registering your works.* At some point in your career, your music may become published, broadcast, or licensed. This chapter will provide a brief overview of how royalties are collected for your published works.

Companies such as BMI (Broadcast Music Incorporated), ASCAP (American Society of Composers and Publishers), and SESAC (Society of European Stage Authors and Composers) are known as *performance rights organizations* or *P.R.O.s.*

These companies serve as liaisons between copyright holders and the *licensees* who are using their copyrighted works publically.

The specific purpose of these organizations is to collect performance royalties for copyrighted music that is performed *publically.* They do not collect *mechanical royalties,* which are royalties payable for music that is sold to a consumer. They also do not collect licensing fees on your behalf.

It should be clearly stated here that although registration and membership with one of these P.R.O.s is a good preparatory step in your career, merely registering yourself as an artist and registering your music with any of these organizations is meaningless unless you're actively trying to license your music or performing live.

PUBLISHING DEALS

The first step in this process is for you to find a publisher. Music publishers have libraries of music from artists that they use to license to third party *music supervisors.*

Standard publishing deal structures have been known to be based on a 50/50 split in ownership of the song. Half of the song ownership is known as the writer's share, of which you would own 100 percent, and the other half of the song is the publisher's share in which the publisher would own *100 percent of the publisher's share* or the other 50 percent of the song.

If it sounds a little confusing, it is best summarized as 100 percent of writer's share + 100 percent of publisher's share represents 100 percent of song ownership split 50/50.

A publishing agreement will typically involve you submitting an agreed-upon amount of songs to the publisher for a term. During this term, you allow the publisher the exclusive right to publish the songs that are part of this agreement. Should the publisher be successful in placing your music in film or television they will then have the perpetual right to half ownership of that song, and will continue to try to obtain additional placements for this song as often as they are able to do so.

Should the publisher be unsuccessful in placing one or more of your songs during the term, those unplaced songs and all rights attached to those songs will be returned to you and you will retain 100 percent ownership of the unplaced song(s) (100 percent of the writer's share and 100 percent of the publisher's share as well).

SYNC LICENSING

Licensing your music to a third party is most commonly known as *sync licensing*. These licenses are most commonly used for movies, cable television shows, commercials, video games, elevator music, and background music in restaurants, retail stores, skate parks, health clubs, and many other businesses that serve the general public.

As an example, when a movie company or a television series is looking for a song that fits a specific scene they will contact a publisher. If the publisher is able to place your music in this movie scene, you will be offered an upfront licensing fee that will be split between you and the publisher.

The writer's share of the synchronization fees is paid directly to you (the copyright holder) and will allow the *licensee* (person, business, or entity wishing to use your music) the ability to perform the song it has obtained the license for publically in a predetermined format.

After your music is licensed to one of these companies and you collect your upfront licensing fee, you'll be owed a performance royalty for each time this music is performed publically via the media they've embodied your music in or the broadcasting channels they use to play your music.

These royalties are payable quarterly from your PRO (ASCAP, SESAC, or BMI). Keep in mind: you must have these published titles registered with your PRO in order to collect these royalties.

PERFORMANCE ROYALITES FOR LIVE EVENTS

You are also due a performance royalty every time you perform your music live.

Whether you're a headlining act, a supporting act, or a local opener and whether you're playing a small, mid-sized, or large venue, P.R.O.s will collect a performance royalty for you based on the amount of registered songs you perform live. This in itself is another revenue stream for you as an artist. Do not forget about this if you're planning a tour.

BMI Live pays quarterly on songs from your setlist that are registered in their database. You can enter your setlist online by logging into your BMI account or you can use the BMI mobile app. You're also allowed to go back up to six months prior to input data from your previous performances.

Another viable revenue stream within the reach of most independent artists is Internet radio.

ONLINE RADIO AND DIGITAL PERFORMANCE ROYALTIES

Digital performance royalties are collected and dispersed by a company called SoundExchange.

Digital royalties are fees that service providers such as Pandora, SiriusXM, and webcasters are required by law to pay for streaming musical content. These royalties are paid by the services to SoundExchange, and accompanied with playlists of all the recordings played by the service provider.

SoundExchange takes these payments, allocates the fees to the recordings according to how often each song was played, and then pays the featured artist(s) and copyright owners of those recordings. More than 90,000 artists and over 28,000 sound recording copyright owners have registered with SoundExchange. They've paid out more than $1.5 billion in royalties since their first distribution.

Each and every one of these companies are advocates of artists' rights and are very client-friendly.

As you'll see throughout this book, there's much more to this business than just recording and releasing music. Taking the time to follow all of these steps will help you ensure that you get the absolute most out of your creative content and intellectual property.

The reality of this business is that you'll want to have multiple revenue streams set up, which in the beginning will be consistently paying small amounts of money into one combined pot.

As you increase in popularity, these streams increase in revenue and all feed the same account, which will ideally become quite lucrative for you as an artist.

PRO AND ROYALTY COLLECTION AGENCIES

For royalty collection inside the United States of America, any of the following can be used. The first three on the list are performing rights organizations, and the fourth, *SoundExchange*, is a digital broadcasting royalty collection agency that can be used along with either of the first three.

1. The American Society of Composers, Authors and Publishers www.ascap.com

2. Broadcast Music, Inc.www.bmi.com

3. The Society of European Stage Authors and Composers www.sesac.com

4. SoundExchange - www.soundexchange.com

CHAPTER FOURTEEN

COMPULSORY LICENSES AND CLEARING SAMPLES

Another area of music publishing is clearances. Artists who cover or use samples of other artists' songs in their music are legally required to get these samples cleared.

In the United States—and only in the United States—there exists a thing called a *compulsory license.*

A compulsory license allows artists to legally sell their rendition or "cover" of another song based on a set royalty payment scale. A compulsory license is obtainable for any song that has already been previously recorded and sold with the consent of the original musical composition copyright holder.

Unlike a traditional music copyright license, the terms for a compulsory cover license are established by the U.S. Copyright Office rather than the artist or record label. This includes set royalty percentages and payment schedules. Also, a compulsory cover license does not require negotiations with the original musical composition copyright holder. In other words, you can obtain the right to sell a cover version of a song without ever having to gain the consent of the original artist.

The legal statute regarding compulsory licenses is as follows:

> *Section 115 of the Copyright Act provides a compulsory license to make and distribute phonorecords once a phonorecord of a work has been distributed to the public in the United States under authority of the copyright owner, subject to certain terms and conditions of use. Such a license includes the right of the compulsory licensee to make and distribute, or to authorize the making and distribution of, a phonorecord of a nondramatic musical work by means of a digital transmission, which constitutes a digital phonorecord delivery. The Copyright Office's regulations set out in detail the procedures that must be followed to operate under a compulsory license.*
> *See www.copyright.gov/title37/201/37cfr201-18.html*
> *and www.copyright.gov/title37/201/37cfr201-19.html*

It should be noted that compulsory licenses are not mandatory. An artist has the option of negotiating a direct arrangement with the copyright owner to license their music. However, even if the copyright owner is unwilling to negotiate, the licensee can still obtain a compulsory license.

Compulsory licenses will only allow you to sell music with these samples within the United States. This will not authorize you to sell your music with embedded samples in territories outside of the United States. There is no legal provision for a compulsory license outside of the United States; they just don't exist.

There is an intricate chain of foreign Performing Rights Organizations that you will have to navigate in order to secure foreign licensing for songs that are covers or that include samples, and these territories have the right and the option to charge you fees set at their sole discretion.

Even if you are clearing samples directly with a company such as Sony ATV or Universal Music Publishing Group, they will only issue compulsory licenses within the United States. They have offices worldwide, but you will need to deal with these foreign offices individually as I previously mentioned.

COMPANIES THAT WILL ISSUE COMPULSORY LICENSES

There are many companies that will issue compulsory licenses for cover songs including the song publishers themselves. However, if you wish to obtain licenses in a quick turnaround time for a small fee and an agreement to pay a predetermined royalty rate to the composer, you can contact any of the following companies:

- Harry Fox Agency – harryfox.com
- Rights Flow - rightsflow.com
- License Music Now - licensemusicnow.com
- Easy Song Licensing - easysonglicensing.com
- The Music Bridge - themusicbridge.com
- Song File - songfile.com

SAMPLES

Sampling is the process of taking a segment of an existing musical work and incorporating it into a new composition. This is mostly prevalent in rap, hip hop, and electronic music.

Clearing samples is much more complicated than cover songs since they can involve two separate copyrighted works and multiple rights-holders, such as record labels for the *sound recording* and music publishers for the *music composition* and are always subject to negotiation.

Unlike compulsory licenses, if you chose to rework the sample prior to using it you would still need permission from the publisher for your "rendition" of the original derivative work. As Congress has made no provision for this in copyright legislation, your only avenue of obtaining permission to use this sample is to negotiate with the publisher, who has the option and the right to reject your request in its entirety.

If your request is rejected and you still choose to use this sample in your music, you would be liable for copyright infringement and could be sued for substantial amounts of money.

Because sampling is so popular in urban music, many record labels and publishers have contacts who handle these requests.

MOVING THE SAMPLING LEGAL ISSUE FORWARD

There are many people in the industry who recognize the value of sampling and its importance as an ingredient in urban music.

Several discussions on this topic at music conferences have resulted in a push within the industry to make Congress draft a provision in its legislation recognizing this practice and setting parameters for its usage.

However there are many complexities to this issue that need to be addressed prior to even being able to draft legislation for this matter. Until then, sampling any part of any copyrighted song—no matter how short the length of a sample you use—**is still illegal** and an infringement of someone's copyright. If you heard otherwise, **you heard wrong.**

CHAPTER FIFTEEN

THE PRESSKIT

EVERY ARTIST'S PROFESSIONAL CALLING CARD

Having a presskit offers a concise look into who you are as a band in a short summary.

This is the professional way to present information about your act to anyone and everyone in the industry. Booking agents, record labels, music directors, and many others will expect you to be able to deliver this item to them on short notice.

It is, for all practical purposes, your resume.

You're a part of an insane rat race where millions of artists are trying to get the attention of only a few thousand people that can advance their career to the next level. Your first communication with these people is very important.

YOU AND YOUR GROUP ONLY HAVE ONE CHANCE TO MAKE A FIRST IMPRESSION.

We now live in a day and age where you can contact any person in any country with one keystroke and many times your first impression with one of these people will come across on one of their computer screens in the form of an electronic presskit attached to an email.

Be concise and grammatically correct with the information you present. This is such a basic fundamental building block of communication and professionalism that there's really no excuse for making shortcuts here. Communication is a skill in itself and if you present your presskit with horrible spelling and grammar it most likely won't be read in its entirety. If you're sending out a *press release* and it isn't formatted in such a way that's accepted by the Associated Press and other publications, your chances of having it published are non-existent.

The spelling, grammar, and format are merely the delivery vehicles for the content, which is equally important.

Whether the person receiving your presskit is a music director at a college or terrestrial radio station, a booking agent, promoter, record label executive, or a magazine editor, he's receiving multiple emails like yours every day. So when he opens that email, it had better contain some type of successful content if it's going to stand out from the rest. If your story isn't inspiring and has some degree of success to it, then what's the motivation for a magazine editor to print it?

Most magazines are looking for stories to print about artists and bands that are either successful or on the cusp of success. Are you doing anything significant? Is your group even relevant in today's market? Can you consider yourself *visible*, *well-known*, *or trending*? Think about this, because you'll be competing for editorial space with acts that have already become a *household name* or soon will be.

So let's examine the structure of what you'll be sending these industry contacts;

There are a few different reasons for having a presskit, and for each of these reasons, the layout and information may need to be a little different.

DEVELOPING YOUR ONESHEET:

First we'll look at the onesheet, which in a sense is a standalone presskit used for specific purposes. This is a type of summary that focuses on specific information and is generally used for one of the following specific purposes.

This is an integral piece of information for your marketing and it should present itself accordingly. Below are a few examples of what is contained in one of these.

FOR AN ALBUM RELEASE:

This is historically referred to as the onesheet. This is the product information sheet that the record store looks for when they open the box, but it is not a packing slip. It is a summary of the release that the label has prepared. It includes specific information related to that release, such as the artist name, album title, genre, UPC (universal product code), release date, number of tracks, track listing, promoted songs or singles, SLRP (suggested list retail price), album cover artwork, press photo, similar artists (if this is a debut release), a short band biography, recent notable accomplishments, distributor information, and record label contact information.

FOR DIGITAL MARKETING:

This will include all of the information in the album release, but will also require your first week's global sales projections, tour dates, YouTube views, Facebook and Twitter links and amount of likes and followers, pending press, confirmed press, your radio marketing campaign, any TV or public appearances you have scheduled, and your international marketing plans.

This detailed summary of your marketing plan needs to be submitted with your release if you're trying to get front page advertising on digital retail sites such as iTunes and MySpace.

Depending on who you're distributing your digital titles through, this may or may not be available to you.

I'll cover this in a little more detail in the section on marketing.

FOR SELF PROMOTION:

If you're sending out an EPK (electronic press kit) in an email blast or to various sources, you can provide the information such as what's available on the onesheet with the exception of the UPC number, SLRP, and the distributor information. How you present this information is your preference. I personally design these all in Photoshop and my layouts have varied from what you would see in a PowerPoint display to a layout similar to what you may see in a magazine advertisement.

QUICK RESPONSE CODES (QRC)

I've even gone as far as embedding QR (quick response) codes into the design in an effort to give the consumer a direct hassle free link to the point of purchase. You can have a QR code generated for any URL and do it for free online at GOQR.ME.

I have not only gotten a lot of compliments from people who have seen me implement QRCs onto my printed media, but I have also seen them integrate these themselves into their print media, including flyers and business cards.

BALANCE AND MINIMALISM

I have provided the following two images as examples of my graphic design work to provide a contrast in flyer design. As this is a teaching book, I will also share with you a flaw in the layout of the first of the two images.

In an effort to create interest and awareness of the underground artist in the first image, I provided a lot of information on the flyer which was built from a onesheet that I created. However, after an informal meeting with an advertising professional from The Leo Burnett Agency here in Chicago, I was told that this was excessive by design standards and that the piece should have actually had minimal text and information placed on it.

I was told that an ad's primary function is to grab consumers' attention and that if they are interested they will follow through on their own accord.

I defended my position by stating that in order to create interest, information did in fact need to be provided. But after going a little further in the conversation, we came to a point that we not only agreed on, but that I knew all along, and that is that *the majority of the American public is too motherfucking lazy to read*.

Below is the flyer that we discussed, and although I did my best to balance my layout, visually there was just too much information and clutter.

Now here is an example of a onesheet that I designed for a Chicago metal band named Never We See utilizing some of the information that I have provided in this chapter. This was specifically formatted to send to a talent buyer and has a more moderately designed layout.

ASSEMBLING THE NECESSARY ELEMENTS OF YOUR PRESSKIT:

The following guidelines will provide you with some information on the things that should be included in your presskit.

WRITING YOUR BIO:

There are several points that I feel I need to make here. First of all, this is the way that you're selling your act to someone. This is the only information that people are going to know about you, and this may be your first and last interaction with them. Make it count.

Provide the recipient with current and relevant information about your music career only. Avoid information about how you were born into a broken home, the projects, or in a trailer park; this doesn't concern me.

If you're a gangster rap artist, your bio shouldn't tell me that you were charged with a murder rap. I've actually received presskits that read like this. This information is a big red flag about you and tells me nothing about your accomplishments as an artist. Do you actually think that this paints you in a positive light and is going to sell me on you?

All that information tells me is that you're a tough guy. Well, you know what? I know a lot of tough guys too. Many of them are currently in the penitentiary or in the graveyard, which means that I can't put any of them on tour right now. So where do you think you stand when you send me that info?

Even though you may feel the need to let people know that you have street cred, this makes you look like you may become more of a liability than a good investment.

Next, be sure to avoid fluff. The use of multiple descriptive adjectives doesn't make the direct object any more appealing. I don't need to read about how you're destined to change the game or about your "epic, game-changing, powerful new release." I get it; you have a new release. Where was it mixed? Who mastered it? Were they industry names that ring big bells in your genre?

Adding info regarding other people attached to your project is fine, if you do it in passing. Make sure that you don't turn your bio into their bio.

This presskit is how you need to make your first impression. This information needs to be centered on your accomplishments. Have you recently toured to promote this album? Who were the headlining acts? Tell me some factual information that shows me your relevance.

Also avoid phrases like "If given the chance, I will prove that..." Describing yourself in this manner immediately shows that you haven't established yourself as an act yet, and it also directly states that you still have something to prove. I have an immediate mental reaction to these types of statements that makes me inclined to reject the submissions to which they're attached.

An artist that exudes confidence, on the other hand, is someone to whom I may be inclined to respond.

You should also include brief and concise information regarding the members' former projects if they're noteworthy.

Include some of your current project's career highlights and important show dates with well-known acts and any press or awards that you may have received.

If you haven't gotten to this point in your career yet, keep it related to music. How long have you been performing, who did you study under, and is this your debut release? Find a way to make this a short but interesting peek into your life as an artist without grasping at straws just to put something on paper. That will be blatantly obvious to the reader and it will appear that you're trying too hard.

Keep in mind that your bio will *always* be a work in progress. It will be constantly updated as your career moves forward. If your bio lacks content and history at this time, then go out and make some history. Start booking shows, release some music through a distributor, and get involved in as many music-related events and activities as possible because all of these activities combined will help you construct a current and working bio.

You should stay active enough in your career to the point that you can take some of the larger, more significant events in your career and place them in your bio as career highlights.

You'll want to do this in a short summary. Being concise means presenting only the facts and you will not want to send a book along with your presskit; a few short paragraphs will suffice.

Also, do not lie. As tempting as it is to make yourself look better and boost your image in front of industry professionals, just don't do it.

Once the fact-checking is done behind your submission and the information doesn't add up, your credibility is shot. Should you try to submit a legitimate presskit to these people in the future, chances are it will be discarded because they won't waste their time researching you since they'll already expect another bunch of lies.

Keep in mind, a lot of people know each other in this business. So keep your integrity.

PRESS, INTERVIEWS, AND WRITE UPS:

This is your presskit—you should be providing some official press along with it. Bands and artists are asked often for interviews. If you haven't been asked, there's no rule that states that you can't go out and attempt to obtain some reviews, interviews, or write-ups. Providing hyperlinks to your interviews and reviews in your *EPK* will also help you legitimize your act and give the person you submitted it to extra reading to take into consideration.

HIGH QUALITY PHOTOGRAPHS:

When they say that a picture is worth a thousand words, there's a certain reality to that.

When I view a band photo, I look for certain elements that the band or artist most likely never took into consideration when they chose the photo. I've developed a keen eye for this over an extended period of time.

Since about the time I was in third or fourth grade, I began purchasing issues of *Circus* Magazine, which at that early age was the only window that I had into the music industry. This was before the Internet and before MTV, and I found it in the magazine section in my grocery store.

Many of you are too young to remember this magazine, as it printed its last issue in 2006, but it employed some of the biggest names in rock journalism and rivaled *Rolling Stone* and *Hit Parader*.

The iconic band photos presented in this magazine were from the largest touring acts in the industry, and as a child it was easy to get pulled into these live concert photos. They conveyed to me the large-scale production involved in one of these events, and when I see an awesome live photo of a group it's because certain elements have been included in the photo.

Testament performing live. Photo credit: Justin Koteff - Red Flame Photography

LIGHTING AND SCAFFOLDING:

How does this appear in the photo? Are the vivid colors hitting the subject in the foreground without blowing out his image? Are the scaffolds visible in the background of the photo to show the viewer some depth and convey to him that this is indeed on a very large stage? Was there a fog machine on that captured the colors from the can lighting? Were any professional grade filters used by the photographer?

ILL Patientz live in Las Vegas. Photo credit: Justin Koteff - Red Flame Photography

In the following picture you see a prime example of how these same elements are important for band photos even when taken in a more modest sized venue.

AGHORI Live at the Cheyenne Salon, Las Vegas, NV March 1st 2014

THE SUBJECT:

Is he centered in the photo? Are his arms or head cut off? Have you caught him "in the moment?" Is the subject exuding some passion in his performance that was captured in this photo? Is he airborne? How is the contrast and the focus? Was any type of specific shutter speed used to obtain an effect?

Wretched performing live. Photo credit: Eric Munnings-Victory Records

Photos taken like the one above and the one below show how the perfectly timed shot can really convey the passion these artists exude while performing live. In order to capture the right moment, you may need to set a camera in sport mode and take 15 to 30 shots at a time to grab one perfectly timed photo.

Other elements that are critical to getting that shot are the angle in which you choose to take your shot from and the lighting at the time of your shot.

Circa Sik in mid-flight. Photo credit: Justin Koteff - Red Flame Photography

Blood In Blood Out. Photo credit: Amanda Nowman Photography

Wretched performing live at Mayhem Fest. Photo Credit: Eric Munnings-Victory Records

THE FOREGROUND: Can I see that there are people at this event? Can I see that there's a large crowd of people in front of the stage? Is the artist or musician propping up his leg on a floor monitor? Is he engaging the crowd?

Having a professional photo that embodies the elements listed in this section will give the person looking at your presskit the impression that you're at home on big stages and that you've reached a competitive level in your career.

A good photographer will often shoot 150 to 300 photos of you and give you the 20 best ones, which are usually of magazine quality or close to it. The work involved in getting these shots, along with the photographer's artistic eye and his or her experience is what you are paying for.

Dustin Keimig, Lead singer of AGHORI engaging the crowd during their 2014 Southwest Slaughter Tour

174

Islanders vocalist Mikey Carvajal leaning over the barricades to get closer to the audience. Photo credit: Eric Munnings-Victory Records.

Not every photographer has the ability to capture the things that I mentioned in my bullet points, because although they may have taken some classes, if they don't attend live music events often, and if they lack creative vision, then you won't get these types of photos.

I've seen photographers that have only taken close-up photos at large events and I've also seen photographers who have only taken wide angle shots of performers at empty bars with a stage that was only six inches off of the ground. Both of these photographers failed miserably at their jobs and don't understand how to capture images at live events.

THE BAND PHOTO

On the opposite end of the spectrum, you may want to consider attaching a black and white band photo to your presskit. You need to be selective when you do this, because again, first impressions mean everything and people make assumptions based on what they see.

The historic 8x10 glossy photos of the band members from head to toe look like shit in my eyes; there's really nothing artistic about a photo that has the subjects standing side by side and shoulder to shoulder.

Some of these photos look more like a police department lineup photo than a promo shot, and it's my personal advice and professional opinion that you avoid photos like these at all costs.

A good band photo in my eyes has a background with some depth or significance that isn't too busy as to where it's going to take away from the subjects in the

8x10 Glossy Band photo taken in 1996, Photo credit: Revolt Amps

foreground. Band members should be shown from the waist up and staggered in position throughout the photo with shorter members in front and taller members in the back. The picture below with the skull backdrop, staggered members and interactive pose to allow for the logo placement embodies all of these elements.

Promotional photo for the band Protest. Photo Credit: Justin Koteff-Red Flame Photography

This will create a sense of depth and fill up the picture frame nicely. If you're taking these yourself, then take a lot of them. It may take 100 shots or more to get that one perfect photo.

LINKS TO YOUR MUSIC:

When you send out emails and electronic presskits, make sure you have the hyperlinks enabled in the email. We're all creatures of convenience and if I can't click on it and go right to it, there's a 50 percent chance that I won't even bother taking the time to copy and paste the link into a new browser window.

Just as importantly, make sure that the destination URL goes directly to your music and not a landing page. I've had this happen several times when following links to Soundcloud. I ended up on an artist's profile page, was unable to listen to any music, and moved on to the next submission without a second thought. Remember, people are busy, and somewhat impatient. Try to make things convenient and easy for them.

Also avoid providing links to Hulkshare, Dropbox, or other file sharing or downloading sites. If someone who doesn't know you is reviewing your submission, he may be reluctant to download these files because you aren't a trusted source.

Keep it to streaming and direct links to the music. Assume the person you've sent your music to has 50 other emails to look at before getting to his other tasks. Time is valuable, so streamline your presskit.

I myself usually have a huge pile of work on my desk, so when I open your email, I want as much key information in front of me as possible without the need to go hunting.

I've gone over countless submissions and I can honestly say that it takes a very, very short period of listening time to determine if a song is a hit or a flop. Have your best material available for streaming. Long intros are unnecessary. If you're a rap artist, I really don't need to listen to a full minute of you giving shout outs to your boys and claiming your set. I want to hear a song that jumps right in and kicks my ass musically.

I can tell if a song is a hit in three to five seconds. That is not an exaggeration. The right production quality coupled with the right musical progression will jump out at you whether you've heard the lyrics yet or not. If the song is catchy then you don't have to keep listening to determine if you like it or not; you just do. Good music is good music, and hit songs are hit songs.

I'll give every song enough time to go through a verse and a chorus (hook), some iffy songs may get double that time, and I may listen to a second song to make sure I'm drinking in enough of your work to give it a fair listen.

If the song is bad—and I mean garbage—it doesn't take long to figure that out as well.

Bad, redundant lyrics or off-key singing and bad compositions will send your music and your presskit to the recycle bin without much of a chance.

Another thing that will get your submission passed over is if you send me a cover or a "remix."

If a band sends me a cover song, this is worthless to me. All I can ascertain from this is that you can attempt to sound like someone else; whether you do it well or not makes no difference to me. Cover bands are not—and never have been—on my radar, and no label will sign you if you don't have any original material. We want to hear something NEW.

I find it amusing when rap artists promote a new mixtape release and they post something to the effect of, "listen to me fuck up this dude's song." Well you know what dude, you really did. Leave that shit alone; have some pride and send me some original music. When Wiz Khalifa released "Black and Yellow," I had countless submissions over the instrumental for that song. I would hear the first few notes of that song, say to myself *"here's another one,"* and hit the "Delete" button immediately. They beat that song to death and it still kept showing up in my inbox.

If a song is a hit—no matter what song it is—recognize it and appreciate it for what it is. Let it be an inspiration to you and try to write something better.

You should only send original music in a submission. If something you send to a label gets them to call you, they are going to want to release that song. Make sure you have exclusive rights to it. I've contacted artists who sent me hit records just to find out the rights were no longer available. This resulted in the retraction of a potential contract offer. It's the hit song that gets the artist signed; keep this in mind.

CONTACT INFORMATION AND SOCIAL MEDIA LINKS:

With the exception of your home address, I would put every method of contact in here that you're comfortable with (cell phone, email, etc.).

Social media links are pretty much a standard now, as they also allow the recipient a look into your fan base size and your interactions with them along with being an additional platform for communication.

If your presskit is being sent to a booking agent, he may actually place your Twitter handle or other social media information on his event flyers as well.

SENDING YOUR PRESSKIT:

The best way to distribute mass mailings is via use of a bulk email client such as Mailchimp. These automated email clients will send an individual, personally addressed email to each of your contacts, one at a time over the course of a few hours. They cost about $15 a month.

If it's not cost-effective for you to utilize an email client, there's no reason that you can't send the emails yourself.

If you're sending out bulk emails yourself, you can categorize your contacts in your email server by folder. Every email provider has the option of adding new distribution groups to your contacts list. Once you create a group, you can add specific contacts to that group. These groups enable you to send one email to multiple contacts with one keystroke. This can save you hours of sitting behind a computer.

It's very important for me to mention at this time that you need to respect the privacy of your contacts' email addresses. When sending out these emails, you need to use the BCC (blind carbon copy) field. This will hide every email address from public view and your recipients will only see their own contact information in the "TO:" field; you can use your own email address for this if you need to.

Also, in the subject line of your email, it is considered bad email etiquette to use all capital letters; most email that has spam content is formatted like this to grab your attention.

Be sure to proofread every single email you send out. There's a very good possibility that you might send out mail addressed to the prior or wrong recipient when going through the monotony of sending out mass emails.

You don't want to be misidentified as a spammer, because this can very easily have you internally blacklisted by the company's email host that you are trying to contact. Once that happens, none of your mail will get through. Keep this in mind because more likely than not, you'll eventually need to email this person in the future.

Be specific, clearly identify yourself, and briefly state your purpose. Include any time-sensitive deadlines if absolutely necessary. Do this in the least amount of words possible.

The language contained in this subject line determines if the email will even get opened or not.

Make it short, concise, and interesting.

CHAPTER SIXTEEN

THE INTERVIEW

For a new band or artist, getting the news that you will be conducting your first interview is exciting and is always a big deal.

Even for a seasoned musician, the first interview regarding a new project means that you're obtaining press that will enhance your visibility and give you additional content with which to beef up your presskit.

You'll either have an unscripted interview—in which case you'd better think quickly on your feet—or you may be emailed a series of questions which you'll be asked to fill out and return when completed.

Either way that it's presented, it's amazing how many people will actually still fuck this up.

If you're asked a question, give an answer. You should not only just give an answer, but you should give the most in-depth and detailed answer as possible.

It's always better to give the reporter more than he needs for each question; he can always edit extraneous information later to narrow down the interview before he publishes it. On the other hand, one thing he cant do is add depth and content to the answers that you provide.

The last thing you want to do in an interview is give an answer that is only one sentence long.

Or even worse, a simple yes or no answer.

If the answer is a simple yes or no, well then why? What happened behind the scenes to lead you to this decision? Elaborate on this answer with as much pertinent information as possible, because this is all the interviewer has to work with.

Don't assume that he has done—or will do—additional research on you. That research goes into an article, not an interview. Assuming things in any aspect of your life will almost always get you in trouble.

An interview, unlike your presskit, is going to be a little more of an open format so its okay to delve into your personal life or the details of the crazy things that have happened in your past that made you who you are today.

Similar to what I mentioned in the last chapter, this may be the first way that a reader will be able to get to know who you are and what your band does. Make it count. Try to connect with your potential fans and listeners; make yourself interesting enough for them to warrant a desire to follow up on you with additional research.

Do you have a certain member of your group who is charismatic? Does he naturally have the floor when speaking to a group of people? If so, this is probably the guy you want to be your band's spokesperson.

This involves being somewhat of a politician. You need to know how to deflect or redirect questions where the answers could be damaging or may paint you in a less positive light, and at the same time you need to have the ability to go into great detail on the activities and accomplishments that make you look appealing.

Not only is the interview about you, but it's for the benefit of the reader and it's for your fans. Most importantly, it's for the people who haven't yet heard you. These are the people that you want to win over.

You want to get readers to care about more than just your music; you want them to take a genuine interest in you as a person, and you can accomplish this by giving an honest, in-depth interview without being shallow or superficial.

Try to make a positive, long-lasting impression on everyone you meet in your life.

CHAPTER SEVENTEEN
THE PRESS RELEASE

Not to be confused with the *presskit,* the press release is a completely separate tool used for disseminating information to the media.

PURPOSE

Your press release is your official statement or account of any news related to your activities that is edited and correctly formatted in a manner that meets the print standards of newspapers, magazines, and other news media outlets. It is then delivered to them so it can be released to the general public.

CONTENT

The premise of this document is simple in nature. It is composed to summarize the *who, what, why, where, when*, and *how* of your news story.

While drafting your release, you need to ask yourself if what you are writing is actually newsworthy—is there an actual public interest in what you are writing about?

It is important that you critique your story while writing it, because if the answers to the two questions that I asked you in the last paragraph are both *no,* then your chances of having a staff writer or editor publish your story are slim to none.

Also, be sure to focus more on fact than fluff when composing your press release; again, this is an official statement.

GRAMMAR

It is mandatory that you follow the rules of grammar and composition when drafting a press release; failure to do so will result in it being rejected by all media outlets.

If you are unable to do so, hire someone to draft the press release for you and then have it edited by someone else if the writer is not accredited or educationally qualified to handle the job.

All newspapers are written at a sixth grade reading level, and the U.S. Department of Education's National Institute of Literacy released a study in 2013 that showed that 21 percent of U.S. adults read at under a fifth grade reading level. So if you struggle when reading a news article then you shouldn't be writing your press release yourself.

AN ALL TOO COMMON UNACCEPTABLE MISTAKE

One thing that absolutely drives me up a fucking wall is hearing people speaking publicly about their artists and not being able to reference them in the proper part of speech. So, for the record:

- Artist – /ärdəst/ or /är-tist/ singular: in reference to one person.
- Artists – /ärdəsts/ or /är-tists/ plural: in reference to more than one person.
- Artists's – /ärdəsts-es/ or /är-tists-is/ this is bullshit – not a proper noun form: this word doesn't exist in the English language, so stop using this term because you sound like a fucking moron.

Again, I cannot stress enough that this must be done correctly. So if you need to hire someone else to do this for you, get it done right, or don't do it all.

FORMAT

All press releases follow a specific format; this is a standard and uniform format that is widely accepted by media outlets.

- **_Release Date_** – The first thing you should have on the upper left hand side of your press release is the release date. If the press release is meant for immediate distribution, the words "FOR IMMEDIATE RELEASE" should be placed here. If the press release is meant to go out on a specific date after you deliver it, the words "HOLD FOR RELEASE UNTIL [insert date here]" should appear here.

- **Headline** – Similar to a newspaper article, this is a short concise description of the content of your press release. Avoid using all capital letters and be sure to make it sound interesting.
- **Summary or sub-headline** – This is a more detailed description of your headline. You should elaborate on your headline, but do so without repeating the information that was listed in the headline. Magazines and news websites shun redundancies which are also prone to getting your press release rejected by an editor.
- **Orientation** – This is the location and the date of where the news is generated from and appears at the beginning of the body.
- **Body** – This is where you provide the details of your event. You are not writing an article; you are writing a press release. In the first paragraph you should provide the *who, what, where, when*, and *why* of the story. Supporting details and quotes can go into the paragraphs that follow. Your paragraphs should be truncated to four sentences or less and you should avoid referring to yourself in the first person (I, me, we, us). You can see in the example press release below how I avoided referring to myself in the first person.
- **Company or contact info** – The end of your press release should have your contact information to allow people to follow up with you or contact you regarding your release. Since mine was for a product release, I opted to forego including my contact information and instead placed links to where this book could be purchased online, which was what I originally intended.

An example of a press release is provided on the following page.

EXAMPLE

For immediate release.

The Music Industry Self Help Guide. Taking Your First Steps towards Trampling Over the Obstacles in an Independent Market.

The first volume in a series of music education guidebooks that provides valuable resources for emerging artists along with the building blocks necessary to create leverage and equity in their career.

Chicago, IL March 23rd 2014

The Music Industry Self Help Guide – Taking Your Steps towards Trampling Over The Obstacles in an Independent Market is the first literary contribution from author Michael Repel, a longtime working musician and independent record label owner.

After playing with many bands, mentoring artists from multiple genres at music conferences, and receiving multiple submissions from unprepared artists and bands, Repel thought it necessary to provide a book for emerging artists that addressed all of the items that are creating a huge disparity between working musicians and those who are trying to get their foot in the door of the industry.

Deeply rooted in the DIY (Do it yourself) mentality, this book provides a realistic approach to multiple aspects of career development that are overlooked by many entry level and intermediate artists.

With real world statistics, and at times, some hard doses of common sense, this book is loaded with personal experience in addition to the tools and concepts that every artist needs to move forward in the independent music market.

Written in an honest, conversational, thought-provoking, and inspirational manner, this book will eliminate a majority of the guesswork that aspiring musicians will face and prepare them for the realities of today's music industry.

Preview The Music Industry Self Help Guide where it is currently available for purchase: on Amazon Kindle, Apple iBooks, Google Books, Kobo Books, Sony Books, Samsung Reader, Nook, and Blio.

A paperback edition is available for international mail-order on the book's website: http://themusicindustryselfhelpguide.com (282 pages, 6 x 9 US Trade size.) ISBN: 978-0-9915155-0-9

Amazon Kindle: http://www.amazon.com/dp/B00JBNP656

Apple iBooks: https://itunes.apple.com/us/book/music-industry-self-help-guide/id850533215?mt=11

PRESS RELEASE DISTRIBUTION

Once you finish your press release you need to get it to the media outlets. If you have established a mailing list, you can send the release out to all of your industry contacts yourself.

I have without a doubt gotten the most effective results by hand-picking the magazines I wanted visibility in and contacting them directly myself. This has resulted in magazine reviews and on-air radio interviews, and it cost me nothing.

You also have the option of using a press release distribution service that will send your release out for you. I have used a few of these services myself in the past and they have worked for me with limited results.

But be forewarned; just because you paid for a service, there is no guarantee that any news or media outlet will publish your story.

Other companies I have found that distribute press releases—some free of charge—are listed below.

1. newmusicweekly.com
2. marketwired.com
3. free-press-release.com
4. 1888pressrelease.com
5. express-press-release.net
6. newscomm.de
7. usprwire.com
8. prlog.org
9. pressbox.co.uk
10. mononews.ca
11. ereleases.com
12. briefingwire.com
13. send2press.com
14. massmediadistribution.com
15. uwire.com
16. gorkana.us
17. prunderground.com
18. outbrain.com

For a fee, some of these companies will also edit and format your press release for you prior to distribution.

DISTRIBUTING NEWS THROUGH YOUR NETWORK

It's critical that you have the solid online presence established as I told you to do earlier in this book; these will be the places where you disseminate your news pieces yourself.

While the press release has the potential to obtain placement for your news in magazines and in music news blurbs, this will only be seen by the people who view these sites and those with whom they choose to share the news in their networks.

Studies have indicated that more people spent time on the social media sites that I listed earlier in this book than they do on news sites.

It is imperative that you put forth the extra effort to repost your news story on your social media accounts and artist profile pages after it appears on a reputable website.

This will ensure that *your supporters* see the news. These are the people who will repost these news links for you.

You need to face the facts that although this book may be providing you with tools that you may be using for the first time, it doesn't mean that you will be instantly propelled to the front page of *Billboard* Magazine. Many people who don't know who you are will simply overlook your story. Keep in mind, nobody ever picks up a newspaper and reads the entire thing from front to back.

As an emerging artist you will need to push your visibility as far as you can. Until you reach a tipping point, become relevant, and start trending, you can expect limited reposts and limited results from these activities, however it is absolutely necessary that you follow through on this and repost your story yourself on the pages that I told you to create.

Not only will this ensure that your news gets saturated throughout your network, but also because these posts will become archived on the Internet and will come up when people search for you in the future.

If you have this online history by the time you reach out to booking agents, managers, or record labels, your chances of getting a response will increase because these entities will research you

…but if they find nothing, they will assume that you have accomplished nothing.

CHAPTER EIGHTEEN

CONSIGNMENT

Getting your music into a record store has always been a huge deal for up-and-coming artists.

One would think that without having the long-established relationships that record labels have with brick and mortar stores, or having a distributor that is willing to distribute your physical content, chances of obtaining CD placement in the racks of record stores is slim to none.

This, however, is not the case, and this is a revenue stream that you can totally control on your own.

There is a term called *consignment,* which is defined in its most practical application as the practice where you, as an independent musician, consign your CDs and possibly your merch to a record store to sell with the agreement that payment will be made to you for completed sales and that unsold items will be returned to you within a specified time frame.

This can be arranged quite painlessly by contacting your local record store and filling out a consignment form which will include your contact info, artist or band name, album title, genre, Suggested List Retail Price, UPC number, brief description of the product, and release date. This is also the same information that you include on your onesheet as we discussed previously.

If your CDs are delivered to the store prior to your release date, the store will not place them on the shelves until that specified date.

Upon your first delivery, most independent record stores will agree to take between three and five of your CDs and agree to keep them on the shelves for up to 90 days. If your CDs start selling, they will notify you when they are out of stock so you can replenish it, and depending upon the volume of your sales, they may request you to supply them with a larger amount.

BAR CODES

In order for you to sell your CDs (or vinyl records) in stores you will need to have them barcoded. A professional CD manufacturer such as *DiscMakers* will issue you a barcode and a UPC as part of your order.

This allows the store to track its sales and inventory, and in the event that you have your CDs in a chain store, they can transfer copies to other stores they manage if a customer orders one from another location.

You can also register your UPC with Nielsen SoundScan, which allows Nielsen to track your digital and physical sales combined.

In the event that you are in a position to negotiate a record contract with a label in your future, having the ability to present Nielsen sales figures will offer incontestable proof of your ability to sell your music and how many units were actually sold.

FOLLOW UP

It is important that you practice due diligence when leaving your CDs at a store on consignment.

Many of these stores have a drawer full of consignment sheets, and some of the places where I have sold my CDs in the past have completely lacked any form of organizational skills whatsoever.

They also have a tendency to prioritize the content from major labels and major distribution chains. This is because these CDs usually bring in money and need to be replenished at a higher frequency than those of local bands and artists.

My advice to you is to call every 30 days initially to see how your CD is selling; if the store starts moving units of your material and they sell out, than start calling in more frequently.

After all, this is your money that they are playing with; so make sure that you collect your revenue when it is available to you.

CHAPTER NINETEEN

MARKETING AND PROMOTING YOURSELF

ARE YOU DOING EVERYTHING YOU CAN?

Until you have a 5-foot tall powered light box strapped to your back, don't try telling me that you are promoting your act harder than everyone else.

BEING MENTALLY PREPARED FOR SUCCESS

I've mentioned *visibility,* and I've mentioned *momentum*, now let's talk about creating them.

If you're an unproven, unbroken artist, remember this: no matter how much money you have, or what kind of strategy you have, you're embarking on a rocky journey to the top. Make sure you keep your eyes and your feet on the road; if you slip up, there's a strong likelihood that you won't make it any higher up the mountain.

Going from being an unknown, to an underground artist, to a recognized independent artist affects different people in different ways psychologically.

Some artists loosen their grip on reality when they start to obtain visibility or see that becoming well-known is within their reach. They get big-headed, sloppy, lazy, and begin to neglect their obligations to the people that put them there—their management and their fans.

The thing to keep in mind is that even if you appear to be doing big things on the underground or independent music scene, it's irrelevant unless you're selling records and filling venues. Even if you're managing to have an impact in your local independent market, where does that put you nationally? Where does it put you internationally?

Although you think you're the big fish in a little pond, you're actually still a very small fish in an ocean.

Marketing can be done at any time. You'll get no argument out of me regarding this fact; but it should always have a purpose, such as creating a revenue stream like an album release or a live event. In this chapter, however, our focus will be on the marketing that can be done for an independent album release.

Having a marketable record with the recording costs covered, the masters finished, and the copyrights registered is obviously step one, so let's make sure that we have the stage set for this operation.

An initial press release should be sent through your networks alluding to a tentative release date.

ADVANCE PREPARATION FOR YOUR RELEASE

MUSIC VIDEO

Filming a video for your single will create a marketing driver (or platform for which you can use to gain visibility for yourself) for your release. Outside of yourself and your live performance schedule, this may be the single most important marketing tool that you will have for your release.

This platform is your *loss leader* for your album sales; it will cost you some time and money to put a quality music video together but this visual media is the go-to sales driver for album sales.

It is critical that the timing of this video release coincides with your album campaign. Should your video drop on the street release date of your album, you will be able to maximize your earning potential by directing impulse buyers into a point of purchase. This is achieved by simply having a link to where this music is available on iTunes or other sales platforms in the "About" section of the video.

Not only is YouTube now considered a music search engine by some, but it has embedding codes that allow you to repost your music video on your websites, social media accounts, blogs, Facebook groups, and Google communities that you're a member of which can create instant visibility far and wide while simultaneously creating a potential revenue stream from each of the pages where you have posted it.

Artists that don't understand that an album release is about planning and disciplined timing ultimately suffer from lackluster sales. It is imperative that you coordinate all aspects of your strategy if you want to realize revenue and successful results from your release.

Having all of the pieces of the puzzle in your hands and getting them to run together like the gears in a Swiss clock is the only way to bring yourself to the surface of several million other artists who are all trying to figure this game out as they go along.

LEAD TIME

Advance planning is the key to a successful release. Setting a release date for the Friday (the day of the week that all new music is released) four to six weeks from today will allow us plenty of time to organize and execute our *lead time* strategy.

Lead time refers to the period of time leading up to a predetermined and confirmed release date. Once this day is confirmed, an official press release should be sent out through all your networks, including all of your social media and email lists.

You should have your lead time marketing strategy and your album release marketing strategy, budget, and marketing drivers all in place before you even submit your release to your distributor. If you submit a comprehensive digital marketing strategy for your release with your music, you'll have the possibility of obtaining a featured spot on iTunes, MySpace, and other digital music retail sites for the first full week of your release. This was covered in the chapter on presskits

GET YOUR ALBUM REVIEWED

Your presskits should be assembled ahead of this time so that you can attach the UPC codes as soon as they're available and get them out the door. Submit them, along with a formal request to have your music reviewed, to all the magazines, websites, and bloggers you have in your network who actively review music. This will give the magazines the adequate time that they need to review the material so they can publish the album review the week of its release.

Submit your single to Internet, satellite, college, and terrestrial radio stations as well as DJ pools. Having a copy of the *Indie Bible* (an incredible resource guide for emerging artists (www.indiebible.com)) on hand will give you a large and current list of stations that will accept your submissions. Once your submissions have been made, you should make a positive effort to ensure that things start running like clockwork from this point on.

The single that you're submitting to everyone should be the best song on the album, and if it has explicit content you'll need to have a version that's edited for radio. You will severely limit any type of visibility you're trying to obtain if you don't do this. The FCC will not allow explicit content on the airwaves and this rule applies to all college radio stations on the AM and FM dials.

Post your new songs (not all of them) on social media and on all the sites I mentioned in Chapter Eight and begin to hype up the release date.

I placed a strong emphasis on developing a network on these artist websites and social media accounts because without a developed network, anything you place on these sites will be useless if you haven't already created an audience for your activities.

All of your marketing during an album release's lead time should redirect to a preorder point of purchase or a squeeze page that requires a call to action.

THE SQUEEZE PAGE

The squeeze page is a page on your website where you direct all of your traffic prior to an album release. These pages are primarily set up to create an incentive for your consumer. They are an essential part of your lead time strategy and can serve you in many ways.

OFFER FREE SHIT

Everyone likes free shit, so as part of your lead time advertising, offer a free download or free admission to one of your events in exchange for a *verified email address.*

Keep in mind that people will often put bullshit email addresses on your mailing lists at live shows, and if given the chance they will do it online too. There are plugins for your website that you can use to verify email addresses and they will send a response email back to the sender asking him or her to verify that this is a real email account.

The reason for this exchange is because once you obtain a person's email address you can do what is known as *Direct To Consumer Marketing,* which simply means having the ability to email a potential consumer, at will, about any of your updates, This is hands down the most efficient and cost-effective way of reaching people.

Not only should the squeeze page be set up as a place for you to obtain email addresses, but it can also serve you in several other ways simultaneously.

This page can also offer something special that won't otherwise be commercially available such as a preorder bundled limited edition T-shirt, CD, and signed poster package, or something of that nature. Outbound links on the menu bar of the squeeze page can also direct your customers to where they can preorder your digital album.

PRE-ORDER SALES

Amazon.com does preorders for MP3s and for on-demand albums. It's wise to take advantage of this by redirecting some or all of your lead time advertising to your album's preorder page. This will satisfy the urge of any impulse buyers and ensure your revenue for your first week sales projections.

You can also offer a discounted album price the week leading up to a release to encourage presales. This will provide consumers with an incentive to purchase your album and any good digital distributor will be able to coordinate this for you.

During your lead time, this may be the place where you want to redirect your YouTube traffic at least until your release date, where you'll have the option of continuing to provide them the link to Amazon or changing it to a link to iTunes.

SHIPPING THE PRODUCT

Your lead time also buys you a few weeks to place your CDs or vinyl in local brick-and-mortar record stores and to ship your physical CDs and the product information sheets to stores in the other cities where you've successfully branded yourself and created a demand for your product. This can be done either as coordinated through your distributor or through any consignment avenues that you have already established.

The product information sheet along with a summary of your marketing strategy may persuade a record store manager to provide you with in-store advertising if you've included promotional material with your delivery. Record store chains such as F.Y.E. can coordinate end cap displays and in-store promotions such as poster visibility. These, however, will come at a price.

You should keep your product availability centralized to where people actually know who you are. Just because your CD is in a store does not mean people are going to buy it, especially when they've never heard of you. Shipping CDs to places where there's no demand for your product costs money, and unnecessary expenditures can derail a marketing campaign when funding is critical.

GUERRILLA MARKETING

Your street team will be responsible for executing the hand-to-hand direct marketing and street-level promotions of your marketing campaign. This is also known as *canvassing*.

Printers can provide you with discounts for bulk orders. Placing orders of 20,000 pieces and up will make your advertising affordable and provide you with enough material to disperse over a large area.

If you have teams in other cities that are aggressive and can be depended on to do a large amount of advertising, you may be better off sending the digital files to printers in their city. This will eliminate the cost of postage and they can just pick up the promotional materials when they're ready.

In order for them to work effectively, there needs to be oversight, follow-through, and accountability. Successful street teams have a chain of command and coordinators. Materials need to be dispersed in a timely manner for upcoming shows as well as album releases. When managing a large-scale marketing campaign on a national or international level, you'll want things executed with military timing and precision.

If you've been utilizing your social media and email lists correctly, and your street team has been hyping you up, then your fans should be eagerly anticipating your upcoming release.

Always strike while the iron's hot.

MAXIMIZING YOUR EFFICIENCY

Take the time to do dedicated research to make sure that your teams hit target locations and areas.

Hitting your demographic or *target market* in these campaigns is critical to its success.

Promotions in general cost a lot of money, and what looks like a massive pile of promotional material will dwindle away very quickly, so be sure to make every calculated effort possible to get this material to your target consumer.

You can't afford to throw everything at the wall just to see what sticks. Casting too wide of an unfocused effort is just an exercise in futility and will result in a conversion rate of zero. This type of approach will exhaust your marketing budget and supplies and will leave you unprepared should a major promotional opportunity come up such as a large concert or music festival.

I've provided my teams with addresses of certain businesses, dispersal routes, and maps in the past. I've hand-picked my placements by determining the best way to hit my target consumer based on a few simple questions: What's my target consumer listening to? Where does he go to listen to this music? Where does he acquire or purchase this music? Where does he shop? Where is his recreational time spent? What other activities is he involved in?

Identifying all aspects of what defines the subculture of your fan base is an extremely effective way of determining where and how to market and advertise your release.

Sometimes the youngest members of your team can be the most effective. Having someone with a book bag full of flyers, bookmarks, and sampler CDs inside a school with 1,500 impressionable young listeners can create a buzz quickly.

Your street teams should be placing any material you supply them with in these areas, as well as in business districts with a high amount of foot traffic.

Businesses in trendy or 'hip" areas usually always have a designated flyer area or bulletin board where you can place your promotional material oftentimes without the need to ask permission from the owner or store manager.

Your team should also always be handing out flyers at live events within your genre of music including your own shows.

Make it a goal to mirror this effort in every city that you have access to or that your group has been performing in because this is how you will create a demand for your product in more than one market.

You'll also need to take the personal responsibility to always be prepared to further your brand. You should have with you at all times a stack of your band's stickers at every venue you play—whether it's every weekend in your hometown or in every city that you visit while on tour. Hitting up the green room, the washrooms, and the street lampposts outside the venue will ensure that your brand has visibility long after you leave that city for the benefit exposure to the rest of the people that attend shows at those locations.

Independently, some of these things may seem inconsequential to you, so I want you to take a moment to consider what your visibility would be like if you did indeed have all of these platforms running in play simultaneously. These points that I'm presenting are more than just suggestions; they are the critical components of an advertising and marketing campaign that are proven to work and are tailor-made to make yourself visible in front of the people that you want to hear your music.

Your advertising should be made as simple as possible. The general public is too lazy to read and too much text will scare some people away. Just look at all of the advertising around you; it's usually stripped down to one basic message. Use a design that pops and attach limited information to it. Don't clutter it with extraneous information. Make your point and be done with it. If your advertising is visually appealing to your target consumers, they'll follow up on their own.

MARKETING YOUR PRODUCT BY PERFORMING LIVE AND TOURING

Your performance schedule should complement this advertising and also your marketing plan overall because you are the single most important marketing driver for your music and the best way to market yourself is to perform live.

You should have a tour planned for each and every album that you release. This has historically been the standard practice for every album release. If you want to do this successfully, you'll need to be playing in more than one music market. That is a fact.

This ongoing combination of promotions and touring is the essence of branding and is the core foundation of a band's sustainable presence. Never forget this.

Tours are usually scheduled after the release date, and a good way to kick one off is with a CD release party. We'll discuss how to set up a live event later in this book. Invite the key players in your local music market along with any media contacts that you can reach out to and try to get some publicity for your release and your pending tour.

INFILTRATING OTHER MARKETS

Once you're on the road, you'll need to coordinate your tour dates with the local record stores and radio stations if you want extra visibility in those markets. In-store appearances are a great way to connect with your fan base if you've developed one in these cities. This is also a good way to get your finger on the pulse of what's happening musically in that city.

The guy behind the counter at an independently owned record store may be able to provide you with more information about that city's music scene in a few minutes than you could have ever found out on your own.

A majority of the marketing that I do in other cities begins with a stop to a few predetermined spots where I post my notices and ask the locals a few questions regarding the music market that I'm targeting. This leads me to several other locations and events that I wouldn't have known about if I didn't take the time to talk to people.

On-air appearances are another way to create a last-minute boost in attendance at your show in another city. If the radio stations that you have access to are at the college level, you may be able to do an after party on-campus in a fraternity or sorority house and get the word out to the student body that is tuning in. Tapping friends who have gone away to school is also a great way to spread awareness of your release on campus as they're already integrated into the college community.

Perhaps your friends may be the ones who are providing you with the contact information for the radio station at your college. If they aren't, you can refer to the *Indie Bible* and in most cases actually provide your friends with their school's radio station information yourself.

Having teams increasing your visibility in these cities in the weeks leading up to your tour dates should be coordinated with your efforts to secure press in local newspapers, magazines, blogs, etc. Mostly all of these publications and webzines will require at least four weeks' notice of your performance date, so you need to plan and coordinate in advance. Everything needs to run on strict and disciplined timing.

By this time, your album reviews should be published, adding to your confirmed press.

ONLINE MARKETING

In the chapter on building an online presence I told you that the social media and Internet profiles that you need to develop for visibility would also be used as a launch-pad for your marketing campaigns.

Every concert date, press release, album review, interview, and other confirmed press that you can obtain needs to be used to update these pages.

There are platforms that have been created that can allow you to run all of your social media profiles from one source. Companies such as Sprout Social can allow you to manage between 10 and 50 of these profiles from their website. This will help you manage your time more efficiently so you can attend to other aspects of your marketing campaign. Obviously there are fees associated with this, which is just another reason that you need to create revenue streams for yourself.

Beefing all of this up with regional or targeted Internet marketing that focuses on your specific demographic via pay-per-click advertising will leave you with a multi-pronged marketing strategy in place. As you can see by what I've laid out above, these different promotional efforts complement each other. If coordinated and executed correctly, they will provide you with overlapping layers of visibility. Execute this campaign with organization and discipline, because no matter what level you're at in your career, *organization and discipline win*.

MARKETING OVERVIEW

So now you've executed a precise marketing plan on all platforms, have teams working for you in several major metropolitan areas, have confirmed press in a few magazines, have a full performance schedule, and maybe even a regional tour pending if you are not already on one.

At this time you feel like you've done more than every other band or independent artist you know, and at this point, the odds are that you probably have.

So is it time to celebrate?

No.

Besides the fact that the average millennial youth has the attention span of less than 140 characters—which is subsequently the length of a tweet—and the fact that you're in competition with every other musician out there to capture the interest of someone's limited attention span, advertising conversion rates in general are very small.

The reality is that the return rate on all of the marketing and advertising that you've done is going to be well under 1 or 2 percent of your total reach.

ONLINE CONVERSION RATES

In online marketing and pay-per-click advertising (such as Google AdWords) these return rates are referred to as your click-through rate, or CTR.

CTR is defined as the number of clicks your ad receives divided by the number of times your ad is shown. So let's say for example that your ad has 1,000 impressions (is shown 1,000 times) and five people click on your ad—this would give you a CTR of 0.5% (half of one percent.)

Now, once you get people to actually visit your website, the next question you need to ask yourself is: *how long are the people that respond to your advertising actually spending on your site?*

Installing tracking mechanisms on your website such as Google Analytics and StatCounter will give you detailed reports of the visitor activity on your website.

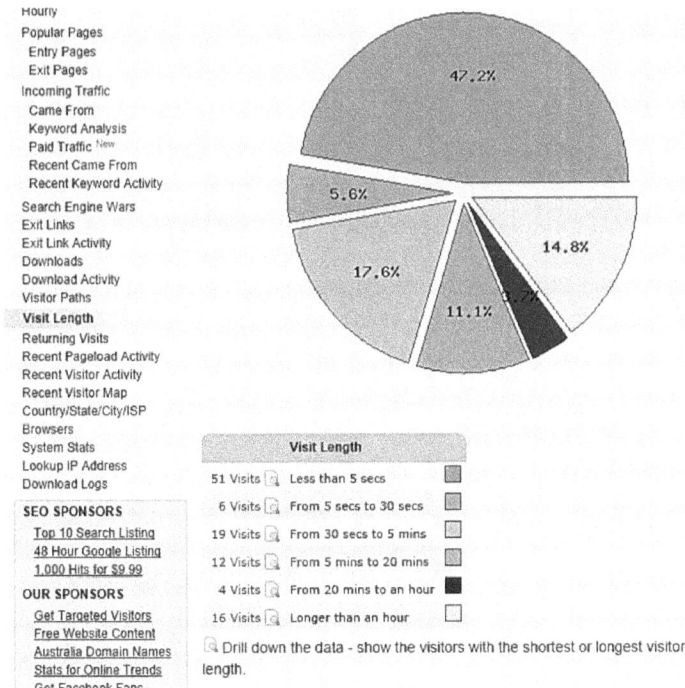

Hourly
Popular Pages
  Entry Pages
  Exit Pages
Incoming Traffic
  Came From
  Keyword Analysis
  Paid Traffic New
  Recent Came From
  Recent Keyword Activity
Search Engine Wars
Exit Links
  Exit Link Activity
Downloads
  Download Activity
Visitor Paths
Visit Length
  Returning Visits
  Recent Pageload Activity
  Recent Visitor Activity
  Recent Visitor Map
Country/State/City/ISP
Browsers
System Stats
Lookup IP Address
Download Logs

SEO SPONSORS
  Top 10 Search Listing
  48 Hour Google Listing
  1,000 Hits for $9.99

OUR SPONSORS
  Get Targeted Visitors
  Free Website Content
  Australia Domain Names
  Stats for Online Trends
  Get Facebook Fans

Pie chart values: 47.2%, 5.6%, 14.8%, 17.6%, 11.1%

Visit Length

51 Visits	Less than 5 secs	
6 Visits	From 5 secs to 30 secs	
19 Visits	From 30 secs to 5 mins	
12 Visits	From 5 mins to 20 mins	
4 Visits	From 20 mins to an hour	
16 Visits	Longer than an hour	

Drill down the data - show the visitors with the shortest or longest visitor length.

StatCounter has a pie graph that breaks down visits by lengths of less than five seconds, five seconds to 30 seconds, 30 seconds to five minutes, five minutes to 20 minutes, 20 minutes to one hour, and visits lasting more than one hour.

You might see that during an online campaign that a large portion of your visitors may indeed be spending less than five seconds on your website.

If this proves to be true, you will need to rethink how engaging your content is because you want to keep people around long enough to make a sale.

You must understand that the amount of people that actually follow your call to action once they go to your website or online music store will be far less than those who actually see your ad in the first place.

To determine the amount of people that actually follow your call to action once they go to your website or online music store is next to impossible, but by following the facts presented above, the formula for trying to determine your sales to online advertising conversion rate would read something like this:

Total amount of advertising impressions shown divided by total amount of clicks divided by percentage of people who spend more than 30 seconds on your site = total amount of visitors who may create a potential sale.

These are the same statistics that successful artists and corporations are beholden to, so make no mistake, if you really want this, you'll need to keep the ball rolling. Only a relentless never-ending campaign of advertising, marketing, and branding will get you the results that you hope to achieve. This is the professional advertising equivalent of keeping up your appearances.

RADIO PLAY CONVERSION RATES

Now up until this point I've limited any reference to radio airplay in this chapter and have kept the scope primarily to Internet and college radio because major market radio airplay is usually somewhat out of your reach. Since this book is primarily for entry-level artists, I was trying to keep the subject matter restricted to the things that you can actually get done for yourself in the beginning stages of your career.

But to further drive home the importance of marketing yourself to your existing fan base and to corroborate the abysmally small numbers I mentioned when describing advertising conversion rates that you can realistically expect to see from your campaign efforts, we will now turn to an excerpt from *Radio Airplay 101* by Bryan Farrish of Bryan Farrish Radio Promotions:

> *We talk to a lot of artists who want promotion, and everyone of them have music on a site somewhere that has a "counter". When they are asked what the AVERAGE number of "views" or "plays" or "listens" they have received (for their best song), the answer is about 200. That's right, 200. And this is cumulative, from day one when they posted it, and is from around the world. That's about one "view" or "play" or "listen" per country. And they've typically had that song up for over 2 years. (Of course, we are talking here about real numbers; not the fake numbers that you can buy).*
>
> *On the other hand, the HIGHEST number that artists typically tell us they've received is 20,000 "views" or "plays" or "listens" for their best song. Again this is from day one (cumulative), and from around the world, and also for about 2 years. This is about 100 listens per country, over a 2 year period. That's less than one listen a week, per country.*
>
> *Obviously, both of the above are miserable failures, since the GOAL OF THE ARTIST was to get LOTS of listens. This, unfortunately, is exactly the problem. The goal should NOT be to get lots of "views" or "plays" or "listens" at all. The goal instead should be to get MONEY; this is so different from "getting listens" that you may even have a hard time understanding the difference.*

The first way to explain this is to look at media facts that pertain to music. Typically, about 0.01 to 0.1 percent (.0001 to .001) of a radio listening audience will buy the music each week. This means that if the total radio exposure of a song is 50 million "listens" per week, then that song will sell 5,000 to 50,000 units each week. In ten weeks, you'd have 50,000 to 500,000 sales. This is why gold records of the past decades took many weeks to make gold; each week they would sell a percentage of the number of radio listens they got from radio.

These of course are major-market high-rotation spins, which generates huge numbers of "listens" weekly (Lady GaGa typically gets 50,000,000 listens per week, per song, per format, from radio, just in the USA). However, medium and smaller market stations, along with major stations that are not spinning as much, generate far fewer "listens" and thus sell far fewer units per week, even though the number of stations may be the same. What makes the difference between selling 5,000 and 50,000 units per week, even though the number of weekly listens remains at 50,000,000? Marketing. But that's another story. For an indie, assume you'll be at the lower level. See www.TopListens.com for snapshot of a week in 2012, and compare it to the sales number of iTunes or Soundscan. You'll see that ALL of the top sellers are getting high "listens" from commercial radio regular rotation. All of them. And keep in mind that digital sales now (2013) are about half of all sales ("physical" CD sales being the other half).

Now comes the "counter". The typical artist has never had any numerical feedback before the counter. No sales tracking, no airplay tracking, no ticket sales tracking, nothing. So the counter looks to be pretty exciting, because for the first time the artist is getting "feedback" on his or her music. So far so good. But the problem arises when the artist makes it their GOAL of maximizing the "views" or "plays" or "listens" on this counter. And the reason this is a problem is because the typical artist reading this article does not have the resources to get enough "views" or "plays" or "listens" to make any sales or anything else occur.

Looking at the example above, it takes 50,000,000 "listens" per week, for one song, in the U.S. only, for a lesser-marketed indie song to sell 5,000 units per week. That's because in lower-rotation markets or *stations, the typical listener will only hear it about 10 total times. So sales are about 0.01 percent (.0001) of the total listens. Using this .01 percent number, the typical artist needs:*

- *50,000,000 "listens" to get 5,000 sales*
- *5,000,000 "listens" to get 500 sales*
- *500,000 "listens" to get 50 sales*
- *50,000 "listens" to get 5 sales*
- *5,000 "listens" to get 0.5 sales (!)*

Compare this to what I said about how many YouTube views the typical artist tells us they have, and you see the problem. The typical artist with 200 views or plays does not have enough for even one sale. And the artists who tell us they have a mega 20,000 views or plays will only be getting 2 sales. THIS IS THE REASON that you don't want to focus any energy on increasing your number on the views-counter or the plays-counter. It won't sell anything, and it will just make you think that your music is not good enough. And of course I did not even mention that most counters are faked now anyway: You can get 1,000,000 fake YouTube views with likes and comments for under $180. Nobody hears your music, but hey, you've now got a big counter.

Now although Farrish points out the futile number of sales you may see from radio play, this whole excerpt reiterates the actual conversion rates you see in professional advertising.

It also proves how valuable the stability of a homegrown fan base is.

Even though these numbers seem quite discouraging, nurturing and marketing your music to a small and growing dedicated fan base will be more profitable than if you were playing your music to tens of thousands of listeners.

As an artist, you really need to fully comprehend this because it's the support of your fan base that will sustain you until you can compete with these major label artists.

Marketing to your fan base, whom you hopefully can depend on to make some purchases, combined with promoting yourself to the general public in an effort to gain new listeners and fans during an album release is also a continual branding of you as a product, and the whole process is absolutely necessary.

Without visibility there is no awareness, and without awareness there is no interest. Without interest there are no sales, and without sales there is no additional money to reintroduce into the advertising campaign. You'll need to keep this wheel turning over and over again and it takes cash to do that.

So let's say you're the one artist who actually highlighted everything in this chapter and followed this plan to the letter. You booked all the shows and scheduled all the dates that you could have had, you're on the road home, what's next?

Do it again.

Remarket yourself for the same release. This is your album; get people to hear it.

Take your time and operate with precision.

Get to places where you didn't go the first time. There are so many music festivals and conferences around now that there is ALWAYS some type of marketing to be done.

Start scheduling another tour; play other regions. Have you covered that? Then it's time to get a passport and play another country.

Marketing has a beginning and middle, but doesn't have an end. The longer you market your product for, the longer you will reap success from it.

This is primarily why labels outline terms within their contract that are usually from a year to 18 months in length. Once the album drops, it takes the artist time to tour through several cities, regions, and countries to market the release. It's the continual ongoing strategic push for each album that makes it sell successfully.

A large reason that some of today's artists are failing is because they believe that releasing large volumes of music will advance their career further than the repetitive ongoing push of one album for an extended period of time. This is not how it's done.

FOLLOW THROUGH

Running through your marketing plan from start to finish is extremely important; some people start out very focused and begin to lose their intensity or enthusiasm after they get midway through the plan. This is a fatal error. Give as much passion to the end of your plan as you do to the beginning and there will be no failure. Even if the plan is mediocre and has a few flaws, you'll see some form of results if you stick to it from beginning to end. Do not ever half-ass your own strategy.

Once you've run through your plan successfully from beginning to end, it's then time to refine and recycle the original plan. Take the points that worked well and elaborate on them. Take the things that didn't work so well and run a full analysis on what went wrong. What did you miss? Who didn't follow through with a task? What could have been done better? Should one aspect of the plan have been scrapped?

You're in control of your plan, so control it. If you're unsure of something, stop being a pussy and make a fucking decision. This is what leaders do.

If it turns out you made the wrong decision, at least you exercised the ability to make one.

Chalk it up as a learning experience.

SUMMARY

Your marketing plans and strategies will evolve over time and become more refined, more efficient, and more effective. Each consecutive plan will be more organized and effective than the one before it. This is how your strategy evolves over time, and it's done by learning from your mistakes and putting in the work. We already covered this lesson in the introduction of this book.

Just remember to aim for your target market and keep in mind that you will need to be able to sustain some form of consistency throughout all of this.

The average person sees more than 3,000 advertisements per day from all platforms; you will need to be consistent enough to make your branding efforts stick out of all this visual clutter.

Throughout all the marketing, touring, interviews, and other methods of creating visibility and awareness of what you are doing, you should ask yourself this question:

Has your group managed to create a *buzz* or not?

This one term alone is how you can gauge if your career is moving upwards or spiraling downwards and it is one of the most important terms in this industry.

CHAPTER TWENTY

MUSIC CONFERENCES

The author, Mike Repel, speaking at the 17th Annual Millennium Music Conference.

If you are an independent artist and you have not yet attended your first music conference, I can't think of a better way for you to expand your horizons than to attend one.

Conferences usually last several days, and this is a more than adequate amount of time to get several things done.

I have been to several of these throughout the United States and have brought something positive back from every one of them that has been an opportunity for growth or that has strengthened me.

PANELS

Outside of a college degree from a media school like Columbia, there's no better way to get a condensed understanding of what is currently happening in today's industry than attending a few panels at conferences, which have several current industry professionals on them.

Label reps, big name artists, PRO members, technology company employees, tour managers, publicists, music industry attorneys, and other professionals share their knowledge in the forums and usually always allow for some Q&A where you can ask them a direct line of questioning related to your situation.

Most conferences have several panels of different subject matter running simultaneously; this allows you the ability to pick and choose which panels and topics you wish to attend.

ONE ON ONE MENTORING SESSIONS

Select music conferences offer mentoring sessions for artists. You may need to sign up or register for one of these in advance, but that's usually just prior to the session on the same day,

When registering, you are able to select from a list of people to talk to. These mentors usually cover every facet of the music industry. Publishers, mastering engineers, label execs, brand consultants, touring musicians, and managers are examples of the people that you will have the opportunity of speaking with one on one.

You can ask these people anything you wish, and you have the ability to steer the direction of the conversation to suit your needs so you get the advice that is specific to your scenario.

These sessions last about 15 minutes on average, which is plenty of time to have a discussion, but it's my recommendation that you jot your thoughts and questions down beforehand so you enter into the session organized and prepared in an effort to get the most out of this individualized opportunity.

NETWORKING

Getting out of your local music market where everyone knows each other, traveling, and meeting new people can be a great opportunity for growth. By attending these conferences you can meet professionals from different regions who you may not have had access to in your town or city.

Business in general is built on interpersonal networks and the best way to create these is to meet people in person. As it has been said, *the size of your network is equal to the size of your net worth.*

These conferences have been referred to as one big schmooze fest and if you use your time efficiently, you may find that after a few days you have a pile of business cards and an equal amount of leads to follow up on.

EXHIBITOR AREAS

The exhibitor areas at a music conference are primarily booths set up in a trade show or convention type of display or layout. Products, technologies, services, and other industry support systems can be found at these areas within a music conference. You very well may be able to find a distributor, publisher, or other professional service that can help advance your career at these exhibitions.

SHOWCASES

What would a music conference be without music? One of the other things you should know about these music conferences is that most of them have live music showcases that spotlight independent artists.

Sonic Bids and ReverbNation will allow you to apply for opportunities to perform at these conferences. This will give you an opportunity to showcase your talent in front of the very industry professionals you have been networking with. However, with the information provided on the following pages, you may be able to just go book yourself.

PREPARATION FOR A CONFERENCE

I strongly encourage you to print some professional-looking business cards, presskits, and professionally packaged CDs of your music before you arrive at a conference.

You will want to have presentable promotional material on hand to make a good first impression; remember, your brand is your image and your image is your brand.

Make sure you have an adequate supply of these items as well. As a rule, I would bring:

- **No less than 250 business cards** – these are for people you are making direct person to person contact or face time with.
- **No less than 1000 flyers** – more if possible. Place these things in and around the conference and wherever you go; you don't know the next time you will be able to create visibility in that city.
- **No less than 100 stickers** – place them where they will get noticed and where they will remain. Usually the venues that showcase the conference artists and bands are a good place to start.
- **No less than 25 presskits** – not everyone is going to require these or even want them. Let people know you have them, but don't force-feed anyone your material, because you don't want to run out and then meet someone who wants to help you.
- **Bring sufficient copies of your music** – The amount of music you bring is really up to you, but it should coincide with what your goals are. If you want to give out copies of your music to everyone, that's fine, but if you are on a budget then bring less and be sure to know ahead of time who you intend to give the copies to (perhaps only A&R reps or booking agents or magazine editors, etc.). Again, not everyone is going to require or even want a copy of your music, and sometimes people just accept them so they don't appear to be rude *(especially if your packaging looks like shit)*.

I also like to bring other miscellaneous customized items with me to increase my brand visibility such as keychain bottle openers, lighters, guitar picks, and other practical items that people will use or hold on to and may follow up on at a later date.

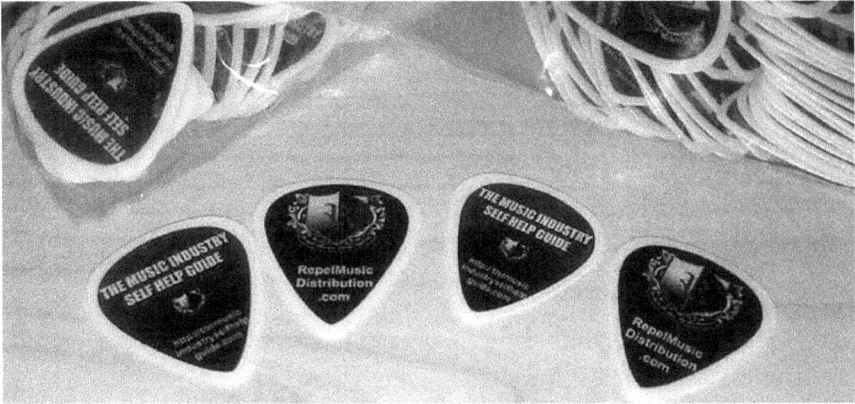

Some practical and presentable promotional material I took to L.A. with me for IES.

You will meet a lot of people over the span of a few short days. If you are actively networking, the most likely outcome of this is that your contact information along with your packaged music and/or presskit will end up in someone's tote bag with similar content supplied by other artists, bands, and industry professionals—and it won't be followed up on immediately.

After a conference, most of the people that you meet will go back to their office and will need to get back up to speed on what they have missed while attending the conference. Follow-up emails and calls happen, but not always immediately, so don't hound your new contacts.

SPONSORSHIP DECKS

If you have It within your budget and would like to have ongoing visibility throughout the conference, you can contact the organizers in advance and request a *sponsorship deck* (sometimes called a *marketing deck*) pricing guide and become a *partner* of the conference.

The deck will give you several options to create visibility for your brand. Some of the common fee-based placements are as follows:

- **Website Listing** – *Usually logo placement and a link to your site*
- **Email Blast** – *Press release or other related news to the conference mailing list*
- **Grab Bag Inserts** – *Placement of at least one item in guest bag*
- **Lanyard** – *Logo placement on the fest pass that people wear*
- **Program Guide** – *Print advertising in the conference program booklet*
- **Exhibitor Booth** – *Your own table to sell your wares*
- **Signage** – *Banner and sign placement throughout the conference and/or venues*
- **Showcase Sponsorship** – *Usually a specific event will be named after you or your company*
- **Radio Advertising** – *You or your company's name mentioned in any radio advertising for the conference*
- **Stage Sponsorship** – *The stage will be named after you and you may also have the option of hanging your banners on it exclusively.*

The examples above were listed from lowest to highest in price range. Some conferences (or festivals as well) also offer Bronze, Silver, Gold, and Platinum sponsorship packages that include several items from the previous list and include VIP passes for you and your staff. Sponsorship levels can cost as little as $150 on the low end and can exceed $120,000 on the high end.

YOUR DEMEANOR

How you carry yourself at a conference is very important to what kind of forward momentum you will obtain. You will be meeting many important people, from major label artists and representatives to business owners and more. It's imperative that you remember that these are all normal people like you. If you want to have a real conversation with any of them, you will need to wipe all fear and intimidation out of your persona and remember not to place any of them on some imaginary pedestal with your hand extended like you want to cradle and massage their testicles.

By following this advice, you will get much farther and it may actually open some doors for you and perhaps even allow you to make some friends.

LIST OF CURRENT MUSIC INDUSTRY CONFERENCES

- **A3C HIP HOP FESTIVAL & MUSIC CONFERENCE** – Atlanta, GA. *A3C, known as hip-hop's annual pilgrimage, is held in early October. This festival takes over most of the live entertainment venues in Atlanta and includes a conference of urban industry professionals and upwards of 500 live concert showcases of well-known artists and emerging artists alike.* www.a3cfestival.com
- **ADE** *(Amsterdam Dance Event)* – Amsterdam, The Netherlands. www.amsterdam-dance-event.nl
- **ASCAP EXPO** – Los Angeles, CA. *Held in late April.* www.ascap.com/eventsawards
- **BIGSOUND** – Brisbane, Australia. *International music industry conference held in early September in Australia.* http://www.qmusic.com.au/bigsound
- **BILLBOARD COUNTRY MUSIC SUMMIT** – Nashville, TN. *Held in June.* www.billboardevents.com/country
- **CMJ MUSIC MARATHON** – New York, NY. *Held in mid-October.* www.cmj.com
- **CMW** *(Canadian Music Week)* – Toronto, ON. *CMW is a music festival and conference held in early May.* www.cmw.net
- **DEWEY BEACH MUSIC CONFERENCE** – Dewey Beach, DE. *Held in late September.* http://www.deweybeachfest.com/dbmc
- **IES** *(Indie Entertainment Summit)* – Los Angeles, CA. *Four=day event held in the first week of August in North Hollywood that focuses on helping artists obtain success within the independent market.* indieentertainmentsummit.com
- **ILMC** *(International Live Music Conference)* – London, UK. *ILMC is held in the beginning of March and focuses on the live music sector of the industry.* www.ilmc.com
- **IMS** *(International Music Summit)* – Ibiza, Spain. *Held in late May.* www.internationalmusicsummit.com
- **MIDEM** – Cannes, France. *Midem is held the first week of February and is an international destination for industry*

professionals that includes a tradeshow and live concert showcases. www.midem.com

- **MMC** (Millennium Music Conference) – Held in late February, this conference holds a series of panels, one-on-one artist mentoring sessions along with showcases all over Harrisburg's live concert venues. Harrisburg, PA
- **MU:CON -** Seoul, South Korea. www.mucon.or.kr
- **MUSEXPO -** Hollywood, CA. Held in the first week of May. MUSEXPO www.musexpo.net
- **MUSIC BIZ CONFERENCE -** Los Angeles, CA. http://musicbiz.org
- **MUSIC MATTERS** – Singapore. Held in late May. www.allthatmatters.asia
- **NAMM -** Anaheim, CA. The NAMM show is the music products and gear tradeshow that is held around the last week in January and showcases the newest gear and technology on the market. www.namm.com
- **NEW MUSIC SEMINAR -** New York, NY. Held in early June. www.newmusicseminar.com
- **NXNW** - (North By Northwest) – Toronto, CA. NXNW is a music, tech, film, comedy, interactive, and culture festival held the third week of June. http://nxne.com
- **SXSW** (South By Southwest) – Austin, TX. SXSW is held the first week of March and is the largest music conference in the U.S. This conference has programming for music and film and is also well-known for a myriad of live performances and after parties surrounding the convention. www.sxsw.com
- **TAXI ROAD RALLY -** Los Angeles, CA. Taxi holds its conference in November. www.taxi.com/rally
- **THE GREAT ESCAPE -** Brighton, UK. www.greatescape.com
- **YELLOWPHONE MUSIC CONFERENCE** – Milwaukee, WI. Held on the second week of September and focused on helping up-and-coming artists.
- **WMC** (Winter Music Conference) Miami, FL. Held in late March. www.wmf.com
- **WOMEX -** Cardiff, Wales. WOMEX is a five-day event held in late October. www.womex.com

CHAPTER TWENTY-ONE

WORKING WITH LABELS AND MANAGEMENT

Many of you artists hear that there's going to be an A&R representative from a label in the audience at the club you're performing at and think that Jesus Christ himself has come down from the heavens to admonish upon you a magical life-altering contract that will miraculously elevate you to the top of the Billboard charts and shower you with wealth and fame while invoking an army of minions to attend to your every whim.

The fact of the matter is that a majority of you don't even know what the title "A&R" stands for, and few of you even know what the job description is for that title.

In an effort to help you establish some bargaining power should you meet any official label rep, I'd like to reiterate some important points that I made earlier in this book. You'll need to work, nobody owes you shit, and nobody is going to care if you're successful or not more than you are.

YOU NEED TO HAVE A FAN BASE

Before you get signed or can obtain management, you'll need to have an established fan base already.

Contrary to what you may believe, it's not a record label's job to create a fan base for you.

If people aren't interested in your music and aren't buying it, labels aren't going to be interested in you. Labels need to see that you can create revenue and have the potential to create more revenue. They in turn advertise to your fan base and get the music to places where consumers can acquire it physically or digitally.

Naturally, with all of the priming and primping that they will put into the advertising for your product it will attract more visibility for you outside of your fan base, but this is to reinforce and build upon what you've already started.

If a label launches an advertising campaign to further your brand visibility to people outside of your reach, it's depending on generating revenue from your existing fan base to cover those expenses This is the exact reason that a label will try to calculate your first week's sales projections; it serves as a barometer of what kind of profit or loss margin they will be receiving.

Every step a label makes on your behalf requires time, money, and manpower. If they can't project a positive return on their investment then they're looking at taking a loss. You need to have enough of a buzz to either lower or justify the risk threshold that's involved in investing capital into your project.

SO WHO IS ACTUALLY MAKING MONEY?

According to the Recording Industry Association of America (RIAA), approximately 90 percent of the records that are released by major recording labels fail to make a profit. These companies aren't independently wealthy and have massive overhead that needs to be covered solely by the money spent by the fan. The major labels spend billions (literally) running a corporate machine that barely breaks even. Their operating expenses alone are around 95 percent.

There are a lot of misconceptions about this industry on the behalf of new or naive artists who think that signing to a major label will be the answer to all of their prayers, but in reality a staggeringly large majority of releases will fail to make any significant sales at all.

In testimony to Congress, Hilary Rosen of the RIAA provided industry evidence that more than four out of five releases fail. She combined major label and independent figures, but this is what she said:

> "Typically, less than 15 percent of all sound recordings released by Major record companies will even make back their costs. Far fewer return profit. Here are some revealing facts to demonstrate what I'm talking about. There were 38,857 albums released last year [1999], 7,000 from the Majors and 31,857 from independents. Out of the total releases, only 233 sold over 250,000 units. Only 437 sold over 100,000 units. That's 1 percent of the time for the total recording

industry that an album even returns any significant sales, much less profit."

These statistics show slightly larger sales than the similar breakdown that was provided in Chapter 1, in part because they're from nine years earlier, but they still corroborate the narrow margins at the pinnacle of this industry.

To look at the big picture, during the 2003 Future of Music Coalition conference, Jim Cooperman of BMG stated that a major label act has to sell 2 million albums to break even. If Cooperman's calculations are accurate, this would mean that only 0.2 percent of all releases break even.

To many of you, these figures may seem overtly one-sided, and in the past I may have taken that position alongside you. However after financing advertising campaigns for artists that I've personally worked with, I can tell you that these costs go up quickly and the majority of expenditures that the label spends are indeed on the visibility and exposure of the artist. By budgeting your own marketing campaign, you'll have the opportunity of seeing this for yourself firsthand.

This reality results in a very fine line that divides the artist's frustrations with a record label for taking a lion's share of the revenue from their release and the label's frustration with an artist's inability to create revenue when listeners or consumers aren't purchasing their music.

This is the same fine line that makes artists distrust labels and also the same fine line that prevents labels from just going out and signing every band that sounds good.

At the end of the day, you need to realize that this is a two-way business relationship.

You are using the label to finance your visibility and your increased access to customers along with the potential to earn money; and the label is using you and your music to make a profit.

If you plan on making any money at all in this industry, your pay will be based solely on the amount of fans that you have who are willing

to spend the cash it takes to buy your album and your merchandise or pay for a ticket to see you perform live.

That's where the money comes from, not from anywhere else.

The payment that you'll receive for album sales is going to be a percentage of the net revenue received by the record label from its distributors, who take a percentage after the record store chains and digital storefronts take their cut.

The current statutory rate for mechanical royalties as set by the Copyright Royalty Board is 9.1 cents per copy for songs five minutes or less. That's the base rate that you'll be paid for your CD sales. You may think that this is a limited amount until you understand the mechanics of what needs to be funded behind your album release.

CALCULATING THE COSTS

The costs of advertising your music alone involve the work of photographers, videographers, graphic designers, marketing teams, publicists, tour production agencies, accountants, market analysts, promoters, and marketing and advertising executives. These costs also include placement of advertising materials, manufacturing of promotional materials, and radio promotions.

Now we move on to operating expenses, office space, phone and Internet bills, electric and gas, transportation, lawyers, and executive and employee pay, to name a few.

Tag on the recoupable costs of producer royalties, studio time, mastering, rights and licensing, CD manufacturing, and shipping and you see the total expenses that the label is putting into *you* and *your music.*

In order for you to get paid, you need to have enough fan support to purchase enough copies of your album to cover the recoupable expenses first.

In order for the label to make any money, it will need to have sold enough units to your fans to cover what it has spent on the other non-recoupable expenses related to your release.

This is becoming even more difficult now that streaming makes up such a large portion of how music is consumed.

So once again you see that the manipulated numbers of your video plays and large amount of free downloads that you accumulated or paid for really don't mean a fucking thing.

If you can't turn music into sales before presenting yourself to a major label then there is a good possibility that you're just spinning your wheels. If you think you're just going to sit around and not do shit either, then you're just going to develop a bad name for yourself in what you will find is a smaller industry than you think.

NEXT UP – ARTIST MANAGEMENT

Many artists believe that their manager will handle everything and that they aren't required to do work on their end. These artists are obviously not yet ready to have access to this type of support. They haven't yet undergone the self-development necessary to give a manager something viable to work with. Artists shouldn't be seeking out management until they're creating revenue or at least some form of demand for themselves or their product.

But yes, you can pay for management right away if you wish. Some dirtbag with minimal qualifications will take your money; that's a guarantee. I've contacted managers like this in the past who require fees of about $300 a month for extremely limited services such as email blasts, limited promotion, and perhaps some show placement. This phone call usually ends when I ask this self-proclaimed manager if the artist will be able to recoup his monthly fees from compensation from the live performances that the manager is going to place him on.

No matter what stage in your development you are, you should have a realistic expectation of creating some form of revenue stream for your out-of-pocket expenses. That's Business 101; and why wouldn't your manager want to create these revenue-generating opportunities for you? After all, it will help him ensure that he is going to get paid, right?

There are on the other hand, more *professional managers* who will assess your situation and will decline your money if they feel you aren't ready yet.

This is because these managers stand a better chance of long-term employment and quite possibly a secured revenue share with an established client than they do with emerging artists who may not yet have the ability to generate enough revenue to pay them for their services. In reality, they don't want a loser on their roster or resume. They have a reputation that they worked hard for and will not work with just anyone.

If you're denied management, be sure to *listen to what they tell you.* Their specific reasons for refusing to take you on as a client are going to be the exact things you'll need to work on as a developing artist.

Sometimes you'll need to keep your mouth shut, your ears and your eyes open, and watch, listen, and learn what's going on in your career. Don't ignore the people who are trying to help you. This industry is full of people who refuse to listen to anybody else and if you're one of them, you should take the time to think whether or not you would be making things easier for yourself if you went along with the program.

ARE YOU WORTH THE FRUSTRATION?

I've spoken to countless artist mangers and management firms alike that have begun to migrate away from this type of hands-on management because they're tired of working with the artists themselves. There's not a lot of money in this area of the music business and it's not worth the frustration of dealing with a lazy artist who can't work with his own team because of his own arrogance or delusions and visions of grandeur.

Lack of follow-through and ambition are a sure way to get people to lose faith in you quickly, including whatever fan base you've created. This also includes investors and sponsors alike, who will both pull out of a project if they deem it to be a waste of time and resources.

Labels and managers aren't into parenting; they're into making money. If you're shown the ropes and told what is expected of you—especially if it's contractually—it's your obligation to follow through on it. Whether it's a deadline for an album, production for a music video, or even your assistance in marketing your album, these things need to be on the top of your list of priorities.

Having the foundation that I've urged you to develop throughout this book should give you a better understanding of what will be expected of you if you make it this far, because now people are introducing money and manpower into your project. This means that everyone, including you, will be expected to produce results at the peak of their ability.

These people are trying to help you sell *your music*, and if you show no desire or ambition to do so, they'll lose their desire and ambition to help you.

If you've hired a manager and won't listen to him, coordinate your efforts with him, or follow through with getting him the things he requires in a timely fashion, then why did you hire him?

Your management team or your label can coordinate a lot of things for you with your tour schedule or performance dates and their marketing campaign for your release; this is a coordinated team effort where each party complements the other's actions and it increases the effectiveness of everyone's efforts on all sides. You should be working hand-in-hand with your manager or your label if they are being proactive with you. Communicating with them, following through on leads, and confirming your availability should be the first things on your priority list. They're trying to create visibility and awareness for you and your brand. Any cooperation needed by these parties is for your benefit in the long run.

Many times, artists will see things happening for them for the first time in their career and it will blow up their ego and affect their thinking.

Although you may be seeing the fruits of the management team or label's efforts, it's going to take a lot to break you as an upcoming artist besides a write-up in a large magazine or some Internet publicity, or a few large shows and some music industry events.

If you don't understand the concept of *momentum* and the need to remain visible, accessible, and available at all times then you aren't going very far in your career.

Momentum is created by your visibility and this is the one ongoing thing that you need to focus on. If you don't maintain and increase this constantly, you'll never get above the pile of artists that are all doing this as well. It takes relentless and maniacal marketing on all levels to achieve this.

Please don't misconstrue the notion that your visibility at music industry networking parties is more important than performing live on a regular basis. Making new connections with industry contacts is important, but if you don't think that your fan base is just as important to your career as these other people are, then you are sadly mistaken, because even if you have a strong team behind you and access to every industry professional and CEO in the business, if you aren't marketing yourself by performing live and connecting with fans on a consistent basis then all the help and contacts in the world won't be able to make you successful.

Make the time to attend to all of the important aspects of your career, especially your fan base.

There's a lot of work that needs to be done, and you're an essential part of it. If your team is breaking their backs to create awareness, visibility, and sales for you and you don't want to carry any of the weight of the load, then what motivation do they have to keep going?

I've found very few people other than myself in the independent side of the industry that take such a maniacally aggressive approach to getting things done and I see one common denominator among all of us: we do the work. We do the tedious little work that no one else has the patience or the desire to do. We shoulder the weight of this burden because we know no one else is going to do it either correctly, in a timely manner, or at all. Perhaps they don't share a common vision, understand a strategy or much less give a fuck, but one way or another, the work needs to get done.

Since I've entered this business, I've developed a newfound respect for every supervisor and boss that I've ever had since my first job. No matter what their disposition was, I've come to realize they all have had one thing in common. They just wanted to see a job well done, and many of them may have had a shitty attitude due to the less-than-stellar performance of the people they were relying on to get the work done.

Many labels and management companies that I've spoken to all share the same exasperating problem with their artists. The artists are

stubborn and think that nothing is their job and they shouldn't have to do anything beyond the bare minimum.

Some of these problematic artists are convinced that they don't need to do anything except record and perform live, and some fall short on even meeting these criteria. Many artists have the erroneous belief that they aren't required to be involved in their own career and that everything will be handled for them.

The million dollar question here is: handled by whom?

Unless you're bringing in big sales numbers, don't kid yourself into thinking that other people should work on your career harder than you should work on it yourself.

Until your music is creating enough revenue to generate a payroll, it's going to be challenging to keep people interested in volunteering their valuable time and money towards pushing you in a forward or upward direction, especially if you won't lift a finger to do anything yourself.

But not all artists are like this either.

I know several bands that handle their own national tour booking, merchandising, and publicity, and many of them are unsigned and not even looking for a deal. They're building a following on a day-to-day and show-to-show basis, and are relying on no one but themselves.

As your fan base increases along with record sales, show attendance, and merchandise sales, you'll have more expendable income to hire a manager, and it will be more feasible to do so. At this point he should be able to do something for you.

In the rapidly growing independent market, a working artist should focus on building a strong, competent team around him.

Picture a wheel. The artist and his music are the axle, and the label, booking agent, publicist, manager, tour manager, and street team are all spokes on this wheel that support the axle. Each entity has its own independent function and they complement each other, therefore forming a wheel. Without all of these spokes in place and working together—or with one of them showing evidence of being weaker than the others—the structural integrity of the wheel becomes compromised, which results in the rim bending and the wheel running off course.

But the wheel itself cannot function at all if the axle—or the *artist,* in this case—is the dysfunctional component. When an axle fails, it's not uncommon for the entire wheel to detach itself and roll away.

In this industry there is a relentless never-ending workflow that needs to be attended to. Some people, such as myself, take on multiple functions and wear many hats in order to chip away at this pile of work, which is fine, but how efficient is this? It's very time-consuming, but you may actually need to do this stuff yourself because ***it's extremely hard to find competent and capable people who can successfully complete a challenging task.***

This is the realistic picture of what needs to be done in order to cover all your bases. It takes a developed artist to gain the attention of a major label, and an independent label as well, but even though we live in changing times within the industry, it's in your best interest to utilize and develop every piece of leverage that I'm presenting to you if you want to obtain a real edge and stay in front of the curve of the other artists who are trying to make a break in this industry.

The statistic that I hear repeatedly is that most labels are looking for an artist whose album will sell 15,000 copies in the first week of its release. Most major labels have adhered to a practice where they only sign solicited artists that have a discography behind them and a history of making sales. These are the working artists that have put out albums and sold them to the following that they have developed over time.

Your time and tenure with an independent label or as a successful independent artist is the barometer on which a major label is going to judge you.

Realistic sales that are tracked by a Universal Product Code and through Nielsen are the stats that labels are going to look at.

Your sales history will far outweigh your amount of social media followers, YouTube plays, and free downloads, because as I said before, everyone in the industry knows that these numbers can be inflated. Trackable sales, on the other hand, cannot.

Major labels have been known to spend up to $1 million on artist development and another $1 million on marketing an album release.

If I had to invest $2 million on someone, I'd use it to develop the artist with the solid fan base, a good work ethic, winning "can do" attitude, and history of sales.

Investing time and money into an artist who won't lift a finger for his own advancement is a dead-end path and is nothing more than a liability.

Many labels have different business models, but at the end of the day it needs to be a profitable business, and so should your band or act.

Your act is not successful because you were hosted in a magazine, played a big show, or had your video hosted on some popular website. You can pay to play, pay for visibility, and pay for everything as you go along. This is also a *have money will travel* industry, and you can keep spending until you don't have another dime.

Once that happens, what *foundation* have you established to fall back on? Without fan support and some kind of revenue coming in, your existence as a musical act is just a flash in the pan.

Having a network and a following can sustain you should you lose managerial or label support, and following the steps I have laid out in this book will help you do that. The only thing required is that you've got to want to do it.

If you're currently unable to promote and exploit your music easily because you haven't created or figured out how to tap into an extended network, you should be able to find people who will promote you for a fee. Can they do it effectively? Some yes, many no.

WHEN WILL I BE READY?

At some point in time, you may need to utilize these companies, whether they're marketing firms, publicists, promotion companies, or booking agents and tour managers. You owe it to yourself to do extensive research on the people that you're giving your money to. Make sure they're the right fit for you across the board, and that they can deliver on what you're employing them to do. Explain your vision to them and see if their services can move you in the direction of your goals.

I highly recommend that you choose a firm that has already established itself within the music industry and has a client list specific to your genre. Other firms or agencies from outside the music industry will miss the slight nuances that established companies will identify and target or choose to avoid altogether based on their understanding of the current market trends—trends which you yourself need to make it a point to learn to recognize and understand.

Before you even hire a company to do these things for you, ask yourself these questions to see if you're even ready to take this step:

What is it about me that I am paying this company to promote? Have I developed my product and my brand to the point where I require these services? Have I developed a following and some brand recognition abroad so people can identify with the publicity I am getting from these agencies?

And most importantly:

Do I stand the possibility of monetizing my product as a result of these promotions?

The point of the last paragraph is for you to ascertain if you're active enough in your career to even benefit from the services that you're paying for, because if you aren't, you'll be unhappy with the results that you receive.

For instance, let's say you've hired a manager, a promoter, or a publicist.

For the purpose of making my point, we'll just say that you have a publicist. You've paid him a fee and you're aware of his ability to place you in several of your favorite magazines, yet he hasn't. You naturally become upset with him and want to sever your ties with him, but the reality is that because of your inactivity and lack of recent accomplishments, there's actually nothing that any magazine can write about you and it is completely unrealistic for you to believe that there is.

You're simply not newsworthy and your publicist knows this—you have tied his hands behind his back and severely diminished his ability to obtain any press for you.

Following the guidelines I'm laying out in this book will make your brand easier to promote and will help you reap more success from the visibility that you'll receive from the services these agencies can provide you.

I purposely avoided using a publicist for the entire first edition of this book. I made a conscious decision to create as much visibility and awareness for this work before hiring someone to do it for me, and I did it by following the steps that I have shared with you.

Why did I do this?

Well, the answer is simple:

As an unknown author, I wanted to take some time to develop a solid foundation for this book first so I would be sure that I was giving the publicist something he could actually work with. That is, if I even decide to use one at all.

As you can see, no matter whom you have working with you or working for you, you'll need to be proactive if you intend on being successful. Complacency and ambivalence have no place in this industry, and if you lack a maniacal passion for doing this then maybe you should get settled into a factory job and stop fantasizing.

By the way, A&R stands for artist and repertoire.

The job description of an A&R is as defined below:

"A label representative who is responsible for scouting new talent while also performing a myriad of tasks related to that of artist development;

but whose primary function is to smile and nod while new artists tell him old lies."

CHAPTER TWENTY-TWO

THE BAD PROMOTER

THE VULTURE ON YOUR BACK

*I have witnessed some independent music markets
that can be best described as
"A barely functioning, loosely knit catastrophe."*

I'm going to start this chapter out by saying that there are people in this business that just shouldn't be here.

Not all promoters are bad—and I personally know some damn good ones—but the ones that are bad are nothing more than a dysfunctional liability.

This chapter will outline some of the things that these promoters are doing wrong.

It's a problem when the people who are controlling the money for live performances don't know what they're doing.

Unfortunately these problems are more apparent in some genres of music than others—hopefully it's not yours. If it is, then hopefully this chapter will give you some insight on how to avoid these problems and these problematic promoters.

For instance, a lot of you independent rap artists have been getting fucked over for far too long in your relationship with certain promoters that you've been dealing with.

Outside of rap music, I haven't been involved with one other genre of music that has ever charged bands outright to perform.

I'm not saying that it doesn't happen, it just doesn't happen to me— or anyone that I know, for that matter.

But in rap music this is happening constantly, and I'm not talking about paying for tickets for resale either; I'm talking about just outright payment for show placement.

I've been in hardcore and metal bands and I have a long history with punk, rockabilly, and ska bands along with the multitude of musicians that I know that are in classic rock and heavy metal cover bands as well as jazz and blues bands and *not one single musician that I've come across has ever had a story about paying to perform.*

As a matter of fact, many underground bands have musicians that moonlight in cover bands to supplement their income, because *cover bands consistently have gigs and always get paid pretty well*.

The rap music genre is long overdue for a cultural revolution when it comes to event management and show promotions and now is the time for you to move in and change the status quo for yourself and for the generations of artists that follow.

The next chapter of this book will show you how to work around thieving promoters and empower you to clear the way for a new era where all independent artists get paid to perform.

A lot of you constantly claim that you're going to change the game.

Well, this is your chance.

If you want to succeed in ushering in this new day then you'll need to take the personal initiative to lead by example just as any other great leader throughout the course of history has done. Somebody needs to step up to the plate and do this now because there are currently more nightmare stories about promoters than there are promoters in this business, and that's because one bad promoter will continually mismanage events, promotions, and payouts.

The only real difference between the people you meet in prison and some of the people you will meet in the music industry is that the people in the music industry are better dressed.

Promoters place themselves as the liaison between the club and the live acts. Some are collecting money from both sides and sometimes even collecting three streams of revenue a night. There's usually enough money to fairly compensate the local acts that are the lifeblood of the promoter's existence, and they very well may not be getting paid a dime. He may be collecting money at the door, getting a percentage of the bar, making the artists sell tickets, or even charging them outright just to be on the bill.

There is a term in this industry known as PAY-TO-PLAY. It is hands-down THE SINGLE MOST DESPISED PRACTICE that exists among working musicians.

I've recently represented a few rap artists. Every so often, I get last-minute text messages from promoters for shows that have had zero promotion offering me five to eight minutes of stage time to open up for a well-known or soon-to-be-well-known act. The promoters always ask for an exorbitant fee, which has ranged from $100 up to $800 for the same amount of stage time. As I read these messages, I can't help but think to myself, "*is this person fucking nuts?*"

Unplanned, last minute, fly by the seat of your pants event promotion is not a class they teach in Harvard Business School. The promoters that do this are a joke and seldom can run an event successfully from start to finish, but if there's a dollar to be made, you can bet there will be somebody spinning his wheels trying to get his hands on your money.

Just as I spoke about delusional artists who feel entitled to the spotlight in the introduction of this book, don't think for a second that there aren't promoters out there who don't feel entitled to every dime that they bring in that night. The reality is that without your act, and other acts like yours, this promoter wouldn't be able to make a penny.

Some promoters may tell you that for the money you're spending you'll receive great "exposure."

This is a crock of shit.

You are a performing artist.

Every time you get on stage, it's exposure.

This is what the entire live music industry is based on.

If it wasn't for the exposure, you wouldn't be performing live, and the whole reason you're supposed to be getting paid is because you are the one who is providing the entertainment to a room full of people.

Any promoter that will try to dispute this fact with you should be avoided at all costs.

Let's look at another example of event mismanagement.

I was just recently made aware of a promoter who's charging non-headlining acts an additional fee for placement on the flyer of the show that they're already performing on.

This guy doesn't know what he's doing; he's more concerned about making a quick buck than having a successful event and he's doing nothing for the growth and visibility of the acts on his event. He's a promoter; it's his job to list every single act that's on the bill, along with the show date, time, location, cost, and age restrictions.

That's what promoting is; it's not just about the headlining or touring national act. Creating visibility for locals is often what creates a draw, and attending to the growth and development of these local acts by giving them that visibility will actually keep him in business over an extended period of time. Unless you're a last-minute addition to a show and the flyers and posters are already printed, your name should appear on that flyer.

Also, if you have an official logo, that logo should be what appears on that flyer. Under most circumstances this is standard and any worthwhile promoter is already doing this without the need for you to ask.

I've personally never had to deal with any of these problems, which just means that I was lucky to have had good promoters and stand-up people in my network. I can tell you with the utmost sincerity that there hasn't been one time that my band has performed where we didn't receive some sort of compensation. Whether it was cash, food, beer, or a combination of all three, we ALWAYS walked away with something. When I combined that with my merchandise and CD sales, there were some nights where I actually did very well.

One thing that some promoters fail to realize is that it's actually the draw from the local acts that ensures that the touring bands' guarantees are met. Without the locals being proactive in bringing their friends and fan base to an event, the show will be a bust. If it is, the promoter had better have money in his reserves to pay the touring act or any headliner that requires a guarantee.

Promoters that don't know what they're doing are just in the way and should be cleared out of this industry; they're poisoning the reputation of those who do this job with integrity.

There are a lot of good promoters out there and they make sure money gets dispersed the way it should after a show and there a few different ways that they determine this, which we'll discuss in the next chapter.

It's been my experience that the promoters who do this as a part of a community or a tightly knit music scene, and who are actually honest and fair with the bands and artists, outlive many fly-by-night promoters because they build a solid reputation and word gets around, even on a national and international basis. Traveling acts know that this person is well-established and has a reputation of paying out without hassles or bullshit and that they can count on a well-promoted show for that date on their tour.

One of these such promoters—whom I have also had the distinct pleasure of working with—is Shane Merrill of Empire Productions, Chicago's premiere independent metal and hardcore show promotions company.

Merrill, who has been booking shows since 1997, has developed a long-lasting solid reputation as the go-to guy in Chicago for touring bands and had this to say when I asked him the difference between a good and a bad promoter:

"More than anything, passion separates a good promoter from a bad one. With passion, the bands are the focus, and everything else falls into place. Without it, you always have to worry about what brought the

promoter to the table in the first place. If it wasn't a passion and love for the music, they aren't there for the right reasons and therefore can't be trusted."

Unfortunately there are many unskilled, inexperienced, and completely unscrupulous promoters within the business who lack any sense of advance planning or organizational skills.

Unorganized events, especially ones that you have the unfortunate luck of coming across when you're on the road, can go seriously wrong for you and any other artists who just wanted to get out and obtain some visibility for themselves or even possibly catch their break.

If you're being charged money to perform on one of these events, you may be entering into a haphazard situation. So be aware and play at your own risk.

There's a larger likelihood of this happening to you if you're working with people outside of your direct or trusted network. It doesn't happen all the time, but on occasion, it does, and when it happens outside of your hometown, it can put a financial burden and unnecessary stress on you.

For instance, it's becoming a well-documented fact that independent promoters from everywhere are crawling out of the woodwork every winter and attempting to host some type of *pay–to-play* event in Austin, Texas during the South by Southwest (SXSW) convention and festival.

Many of these events aren't even sanctioned by SXSW or affiliated with it in any official capacity; and at times, this is where things go seriously wrong.

The allure of having the ability to perform at such a large festival is tantalizing to an emerging artist and is the exact thing that promoters are capitalizing on. Unfortunately for the unknowing or inexperienced artist, this comes at a price; and on a growing number of occasions promoters are proving that they are unable to deliver

These promises are made to artists not only by event promoters in Austin, but by promoters in their hometowns as well, which creates a nationwide roadmap of costly potholes and hurdles that an artist must avoid while trying to obtain placement on this festival.

There is a story of a promoter who recently brought a coach bus full of artists from his city to perform at a bar just outside of the conference and failed to do any advance promotion in Austin whatsoever.

There are multiple advertising platforms available to everyone during this festival and SXSW sends out offers very far in advance looking for people who want to advertise on the official program material; this is in addition to any independent marketing that people can do for themselves.

It is alleged that this particular promoter charged these artists a nominal fee to travel to and perform in Austin during SXSW, but he didn't invest any of the money into campaign management, advertising, marketing, or promotions.

The outcome was that nobody showed up to this event. He didn't even have people stationed outside to direct foot traffic into the club.

The only people that attended that event were the artists that came to Austin on that bus. They traveled a long distance only to perform in front of the bartender and the people from their hometown that sat next to them on the drive down.

This is almost as sad as it is laughable.

Always know the capabilities and reputation of the promoters that you decide to work with.

I have been made privy to other unorganized pay-to-play scenarios like this where large amounts of money appear to have been misappropriated and went unaccounted for.

One of these reported events, which was also during SXSW, was managed so poorly that no advertising was done; the original date was postponed by a few days, and the fee to rent the venue was never paid. Complaints of trespassing and other minor infractions combined with the presence of the local authorities dictated the premature conclusion of the event, and the artists who didn't get to perform were never reimbursed for their deposit.

Just as is the case with many poorly organized events, there happened to be no performance riders in place, and no agreements that were enforceable. It was suggested that fear of stepping on toes or making waves within the industry prevented any litigation (or any resolution whatsoever, for that matter) from ever arising.

This in itself is a huge problem because not only does this send a message to the promoter who fucked everything up in the first place that this kind of reckless event organizing is acceptable, but it also emboldens and enables this promoter to pull some bullshit like this again.

To compound these problems for the artists that traveled long distances and lost their money attempting to be on this showcase, not only were they unable to perform, but unfortunately they also had to eat their travel expenses. Hotel lodging is at a premium during this event and the estimated out-of-pocket expense for each artist was around $2,000.

As for the disheartened artist with the overdrawn checking account and the deflated hopes of obtaining visibility and recognition, he is left on his own to grovel somewhere while someone else is counting money in more of a cheerful setting.

I'd like to be perfectly clear by saying that the South by Southwest organization cannot be faulted for what opportunistic promoters due outside of the official festival, and for the most part the festival is a great experience for all that choose to attend. The message here was not meant to vilify SXSW in any way, but to merely educate you as an artist on what to look out for when traveling outside of your local music market and getting involved with promoters from other cities while navigating offers surrounding or encompassing large festivals or any events outside of your hometown.

If you actually want to perform at SXSW, I recommend that you either contact the organization directly or submit to perform on ReverbNation or Sonicbids.

Whatever showcase, concert, or live appearance you are considering being a part of, you should do enough research on the event to determine if it appears to be on shaky ground before you commit to anything. See if someone has had the foresight to place an event listing and do some official advertising by the time you're offered a spot on it.

Find out if the venue even has a public place of amusement license to ensure that the place won't get shut down if the authorities happen to show up.

Throughout my 25+ years of involvement in live music, I can say that things like this usually don't happen, they really should never happen, and to ensure that it doesn't happen to you, always be sure to check the reputation of the people you're dealing with.

Do an Internet search of the name of the promoter or the booking or promotion agency before agreeing to anything.

If you can't find anything on this person or agency, then they aren't established as a business, they've done nothing legitimate, and have created no press for themselves or the shows they claim to have put together.

Did the promoter even have a business card to give you?

Think about it:

If the company can't even promote itself effectively then how can you expect it to create exposure for your event successfully?

When doing your research, type this in your search criteria: "[ACME PROMOTIONS] BAD REVIEWS." You can do this for any company in any industry and it will make any dirt on these companies come to the surface.

There are many promoters in this business that simply have substandard business practices and it will take you some time to learn what to avoid and how to feel out these people and these practices for what they are worth. Obviously this chapter's intention is to give you a head start on this because a well-informed artist is less likely to get fucked over.

All promoters should have an extensive database of contacts. Once they put a show together they should, at the bare minimum, be sending out email blasts, utilizing social media, printing up flyers and posters, and handing out flyers at the concerts leading up to the show they're organizing.

If they aren't involved in actively promoting their event, fuck 'em; read the next chapter and do it yourself.

CHAPTER TWENTY-THREE

GO BOOK YOURSELF!

BOOKING THE GIG YOURSELF
AND SIDE-STEPPING THE PROMOTER

One of the most common questions I hear to this day in the music industry is, "can you get us a gig?"

There's a whole segment of this industry that exists because of this question. After reading this chapter you'll have the ability to either sidestep this segment of the industry or become an active part of it.

SECURING THE VENUE

A common misconception is that in order to play somewhere you need to book the show with a promoter.

This isn't true at all.

If you want to play at a local bar or club, *YOU DO NOT NEED TO* talk to the promoter, the bartender, or the club manager.

Go directly to the owner of the establishment if you have the ability to do so. The bartender may redirect you to the promoter or he may tell you the club is unavailable to you at all.

This is where many artists shrug their shoulders and walk away defeated.

The biggest problem with people today in general is that they ARE willing to take NO for an answer.

If you can't achieve your goals with a direct approach, then rethink your strategy and find an alternate way to achieve your goal.

Call the bar and ask to speak to the owner, but don't volunteer any information to anyone about your reason for calling until you get the owner on the phone, as this will eliminate any possibility of somebody blocking your efforts because they want a cut of your proceeds. Once you get him on the phone, state your intentions and let him know your tentative date. If it's available, then lock your date in with him. In smaller bars and clubs, this usually isn't too difficult.

In larger venues, the person you'll want to contact is known as the talent buyer. This is the person who locks the dates in for the promoters, who in this case, is you.

It's imperative that you don't sound timid or are at a loss for words when you make this call. Have what you need to say rehearsed in your mind and on the tip of your tongue because if the person you're talking to senses that you're in over your head or that you don't know what you're doing then your opportunity ends here and they won't bother with you again, at least not in the near future. So speak your business with intent and confidence.

From this point forward, you'll begin negotiating the terms of hosting your event at this venue.

NEGOTIATING THE AGREEMENT

In larger venues, the person you'll want to contact is known as the talent buyer. This is the person who locks the dates in for the promoters, who in this case, is you.

A commonplace arrangement is for the establishment to keep the revenue from the alcohol sales and the band or promoter to keep the revenue from the admission at the door.

This is the first thing you should ask for, because it gets you the club free of charge and eliminates all of your overhead.

If the club is large enough, the owner may counter your proposal with one that includes a fee to cover the costs of security and the sound engineer. This fee can range from $350 to $500, and is this isn't unreasonable. The club will usually be lenient enough to accept a down payment with the balance due the night of the show. Clubs are also realistic enough on some occasions to agree to accept the payment later in the evening because they realize that you won't have the balance until enough paying attendees come through the front door.

To give you a current and realistic idea of how you can expect a concert venue to respond to your inquiry, I've asked Elle Quintana, talent buyer for Reggie's Rock Club & Music Joint in Chicago to share her position on the matter:

> "There are a lot of different factors that decide how bands get paid out. For Rock Club, there is always a room fee. For an all ages show, it's usually a bit more. Same with hardcore or some hip hop. We need to have more staff and security on site which costs us more money. If it's a national, we agree on a guarantee amount which comes out of door to pay the band first, then expenses come out of door (sound, security, staff, support, airfare/hotel) and then the band gets 80 percent of door after that and club keeps 20 percent. If it's Music Joint, we give the bands 100 percent of the door, shows are always 21+ and we feed the bands and give them food and a place to crash if they need it."

Elle has also mentioned that everything is subject to negotiation on a case-by-case basis.

Developing a relationship and a reputation with this club owner may create additional perks for you once you can prove that you can manage successful events. This doesn't only mean having a great show, but the ability to keep the register in the bar ringing as well. If that bar is consistently profitable after several occasions, you may be able to negotiate a stake in the alcohol sales for the evening. A usual percentage that I've seen agreed upon is usually 10 percent. Bands will also want to drink for free, always. Ask the owner if each act can have a few pitchers of draft beer. The owner may in turn offer a few drink tickets for each member. If you have a touring act coming into town, see if it's possible to get them a hot meal. This will help alleviate some of their traveling expenses and make you look good as a promoter at the same time.

When negotiating the above mentioned terms, you'll need to keep this in mind;

This is a cash-driven business and the club WILL NOT offer you a cut of its revenue from liquor sales; it's going to be up to you to have the balls to ask them for it.

Small bars may be more apt to agree to revenue splits on liquor sales than venues will, but you won't know until you ask.

Be assertive, don't hesitate, and don't balk; this is a concert venue, a club, or a bar. It's not some magic castle that only certain people have the keys for. It's an empty room with a stage and some barstools, that's it, nothing more.

Furthermore, if you're trying to book your show on an off night, which is pretty much any day besides Friday or Saturday; you'll be much more likely to get a club owner to agree to most of your terms. The ball is in your court here, because if he doesn't agree to you receiving a percentage of his alcohol sales and you don't perform there, the club will stay empty and he'll make no money at all. The club owner is fully aware of this.

Always remember that everything is negotiable and nothing is off-limits.

Your event makes the club money, not the other way around. Don't ever forget this.

Now that doesn't mean that it's okay to get cocky and become confrontational with a club owner over an open night either; learn the art of negotiation and always talk to these people as if you'll be doing business with them again.

This same plan of attack can be easily applied to mid-sized and larger venues, in which case, as previously mentioned, you may be dealing with a talent buyer as opposed to the owner.

Everything is usually negotiable to some point, and if you have a good reputation the venue's staff will usually be very accommodating.

To this day I'm able to get a venue that holds 350 people with no questions asked and no money down. It takes time to get to that point, but if you play your cards right you should be there in no time.

LEAD TIMES AND PRINT DEADLINES

Once you have an agreement in place with the venue and your *tentative date* becomes a *confirmed date,* you're pretty much on your own. It's your show.

In order to effectively promote this show, you should give yourself adequate time to promote it. I recommend five weeks of lead time. This will leave several weekends for you and all the members of the bands on your bill to go out and promote the event. Obviously most people go out on Friday and Saturday nights, so having this additional lead time will give everyone plenty of time to make their rounds and get the word out.

The venue will place the performers' names from your show on its marquis if it has one and will most likely post your flyers in its establishment. They will also place your event listing on their website and in any monthly show listings they have in local newspapers and publications. Some of these publications and websites will also require at least four weeks of advance notice. Magazines and monthly papers have a print deadline that they must meet as well, and that is well in advance of the date that the paper hits the stands. This is why I use five weeks as a rule. It allows for these timeframes and deadlines. If you're able to get this additional visibility from the club then this will be about all you can expect from them as far as promotions are concerned.

A small bar that consistently has live performances may have event listings as well, but don't count on this publicity. Although you may get this additional visibility, it's your obligation to yourself and the bands that you have booked to manage the promotions of this event yourself.

After all, the club is not the promoter—you are.

Running your show efficiently is going to be entirely up to you. If you use the guidelines I present to you in this book without skipping any steps you should do well with your event.

Usually you will have a touring act that needs a show in your city or some local artists or bands in mind before approaching a venue. Once you have a few groups in mind and a venue locked in with a confirmed date it's time to get to work.

You now need to confirm and lock the bands. Ask the bands to make sure their members don't have any outstanding obligations that day. Believe me; someone will always forget that they had something to do. The last thing you want to have happen is to print up flyers with bands that aren't performing. Yes, it does happen; but if you adhere to certain standards it will be less likely to happen and may be prevented altogether.

With show promotions come costs, so I'm now going to present to you a common scenario that will help alleviate some of the financial risk of you doing this on your own:

COVERING THE GUARANTEE

If you're going to host a touring act or need to pay for a headliner, you need to make sure that you can deliver on your promise to pay their guarantee. Between the cost of the venue, the headliner's guarantee, and the cost of your promotions, you've accepted a decent amount of risk and responsibility.

You'll need to have some reserves on hand to get the ball rolling, such as a down payment for the venue, an additional down payment against any guarantees that you need to pay out, and enough cash to print up flyers, posters, and tickets.

Having the bands pay for the tickets in advance will allow you to make the money you need to cover your upfront costs. If you give each act 30 tickets for a few dollars under the face value of the tickets and the bands in turn sell the tickets for full face value, you will put them in a position where they'll stand to make a profit after they recoup their expense of paying for the tickets.

For example:

- you give the band 30 tickets that have a $10 face value;
- you charge them $7 a ticket ($7 X 30 tickets = $210).
- They sell all the tickets for the full face value of $10 ($10 X 30 tickets = $300) and they make a $90 profit for themselves. If they sell additional tickets, they make even more.

- Upon receipt of the tickets, the bands pay you $210. If you have five bands, you have just made $1,050 towards your expenses. Spend this money wisely and use it appropriately.

Some may argue that this is the formula and framework for pay-to-play, and although it doesn't call for the outright payment for performance slots, it does raise some ethical questions among long time participants of the live music industry who don't believe that any up-front payment should be made by the bands who are providing the entertainment.

Unfortunately, ethics don't run very high among many fame seeking musicians anyway, and until you find artists that you are sure have a dedicated following, this method of booking shows will insulate you from any financial burdens you may incur due to overprojecting event revenues based on performing artists lying about the size of their fanbase.

This isn't the only way to promote a show, but if you haven't established yourself as a promoter, and are unsure of the reputation of the acts that will be performing on your show, this is your best bet. Otherwise, if things don't work out, it's you who will be paying the venue and the guarantees.

This type of business model is becoming more and more prevalent in today's industry, and although it may be an unpopular format to many seasoned musicians, this book was written to give you, the individual reader, a leg-up on the current industry practices that you will encounter. So in an effort to empower you to pull off a successful live event on your first attempt, I have included this detailed scenario because I can guarantee you that when artists find out that you're hosting a live event, they'll want to perform. I can also guarantee that they'll tell you that they'll pack the house. They will blow more smoke up your ass than a fog machine to get on the bill, and some of the artists may not have any real following at all will actually eat the cost of the tickets just to perform.

You can pre-screen your acts by simply checking the amount of followers they have on their social media pages for their bands. If they have no followers, no page likes, no friends, and no song plays then they probably won't bring anyone through the door of the club.

You can also give artists additional incentive to sell tickets by offering the better slots in the lineup to those who sell the most tickets.

Once you know that the bands you're working with can bring a consistent draw, then it's not necessary to have the bands purchase tickets in advance. Keep in mind though, every band, every promoter, and every club will have a bad night from time to time, so be prepared for this.

Another option for you if you're just getting started and want to find a fair way to disburse payment amongst the bands that performed is to run a tally at the door of who is coming in to see which band. Set a fixed amount you will give each band per person and multiply it times the number of people that came to see each band. For small shows of less than a few hundred people, this is by far the fairest way to compensate the bands.

It's as easy as that.

PROMOTING YOUR LIVE EVENT

As a small independent promoter, you still have the option of selling tickets in advance online. Even though your events may not yet be big enough to use Ticketmaster, there are other ticketing companies that will allow you to sell tickets for your event online.

- Ticketfly.com
- Brownpapertickets.com
- Ticketweb.com
- Eventbrite.com
- Eventful.com

All of the companies above are available for use by independent promoters and bands. They'll also enable you to add a purchase link to your online promotions for the event including your website, social media, and anywhere else you can use HTML embedding codes or are able to paste your links online.

Creating an event on Facebook has become a very common method of online concert promotion; you can invite all of your friends to the event in one sitting and your ticket sales link can be posted in that event as well. Utilizing all of your social media platforms and Web pages is also a standard method of show promotion. If you're not doing this already, you're way behind the curve.

You should have an email list strictly for band info and news established by now. I covered how to do this in the chapter on building a support structure. Make sure the show information gets out to all of these contacts.

Email your local newspaper the information and see if you can get a write-up.

Contact any bloggers that you know that cover your genre of music and ask them to post your flyer or event listing.

Text message the show info with the ticket purchase link to everyone in your phone that you would like to invite and be sure to get your flyers out.

Disperse your flyers to as many people as possible *that you think will be interested.* Don't go on a mad dash to get rid of them; you have five weeks. Place them where it counts, and in the hands of those that you think have a good chance of showing up.

As I stated in the chapter on marketing, printing companies give discounts for larger orders. I personally would never order anything less than 5,000 flyers based on cost alone.

Just make sure that your flyers have all of this information on them:

- Name of headlining act
- Names of all supporting acts
- Name of venue
- Address
- Date
- Time

- Cost
- Age restrictions
- Alcohol or drink specials
- Contact information (make sure they don't get lost)

If you have room, put the website addresses for the bands under their logos so people can check them out in advance. I take this extra step because it creates a level of convenience and ease of access for the potential concertgoer to listen to bands he may have not yet heard, which could result in better attendance, which results in more revenue.

You can also offer free or discounted entry for the ladies, as it's no secret that if you have a lot of women attending your events you'll also get a lot of men to show up. For that matter, have a wet T-shirt contest. If you do, make sure you put that on the flyer as well.

Make sure you have your flyers with you at all times in the weeks leading up to your event. Whether you're going to a bar, a concert, a block party, or a barbeque, everywhere you step can become a potential promotional opportunity.

Always be prepared, because successful people are always prepared.

There are many other conventional and unconventional ways to promote a show. Be inventive and be aggressive; the success of your event depends on it.

The one repetitive message that I keep trying to get across in this book is that you should always be willing to do a little *more* than what's required of you. That's what will put you ahead of the crowd and the competition every time. Keep this in mind because if you can prove that you can successfully promote shows on a continual basis you'll eventually place yourself in a position where big-name touring artists are contacting you for a performance date in your city.

Once this happens, you've effectively leveled the playing field.

Please keep in mind that you should run your live events with a sense of integrity and a moral obligation to pay your performing artists. The whole reason I've written this chapter is so you could avoid getting screwed over by the fast-talking shyster promoters that exist in this industry and create a revenue stream for yourself.

If you perpetuate the same business practices as the people that have taken your money in the past then you're no better than they are and you're not part of the solution—you're just another part of the problem.

CHAPTER TWENTY-FOUR

PERFORMANCE RIDERS AND GUARANTEES

We briefly covered some nightmare scenarios that have happened as a result of having no written agreements in place. Now we'll discuss how to put an agreement in place that will ideally prevent these things from happening, or at the least hold the responsible party financially liable for your out-of-pocket expenses and guarantee should the promoter be unable to deliver on his end of the agreement.

If you're traveling anywhere out of your immediate local area and need to cover the logistical expenses of moving your band and your equipment around, I highly recommend you present a performance agreement and rider that contains a compensation clause to the talent buyer or promoter that you're dealing with.

Your expenses traveling out of town will usually consist of missed days at work, a 4X8 trailer rental, gas (or perhaps airfare and car rental), hotel, and food. Whatever it costs you to get to your destination, it will cost you to get back. So in most cases, you are going out on a limb financially.

The guarantee that you're offered often won't cover all of your expenses but will definitely help offset them. This is where merchandising helps a band greatly. The revenue from a merch table can offset these expenses to a break-even point or—in the best-case scenario—make the gig become profitable.

Should the show get cancelled for any reason whatsoever, you'll receive no pay from any source and will absorb all the costs yourself.

These things happen; sometimes they're unavoidable. Fights break out, liquor licenses get suspended, fire marshals close venues down for being over capacity, building departments close venues for public safety issues, clubs get double-booked, and the list goes on.

In an effort to protect yourself from any loss of revenue or visibility due to not being able to perform, you need to have a performance agreement, rider attachment, and monetary guarantee in place.

This documentation, if drafted correctly, will hold the talent buyer or promoter responsible for things falling apart on their end. It will also hold you responsible for arriving and performing at your engagement.

If you decide that you want to start promoting shows, you'll be presented these same types of agreements from certain artists, so get familiar with this chapter; it may help you land the act that you want to have headline.

There are a few separate parts of this documentation that are separate pieces of the whole agreement:

1. THE LIVE PERFORMANCE AGREEMENT – This is where the basic stipulations of the engagement are listed, including your pay. These are all very common in nature and this is the key piece of documentation that you'll need to have in order.
2. THE RIDER AND ITS ATTACHMENTS – The rider (sometimes referred to as the hospitality rider), has additional provisions to the basic agreement. This goes into detail about what the band's needs are. These are listed 1 to 21 and have a section for additional provisions and an example of an added compensation clause for a percentage of the liquor sales attached.
3. STAGE PLOT AND INPUT LIST – Sometimes referred to as the technical rider, this gives the club or the production company the info they need for your stage set-up and exactly what kinds of equipment you are using. This can go into specific detail on compressor and EQ settings and more.
    The stage plot is an actual drawing or schematic of where on the stage the equipment is placed. The stage plot is technically a map that's given to the backline tech, whose responsibility it is to mic up all the instrumentation and plug and pin effects processors.
    These are usually accompanied by the input list and/or technical rider, which gives a detailed list of the name brand equipment that the musician is using and where he has his settings dialed in. These may also include the effects chain details for the vocalist and backup singers for groups that try to sound as close to their studio recording as they can while performing live.

Here's an example of what I request in a performance agreement and rider as well as what it looks like:

LIVE PERFORMANCE AGREEMENT

TERMS

Name of Band or Artist:_____

Name and address of venue:_____

Talent buyer or name of promoter booking event:_____

Date and time of performance:_____

Number of sets and length of performance:_____

Time slot or placement location on showbill:_____

Load in time:_____

Time for sound check:_____

Total compensation:_____

Deposit payment:_____

Date deposit payment to be paid:_____

Artist's Right to Terminate

If artist is entitled to a deposit payment as provided in the Payment section of this agreement, and the deposit has not been paid within the time specified, Artist shall have the right to terminate this agreement without further obligation.
Rider and Attachments

The attached Performance Rider (the "Rider") and any other attachments or exhibits to this Agreement are incorporated into this Agreement.

TERMS OF RIDER

1. Artists and staff will be provided a dressing room Y/N?_____

2. VIP/All Access will be granted to following amount of people_____

3. Hospitality will include food Y/N?_____

4. Hospitality will include beverages in dressing room, including alcoholic and non-alcoholic beverages and water Y/N? Including_____

5. Each Artist requires 3 clean cotton towels can this be provided Y/N?

6. Vendor area will be set aside for Artist and Staff for merchandise sales. If Pre-existing please specify area and display dimensions for vending area._____

If such an area does not exist we request a 10' x 10' area to set up a booth, tent, or tables in a medium to highly trafficked, high visibility area in/on venues landscape or floor plan. Preferably near the front door or in an area which is in line of the access and egress of the performance area.

7. Complimentary tickets and/or guest list will be provided for following amount of non-staff people_____

8. We require our artist's name/logo to appear on all promotional material for this event. We will furnish you with our artist's logo in Jpeg or PDF format unless you require a different format, please give us an email address to send this artwork to_____

9. You will disperse promotional material through all networks available to you.

10. We would like to submit a photo of our artist for flyer and promotional purposes if this is possible   Y/N?

11. The names of artists will be used in all radio   advertising for this event if such advertising exists.

12. If you will be televising commercials can we submit live footage of our artists for this event's commercial, and will you use it Y/N?

13. Will or can you provide us with any media coverage, such as local newspaper, radio, or television interviews/reviews Y/N?

14. We request that you furnish any copies of newspaper clippings, advertisements, flyers, posters, write ups and reviews of this performance to by emailing me at_____

15. Will intelligent lighting or the lightshow be synced with P.A. system?

16. We would like access to your soundbooth and be allowed to work the board with or without your resident engineer during our artist's performance to assure the highest quality sound.

17. Our artist has been billed with_____
and others. He has been booked at large outdoor events/festivals including_____, he has been interviewed on live radio in several cities including_____, and he is a solicited artist with international distribution on our label and has headlined shows on which many Midwest acts have performed. Due to his credentials and experience, we are requesting that our artist's slot be directly before headlining act. Is this possible? If not we would like to request a spot as close to headlining artist as possible.

18. Are there any slots open for any of our other Artists on this playbill? Y/N?

19. Is there an option for a return engagement? If you have one in mind, please specify_____.

20. You will allow us to hang our banners on your stage for the entire evening Y/N?

21. Additional Banner placement will be allowed elsewhere? If so please specify.

ADDITIONAL PROVISIONS TO BE ENTERED HERE:

_____

_____

General

Nothing contained in this agreement or the accompanying Rider shall be deemed to constitute either Purchaser or Artist a partner or employee of the other party. This agreement and the accompanying Rider and exhibits express the complete understanding of the parties and may not be amended except in a writing signed by both parties. If a court finds any provision of this Agreement or the accompanying rider invalid or unenforceable, the remainder of this Agreement shall be interpreted so as best to effect the intent of the parties. This Agreement shall be governed by and interpreted in accordance with the laws of the State of _____, In the event of any dispute arising from or related to this agreement, it shall be heard in the State of _____, County of _____, City of _____, and the prevailing party shall be entitled to attorney's fees.

Artists Name and Title_____

Artist Signature_____

Address_____

Date_____

Purchaser Name and Title_____

Address_____

Date_____

STAGE PLOT AND INPUT LIST

Sample Stage Plot

stage right   stage left

20 AMP 120 Volt AC outlet is
required within 4 feet of every
instrument and mic stand location.

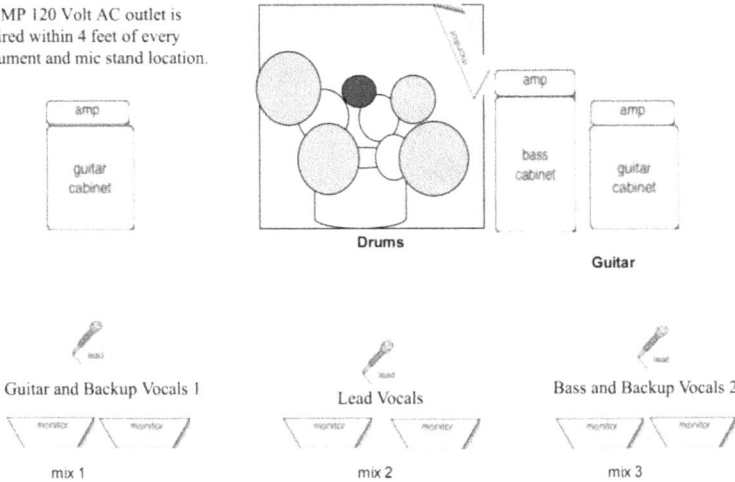

amp

guitar
cabinet

amp

bass
cabinet

amp

guitar
cabinet

Drums

Guitar

Guitar and Backup Vocals 1

Lead Vocals

Bass and Backup Vocals 2

mix 1

mix 2

mix 3

INPUT LIST

CH.	INSTRUMENT	MIC TYPE	STAND	INSERT	GROUPS	LOCATION
1	Kick-In	Beta-91a	xlr	comp/gate	1&2	Drums
2	Kick-Out	Beta-52	short boom	gate	1&2	Drums
3	Snare Top	ATM-25	claw	comp/gate	1&2	Drums
4	Snare Bottom	e905	claw	gate	1&2	Drums
5	Hat	SM-81	short boom			Drums
6	Tom 1	ATM-350	clip	gate	1&2	Drums
7	Floor	ATM-350	clip	gate	1&2	Drums
8	SPDS-Pad	DI	n/a	comp		Drums
9	Mono Tracks	DI	n/a	comp		Drums
10	Oh Stage Right	ATM-450	boom			Drums
11	Oh Stage Left	ATM-450	boom			Drums
12	Bass DI	DI	n/a	comp		SL
13	Guitar SR 1	SM57	n/a		3&4	SR
14	Guitar SL 1	SM57	n/a		3&4	SL
15	Backup Vocal 1	AE6100	boom	comp		SR
16	Lead Vocal	AE6100	n/a	comp		Center
17	Backup Vocal 2	AE6100	boom	comp		SL

We are only carrying a vocal microphone and Dis for samples/spds/guitars.
If available, please have compressors on groups 1-4.

MORE ON RIDERS (*OR MORON RIDERS*)

As the author of this book, I should probably make a public disclaimer absolving myself from any idiotic or childish requests made to promoters on the behalf of any moronic performing artist who may have read this chapter and decided to make an outrageous rider request based on the stupid shit that the media has placed inside his infantile mind.

There will be at least one person who, while reading the 21 rider terms that I offered as an example, will think to himself,

"Oooh, this is where I can ask for an ounce of cocaine on a sterling silver tea service brought to me backstage by a half-naked chocolate-covered midget wrapped in Christmas lights."

No, dumbass, that's not the purpose of this chapter.

There are many stories about outrageous and ridiculous things that artists have requested in their performance riders, and all of these off-the-wall demands have been made based on one historical incident.

While on tour in 1982, Van Halen requested several bowls of M&M's back stage with the mandatory removal of all brown M&M's; failure to do so was to result in show cancellation.

This sparked the imagination of many bands who have concocted many an idiotic rider.

The facts behind the Van Halen story are actually based on purpose and principle, not on some stupid cockamamie bullshit as many of you might have assumed.

During their 1982 world tour, the band felt that if management didn't pay attention to the most minute details of their rider, that things would go unnoticed elsewhere which would result in problems on a larger scale. With extremely complicated wiring diagrams for stage lighting and stage assembly schematics for almost 10 semi-trucks full of equipment there was a natural concern that if something as simple as a few pieces of candy were overlooked that any number of other things could go seriously wrong—some of which could be potentially life-threatening.

You'll be entering into a professional contract with a booking agency or professional stage production company; when requesting your terms it will be in your power to determine if you're respected as an adult or looked upon as a child. Choose your rider stipulations based on professional necessity and choose your terms wisely.

CHAPTER TWENTY-FIVE

DIY TOURING

Rockin Riviera, singer of Chicago Hardcore band NO REGRETS, booking his band's April 2014 East Coast tour during a slow winter night at Chicago's Cobra Lounge.

I've mentioned earlier in this book the necessity of getting your music into as many markets as possible. A good way to rephrase this is to just say that you need to play in as many cities as possible if you want to make a name for yourself.

Now I'm going to outline an easy and realistic approach to this that any artist from any genre can do. This method is so ridiculously simple that you'll be upset with yourself for not thinking of it on your own.

This process will require you to do some work.

Yes, there's that nasty four-letter word again that I keep on using.

However, this whole process will involve nothing more than a little investigative research combined with some basic communication skills, and it can mostly all be done from a laptop.

For the benefit of everyone reading this book, let's assume that you, the reader, are in a new band and you have virtually no network of bands that you play with in other cities. You're the person for whom I wrote this chapter.

If I was in your position, and I wanted to get the word out about my new release by touring—as we've already discussed—the first thing that I would do is jump on ReverbNation.com.

This website is by no means the end-all-be-all of booking a tour online, but it provides you an immediate method and solution to do something that you may have been unable to do for yourself before.

Until a time comes along where you've built up some road experience along with a contact list that includes booking agents and promoters and can establish some other viable options for touring without having someone charge you outright, here's a way for you to get things done for yourself.

ReverbNation is the home base for over 3 million musicians from every genre from all over the world. You can look bands up on ReverbNation by genre, by city, and by local chart position. ReverbNation itself has already done most of the work for you by categorizing bands like this in their database.

I would seek out the top 10 or 20 bands from your genre in each of the closest major metropolitan areas in every direction that are within a reasonable driving distance from your house and start researching them.

I would go on their pages and start looking over their profiles as I listened to their music. The things that I would be looking for would be the following:

- How often is this band performing?
- How many upcoming dates does this band have?
- Do any of these dates fit my schedule?

- How many Total Fans does this band have?
- Does this band have any recent positive press?
- How do they sound? Do they suck? Would I promote them in my hometown?
- What kind of comments are people leaving about them or their music on their page?
- When looking at their live photos, does there appear to be a decent crowd at their shows?

All of the above information can be ascertained in under a minute by going on the band's ReverbNation profile.

ReverbNation is by no means your only option. In Chapter Eight I mentioned the importance of joining groups on Facebook that are specific to your genre of music. Not only are other bands posting in these groups, but also fans, booking agents, and promoters. This is a great way to start becoming a part of a larger network of ambitious working musicians.

Once you find a band that appears to be active in their region or city—and that appears to have a following and good press—send them a message and let them know that you'd like to trade shows with them.

"Trading shows" is a common practice among working bands whether they're in the same city or in neighboring cities. The principle is simple; you book them on your next show in your area, and in turn, they book you on their next show in their area.

Ideally, you want to discuss their travel expenses ahead of time along with yours. Feel free to sign an agreement with them as well to ensure that you start off on the right foot.

This shouldn't be a problem because if you're promoting and booking your own shows the way I've outlined in this book, you should have enough money put aside FOR ANY AND EVERY TRAVELING BAND YOU BOOK. Even if you need to dig into your pocket, make sure you do the right thing for bands that are on the road. You'll want to be treated this same way when you travel away from your hometown. Being in this business is about building long-lasting, positive relationships.

ENTER THE WEEKEND WARRIOR

A good way to start out is by booking your shows on weekends so your traveling doesn't interfere with anyone's work schedules. If you play one city on Friday and another on a Saturday then you've made it to step one.

Weekend shows also have a tendency to bring out a better draw. To help ensure this, remember to plan these dates in advance and use that additional time to maximize your promotional efforts.

So now you've executed this plan successfully with a band in another city. Now do it again with another city in any direction that is of a similar or equal distance to the city you've just done this in.

If you have three or four cities to perform in that you can travel to in under four to six hours in any direction from your hometown then you'll be able to start creating a regional presence for yourself.

This is known as the ripple effect. You start creating a fan base in the local cities closest to you and spread outwards from there.

Getting some notoriety and becoming known in other cities is simply another form of branding. As I've mentioned before, branding is an ongoing process and what you're doing is still considered as marketing yourself, which means that you'll need to make several appearances in other cities before any substantial amount of people really start becoming aware of you. If you plan on doing this for a living, then you'll need to start doing this for a living.

Once people start getting to know you in these cities, you'll need to keep up your appearances in an effort to keep up with your fan support. It's important that you attend to this because if your fan base doesn't grow, it may die. Make sure to book repeating dates.

After you've established a few bands to trade shows with and the number of these bands begins to increase, you can then start booking full weekends.

Play your hometown on Friday, leave Saturday morning to get to the next city, perform Saturday night, and do the whole thing again on Sunday with an attempt to be home before everyone needs to be at work on Monday morning.

There you have it—three shows in three days with expenses covered and nobody missed a day of work. This weekend warrior method of expanding your reach is the standard practice of many independent bands I know, and a practice I've successfully used myself. If you can't make this small step in the development of your group's growth and visibility then you've most likely gone as far as you're going to get in your career and you shouldn't realistically expect much more.

For those of you who've successfully been creating a buzz in several cities, your online fans, followers, and plays should be going up in number and hopefully you've been able to sell your merch at shows. Hopefully your digital and physical sales will begin to pick up and you'll have the means and the desire to expand your reach even further.

If you've tapped into an extended network of active bands by this point in time, you may be able to get referrals to booking agents and promoters. In this day and age, everyone has a Facebook or a LinkedIn profile, and this is where you'll find these people. This whole process really isn't difficult at all and you can do as much of this yourself as you're willing to accomplish.

Keep in mind you can still go back on ReverbNation as well. Look up bands in additional cities and add to your network. If these bands are active but aren't booking their own shows, they probably have the juice to get you on a show and will help set it up for you.

You can also make use of the tools available on the Internet that will help you estimate your driving time to any destination and provide you with a map that you can print out as well.

For that matter you can do all your navigation from your smartphone. Just make sure you have a charger with you at all times. The one time that your phone battery always seems to be dead or dying is when you're on a road trip.

Some of the bands you're meeting may even be a part of a larger network and you will become part of it. This will make your interstate tour planning a lot easier. For now, let's presume that this isn't the case and that you're the one and only person that you can depend on to see this tour scheduled from beginning to end.

Start calculating how many hours it will take to drive from one city to the next when going outside of your pre-existing touring perimeter. Estimate how many gallons of gas it will take you to travel these distances. You can find out how many miles per gallon your vehicle will get by looking this information up online if you don't know it already.

If you're on the Northeastern seaboard of the United States, you've got it made. Every city is a short distance and drive from each other.

Things spread out a little in the Southeast and in the Midwest but are still much closer than the distance between cities once you get west of the Mississippi River. The further west you go, the longer the travel time is between viable cities to play in.

Once you start taking these things into consideration, and have developed a relationship with some solid bands and concert promoters in other cities, you can start working on a budget and attempt to book a small tour, perhaps up to nine days in length.

A nine-day tour is a good workable number because the employed portion of your group will only need to take a week off of work.

You either leave on Friday or do a kickoff show on Friday in your hometown. The fans' support and door money pads up your account for travel expenses and you're on the road later that night or early the next morning to your first out-of-town date.

In an ideal scenario, you're booked every day through the following Saturday night. So in actuality you're looking at a maximum of eight performance dates. The ninth and last day of the tour is set aside for traveling home, but it doesn't have to be.

A band that travels every day and performs every night spends much less money than a band that has days off.

A band with days off starts getting bored and starts fucking off and spending money on bullshit.

For the most part, the van will become your hotel room; most of the sleeping will get done between cities. That is, unless you have that one unruly band member who stays drunk and can't shut the fuck up while everyone else is trying to sleep.

Having a Rand McNally road atlas in the van is a good idea, because when your cell phone battery runs out or you're out of your service provider's area, the only directions you'll get could be from a van full of arguing people who are all pissed off that they're lost and need to be somewhere at a certain time.

Get a full vehicle inspection, a tune–up, and a roadside assistance policy for your vehicle before you leave on any road trip. These expenses combined with the small upcharge on your policy is well worth avoiding costly tow truck, mechanic fees, and rental car costs if for some reason your vehicle breaks down.

You can easily cut costs by having a band go on the road with you to share expenses. Getting a van that seats 15 to 20 people and an 8' x 4' x 8' tow-behind trailer for your equipment, luggage, and merch will get you where you need to go. You may even have enough room left over to stick that drunk motherfucker back there. You can use a hole saw to cut a hole in the floor of that trailer and use a few pieces of PVC pipe and some reducers to build him a self-draining urinal too if you're going to leave him back there for long distances.

Both bands can use a common drum kit. A lot of touring bands strip their larger kits down to a four-piece. There's really no need for a 12- to 14-piece kit with two bass drums and a cage. A double kick petal eliminates that other drum all together. All that other shit is for image and it takes up a lot of space and a lot of set-up time. Guitarists and bassists can use the same cabinets as well which greatly reduces space and weight. The heavier the load that you're towing, the more gas you'll consume.

A pit stop at a motel will be necessary for a shower, but that's about it. You can also do a load of laundry and let everyone check their emails while you're here if the hotel provides a few coin-operated laundry machines and a Wi-Fi connection.

Just make sure someone is in the van or has their eye on it at all times. You don't want your equipment stolen because you stopped for a four-hour nap at some seedy motel that's better known as the Crack Pipe Chalet.

If you're on a budget, stay out of bars and restaurants; these tabs add up quick. Adding a round of shots to the bill can double your tab in some instances.

You're better off buying a case of beer or a 30-pack and taking it back to the hotel room if you must drink.

The whole point here is not to spend more than you're making.

A loaf of bread and a pack of cold cuts can feed the whole team as well. You'll probably get a hot meal at the club you're going to if you remembered to ask for it when you discussed your performance rider and guarantee.

If you're eating meager meals to stay within budget, heed the advice of Paul G. from the Las Vegas-based shock-rock band I.D.S.F.A. and take a few bags of oranges with you on the road.

The oranges make a good snack and are loaded with Vitamin C, which you probably need if you've been partying the whole time.

The bags are also good because they're actually made from plastic netting, and you can put the peels in them and throw them under the seat. The result will be a natural citrus air freshener that will help keep down the stink of several sweaty musicians who haven't bathed since before their last performance.

Soggy corn chips. This is what some people's tour vans smell like. The stale combination of feet, armpit, and ass. Good luck trying to get the cute girl with the pigtails and the fishnets to come and "hang out" with you in the van if it smells like you just walked into Paul Bunyan's damp, musty sock.

Buy the oranges, buy new air freshener trees to hang from the rear view mirror, and buy some adhesive air fresheners as well. This will be your house for a few weeks; try to make it as comfortable as possible.

The more comfortable you make your environment; the further away you'll be from the need to diffuse a nuclear meltdown.

You'll be living in confined quarters for this whole trip. People fart, they snore, they drop snacks and other garbage all over the floor when they're drunk, they burn off alcohol through their pores, they're hungry, thirsty, pissed that the last show didn't pay well, and things can get confrontational.

It's going to take a special kind of patience to drive the short bus long distances while listening to the constant mindfucking that happens when too many alpha males are jammed into the same small container; please keep this in mind.

A good reason to justify a road trip and short tour is if you manage to get yourself booked at a festival. Smart artists and bands book additional show dates around these key dates and connect the dots between each city to and from the music festival they're building the tour around.

FYI – *Going on tour does not mean traveling a great distance to play only one show.* So please don't tell people you're on tour if you only have one date booked. You'll make yourself look like a moron.

ReverbNation and SonicBids are two websites that will allow you to submit your presskit to perform at festivals year-round. These festivals are happening all over the United States and the world and are known to have the potential to put you in front of anywhere from 500 to 15,000 or more people in one day.

The festival itself may be several states and several months away, which gives you plenty of time to pull out a map, see what cities are between your hometown and the city hosting the festival, and begin planning your tour. Use the U.S. Highway and Interstate systems as a guideline in your planning to see which cites you should target and the travel times and distances between them.

Schedule as many performance dates as you can on the way to the festival. Perhaps you can choose a different route on the way home, so you can play other cities that you didn't reach on the way there.

If you follow your marketing procedure or work with established bands or booking agents, you should be fine.

Bands that travel like this are active in their careers; they're go-getters who are out seeking opportunities. You never know who's in your audience or if they're an A&R rep, manager, booking agent, or tour manager who's impressed by your current tour schedule and your work ethic.

This is how many bands get discovered—by traveling and bringing the music to the people, not by waiting around for the people to come to them.

Once you start making a name for yourself in your genre and have fan support, more well-known "national" acts will start recognizing what you've been doing independently and may ask you to go on a tour with them as an opening act.

These tours can last a month or more and are great visibility for you because the headlining act already has an established fan base that will attend their shows.

Your fans, even if you have a limited amount of them, will add to this number of people and potentially help create the possibility of a very well-attended show, which in almost all cases is equal to an awesome show.

Keep in mind that the entire time that you're doing this, you'll have a decent selection of merchandise and a choice of T-shirt sizes with you on the road. Not only will this help spread your visibility and branding, but as I have mentioned elsewhere in this book, sometimes getting paid can be a problem and you'll need to try to create additional revenue to keep yourself out of a bind.

So there you have it.

You've just read the basic fundamentals of do-it-yourself touring.

Outside of my suggestion to use ReverbNation for the purpose of setting up your shows, another way to go about this is to reach through your existing network and see what promoters are booking shows in each city or region. It may take you some time before you've created access to all of these people, but they are there. You'll just need to become well-networked well enough in your genre to obtain access to them.

I can tell you that the information in this chapter is in current practice by many bands. It was in practice by many bands before them for several decades and will continue to be in practice for many bands over the years to come. Many bands will not need to rely on ReverbNation for setting up their whole tours because they're a part of a network of bands within their genre that's been established over a period of time. Maybe you'll become a part of their network or music scene.

Or perhaps you'll create your own network with the information that you've just read and kick off a whole new music scene of your own, becoming known as the person who ushered in a whole line of opportunities for every band that you ever contacted.

It's imperative that you take these steps to establish a foundation for yourself in as many places as possible.

If you can't do this for yourself, you're probably the type of person who's more inclined to provide excuses instead of results and you need to really start thinking about what your goals are.

Either your act is going on the road, or your act is going nowhere. That is an unavoidable fact.

People that get started in their music career at an older age sometimes have a problem with this. They want the magic ticket; they don't want to do the footwork.

They get pissed off when they read the newspaper and see some 18-year-old kid opening up for the big acts on the shows that they feel they're entitled to. Yet what they don't understand is that this young kid may have been building up a fan base on the underground and independent market by touring several years during his high school summer vacations.

It's been my experience that the successful artists who have come up in the industry through a means of consistent sacrifice, hard work, and relentless touring are some of the most humble people I've met.

On the other hand, it's the people that haven't yet made any career milestones that have an ego that can't fit through a doorway.

If you happen to be another Johnny-come-lately, please try to contain yourself because until you've developed a proven track record and the ability to compete with established artists who've been actively building their reputation as hard workers, you really aren't that big of a deal. Get over yourself.

Now in an effort to end this chapter on a positive note and to substantiate most of what I've told you here, I've added a conversation I recently had with Rockin Riviera, the singer of the Chicago Hardcore band No Regrets, who recently just completed their first tour.

I happened to bump into Riviera the night he was booking their next tour scheduled for April of 2014 and asked him a few questions to help give you readers some insight and perspective on independent touring from a band that is currently doing this themselves.

Q. As a new band, how did you set up your first tour?

A. When we set up our first tour, we didn't want to do it alone being as no one ever heard of us, so we decided to bring our brothers in No Zodiac (NZ) out with us. Together, me and Gerardo of NZ put together a route that was manageable and started talking to bands from that area about who books shows in the local areas. From there things started coming together and we did our first tour in the summer of 2012.

Q. What kind of challenges did you face?

A. Being a band no one heard of trying to get kids excited to come out was the biggest challenge cause if there's no kids at the shows, the promoters don't make money to pay us or the venue which in the end we would lose out on our guarantee which forced us to pay out of pocket for our gas.

On top of that, never being in that area before and knowing really anyone, our options were either sleep in the van or having to rent a hotel.

Then there is the band in itself. As my guitarist Jason said, "being in a band is like being in four to five different relationships." You have to learn how everyone deals within themselves, which sometimes causes arguments, and being stuck in a van with each other for five to 10 hours can turn nasty real quick.

Q. What kind of advice would you give a new band that is trying to tour or get beyond their local music market?

A. My advice is unless you are willing to put your whole heart in it, willing to save five to eight paychecks just to spend it all in a matter of days, eat shitty gas station food, and sleep in a van while its 80 degrees outside, don't even bother touring because by the end you will hate it. Don't get me wrong, I've had some GREAT memories and stories that I will remember till I'm old and dead from touring, but with great also comes bad. So give it 100 percent or none at all.

"100 percent or none at all"

CHAPTER TWENTY-SIX

PROBLEMS WITH LIVE SOUND

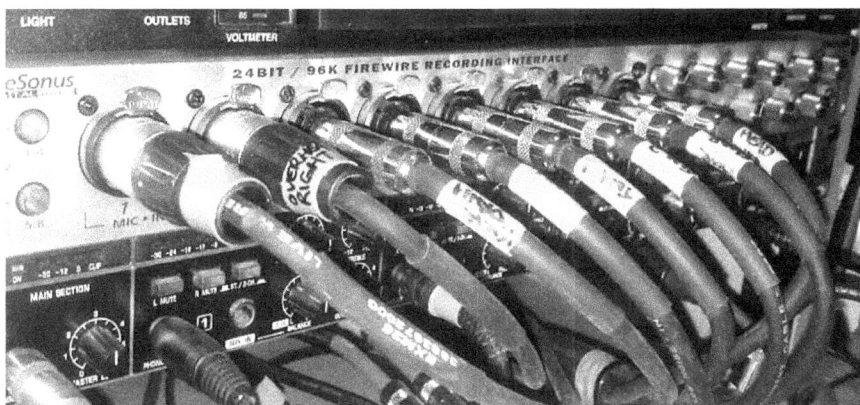

Here's another area in the independent and underground markets where I see a lot of problems that could be easily improved upon.

When performing live, a notable amount of bands and rap artists alike sound anywhere from mediocre to absolutely terrible. I myself have had to walk out of shows on more than one occasion to let my ears rest from substandard audio production. Make no mistake; you can experience ear damage at these live events.

There are several factors that come into play here, and unfortunately several people end up being to blame. Some of these explanations will be for problems that are out of your control but were put here to increase your understanding of the nuances of live sound. Let's break these problems down one at a time and talk about how to correct the ones that we can.

BAD ACOUSTICS DUE TO CONSTRUCTION MATERIALS

I've been in some bars and venues that were not originally designed for live sound. Linoleum or concrete floors combined with exposed brick walls and corrugated metal roofs can create huge sound problems. The limited-to-nonexistent absorption rate of these materials creates an environment where the sound waves reverberate off of the walls and other hard surfaces and will continue to bounce off of other surfaces without immediately dissipating.

Sound in general will reflect off of any surface and continue to travel until it loses sufficient energy to move its wavelengths and begins to dissipate or decay.

These acoustical problems are much more prevalent in venues on nights that have poor attendance because the human body actually helps absorb sound waves; the more people in the venue, the more the residual sound will be absorbed, resulting in less natural reverb.

A good comparison to this and a quick way to understand this issue better is to look at the building materials used in a modern-day movie theater.

Theaters with a good design usually have several very tall, evenly spaced hard acoustic wall panels from ceiling to floor which are raised a few inches from the wall, which allows air to pass through behind the panel while the sound waves travel and dissipate into the fabric of the panel.

Myself and Bob Clayton in an acoustically treated room with open cell foam panels of varying thickness.

These panels, along with open cell foam panels have different acoustical ratings that vary upon thickness and density, which assist in capturing different frequencies. These walls also contain insulation made from cellulose, fiberglass, foam insulation, or preferably ROCKWOOL, which greatly reduces sound.

The theater itself is built with the audience on a slope, which helps with the projection of sound along with the audience's ability to view the screen more clearly. On this slope are seats that are usually tweed or a woven material with foam inserts. The chairs themselves have an absorption rate that helps cut ambient sound.

If these materials aren't present in the room where you're playing or out of budget for the room that you're building, simply hanging thick, heavy curtains along the walls of an untreated room can help buffer sound and reduce natural or runaway reverb.

A flat or corrugated steel or tin roof also creates additional problems as the sound waves that hit it not only bounce directly off of it but also can make it vibrate. This can cause an irritating presence of some high mid-range frequencies and accelerate ear fatigue. The best way to fix this is to install a drop ceiling, as they're well known for their noise reduction capabilities.

BAD STRUCTURAL LAYOUT

Some structures aren't designed with live music in mind. I vowed many years ago never to play at or attend a live performance at a particular venue in Chicago named the U.S. Beer Company; which is essentially a narrow rectangle with slightly curved exposed brick walls. The stage is placed two thirds of the way down the long side of the rectangle, which means that the sound travels the shortest distance possible before hitting the other side of the rectangle, creating an almost immediate bounce-back.

The acoustics are horrendous in this venue and one of their many sound problems could be fixed by relocating the stage.

Sound naturally projects outwards, so if the stage was placed at the deep end of the rectangle the sound would travel a longer distance lengthwise before hitting a flat surface to bounce off of.

Square and rectangular venues create additional problems due to the use of right (90°) angles. These angles are notorious for redirecting and perpetuating residual sound. Without placing large, thick, or dense open cell foam bass traps in these corners you will experience acoustical problems.

On the other hand, if you look at any theater, arena, large concert venue, outdoor amphitheater, or even the Coliseum in Rome, you'll see a different style of design and functionality.

These structures were designed to *project* sound, not contain it. The sound is produced in the center and lowest point in the overall structure, and is projected outwards and even naturally amplified as it picks up energy traveling upwards.

WRONG LOCATION FOR SOUNDBOOTH AND ENGINEER

I've seen the soundboard located in multiple spots since I attended my first concert in 1986. These locations have varied from the side of the stage, to the back of the stage behind the drum riser, to the corner of the front of the venue next to the stage facing the audience and more.

Every single one of these spots is wrong and the reasoning for it is simple common sense.

The sound engineer needs to be in a position where he hears what the audience is hearing.

He should be facing the stage centered mid-position in the venue to get the best analysis of what is coming out of the PA system. Travel to any House of Blues or other large or midsized concert venue and you will see this.

An example of ideal soundbooth placement. Metro Chicago.

When you're equalizing your home stereo you should be doing it from a vantage point that allows you to hear music projected in your direction with no obstructions. You need to hear the sound that is directly coming out of the monitors. This cannot be done from the side or the back of the stage.

Now I do feel obligated to let you know that venues will often have a soundboard in the center of the venue facing the stage *and* a soundboard on the side of the stage. When you see this, it's simply because the engineer in the center of the room is monitoring the sound in the venue that comes out of the *mains* or main PA speakers, and the engineer on the side of the stage is giving the band the live mix that they need in the stage monitors, which are the speakers that face the musicians and are for their benefit only.

THE DJ IS ACTING AS THE SOUND ENGINEER

If you're running a rap show, the DJ is NOT who you want monitoring the live sound quality in the venue.

The DJ's only purpose on that stage should be to deliver music to the soundboard where the engineer does his live mix with the music and any artists and backup singers who are using the other microphones.

Being on the stage is the wrong place to monitor sound for the venue. The DJ can't use his headphones to determine what sound is being heard in the venue in front of the speakers and he can't make that determination with his own ears either because the speakers are not pointed at him. Even if he has monitors on stage, he still can't get an accurate feel of how the music sounds on the main floor of the club.

Another major reason that you have audio problems when a DJ is in control of your sound is because he's using the wrong equipment for the job.

The mixer most commonly used by DJs is made by Numark. These mixers are excellent when used what they are designed for, which is DJing, but they are not built to replace the soundboard for a PA system.

DJ mixers do not have channel strips with individual equalization controls and they don't have a control knob to assign panning. All of these items, along with individual track routing for effects busses, are found on a soundboard. Using the tools available on these independent channel strips in conjunction with the controls on the stereo output channel strip is how the sound engineer achieves his *live mix*.

Using a soundboard in combination with a series of power amps will give you the power and the volume you need to fill almost any size venue or outdoor event.

The size of the room that you'll be able to fill with sound will also depend on the speaker configuration you have for your PA system.

If you're interested in providing your own sound for live events, you should start out by using a pair of cabinets with 2X15" speakers and a horn in each one of them in combination with a pair of subwoofers at the bare minimum. If you don't have enough juice to push the subs, you can get powered subs and that should give you what you need to run sound at a small club or average sized bar. You can add 12" speakers to this configuration to help define the high end but you should not rely solely on 12" speakers for a live PA setup. They won't be able to handle what you are trying to push through them.

Starting out with a small PA system that suits your needs is a good idea if you have the right equipment. You can build a much larger PA system out of the one you have if you start out right.

And if you're a DJ, you can run your equipment through this system as well.

Oh, and a Karaoke machine is not a PA system. Just don't do it. As a matter of fact, don't even think about doing it. Not using the right equipment or using bad equipment are two more ways that you'll compromise your live sound.

THE PERFORMER DOESNT UNDERSTAND FEEDBACK

Feedback is a phenomenon that happens when a microphone's diaphragm comes into direct line with the speaker coils and an audio loop is created. The initial gain or line level white noise from the speakers is picked up by the microphone, amplified, and sent back out of the speaker and back into the microphone and so on and so forth until a loud high-pitched squeal is heard throughout the venue. This squeal remains constant and doesn't dissipate unless the audio loop is broken. If you've never experienced this, you'll know when it happens when you see the people in your audience covering their ears, grimacing in pain, and running for the door in an effort to avoid inner ear damage.

There are certain hotspots on the stage that cause this and they are to be avoided. Some venues mark these spots with an "X" made out of duct tape. The stage manager, backline tech, or sound engineer will be able to tell you about these spots as well if any exist.

THE PERFORMER DOESNT KNOW HOW TO USE A MIC

On many occasions the singer is directly responsible for his audio problems.

There are quite a few things that singers are unaware of when they get involved with a band or as a solo act or rap artist. I would assume it's due to their lack of technical knowledge regarding their chosen piece of equipment—the microphone.

This seems like a no-brainer piece of equipment, but here are a few things you may not have known:

As a vocalist, the most common microphone that you'll come across in the industry and the preferred "house mic" in just about every club is the Shure SM58.

The SM58 is a unidirectional microphone that utilizes a uniform cardioid pickup pattern. The microphone is most sensitive to sound emanating from within this field in front of the microphone and at the same time isolates unwanted ambient sound from outside the field and in the back of the microphone. The following two images display both three-dimensional and one-dimensional images of this pattern.

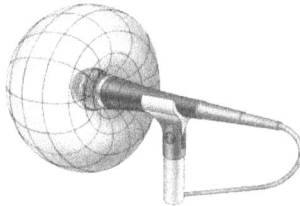

SHURE SM58

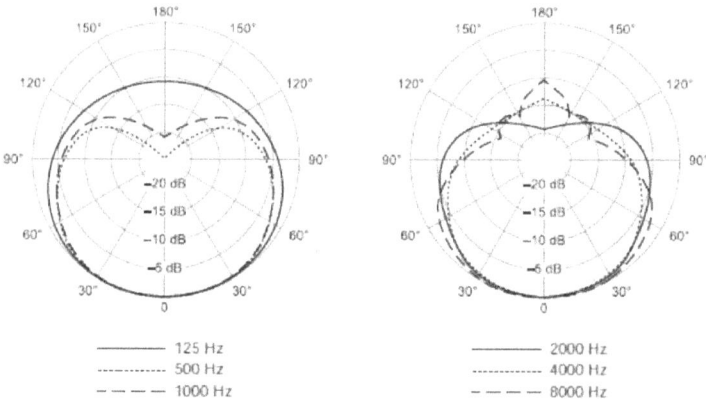

TYPICAL POLAR PATTERNS

Copyright Shure Inc., used with permission

In order for this microphone to pick up the signal placed in front of it correctly, the diaphragm needs to be unobstructed. Holding the microphone on the shaft is the proper way to use this piece of equipment to maximize the quality of sound it picks up.

Gripping the microphone on the grill, or the ball, of the mic is incorrect and obstructs the way the microphone picks up sound. This can also muffle your tone and lower your volume.

Yes, you'll see a lot of people holding the mic by the grill, and vocalists are well-known for doing a lot of posturing on stage, but ask yourself this question:

Would you do this in a recording studio?

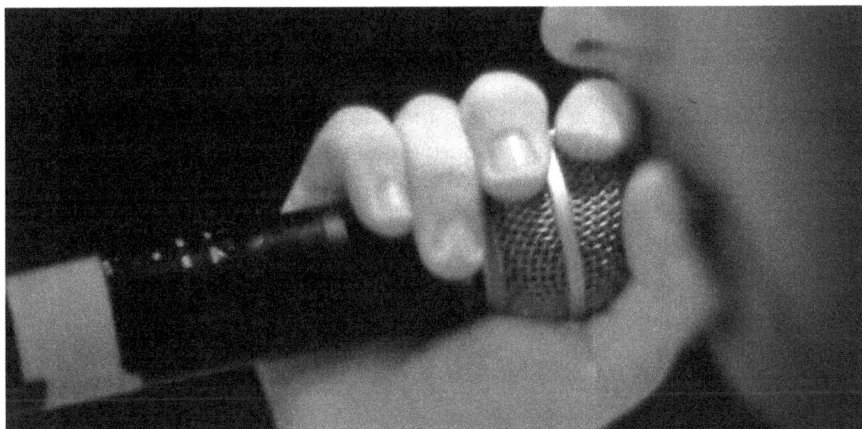

Example of incorrect microphone grip as discussed in this chapter.

Another live audio problem is caused by a technique most commonly referred to as "swallowing the mic."

During live performances, energy runs high and a singer will naturally project this in his vocal delivery. However, without control and restraint it's easy to overcompensate. This results in too much gain entering the microphone, which can make your channel clip, resulting in a garbled, unintelligible vocal delivery.

This happens as a result of the vocalist pulling the microphone too close to his mouth and forcing his volume. Vocalists do this most often when they can't hear themselves and feel drowned out by the music.

Oddly enough, the quickest way to remedy this problem is for them to take their hands off of the grill at the front of the microphone as I just mentioned earlier.

The next time you're at a live show and the vocalist tells the sound engineer to turn up his vocal track, look at how he's holding his microphone; there's a good chance he's obstructing the grill.

If you're a singer, keep this in mind not only for the quality of your live sound, but also because forcing volume from your vocal cords will potentially damage them, especially if you're doing this night after night.

This brings us to volume control.

At certain parts of a song, the music may be relaxed and call for a more subdued vocal just as more high-energy passes in a song require a louder vocal.

You need to know how to control the volume of your instrument, which is your voice. Pulling the microphone away from you will decrease the volume; just as pulling it towards you will increase it.

Singers who deliver a scream at the end of a passage can often be seen gradually pulling the mic away from them to create a volume fade on their vocal while performing live.

If you aren't getting sound at all, check the XLR connection where the cable meets the microphone; it could be loose.

If you're using a wireless microphone system, make sure you purchase a decent one; you really are only as good as your equipment. Get a reliable interference-free system; nothing will throw you off more than hearing a trucker on his CB coming through the PA system in the middle of your song.

Get into the practice of putting a new battery in your wireless transmitter before every performance. This is the best habit you can have. Low battery power will result in signal disruptions and possibly equipment failure.

Also—and I see this a lot—make sure the switch is ON and not OFF.

BAD PERFORMANCE TRACK (RAP ARTISTS)

Many times, I've seen live rap acts where the music is too low, the vocals are too high, and the whole performance sounds like garbage. The group is yelling at the sound guy or DJ to turn up the music and they get pissed at him when he doesn't.

There's a reason that he is not turning up your music track.

He can't.

Although your synth and high hats don't sound loud enough, or are barely audible, every time the bass or an 808 hits, it sends the meter up into the red. Turning this recording up any louder would potentially damage the house PA, and no sound engineer is going to take the risk of causing thousands of dollars worth of equipment damage just because you're pissed at him.

The problem here is in the recording. You didn't use a limiter. You didn't use a maximizer. You may have not even used a compressor.

In the world of audio engineering, there's a term referred to as "headroom." This is the amount of space between your highest volume peak and 0dB, the point where the meter turns red. It's the safety line that the person operating the PA will not pass; it's also the line that you shouldn't pass as an engineer. Sending an uncompressed and unlimited signal that well exceeds 0dB can and will damage your speakers, whether it be in your car, your PA, or your headphones.

A limiter will stop your audio signal at a predetermined volume level and not allow it to go higher. This will help tame those bass notes that are sending the meters into the red. This is controlled by the limiter output.

Limiters also have a tendency to allow the lower volume instruments to increase in volume by raising the limiter input signal.

Bringing the quieter parts of a mix up to a competitive volume is known as raising the floor, which is the lowest volume level in your recording.

Using the limiter alone is not the best way to resolve this issue, but using it in conjunction with a maximizer will help you create a more consistent volume level in your track. This will, however, affect the dynamics of the song, which is the depth you hear in the recording.

Your equalization on the song may have a lot to do with this as well. Many artists and producers have a tendency to overcompensate the bass signal. You should only be hearing a clean knock or bass tone; there should be no buzzing or speaker vibration when these notes hit.

To be specific, you should not hear any distortion of your bass tone. Listen to the bass tone at a lower volume level. It should sound clean, so then raise it up as loud as you can before the signal begins to break up or distort and stay out of the red. Signals only distort when they're clipping.

You'll actually be able to see this if you look at the actual soundwave display on studio. If the soundwaves have a flat top at their peaks, you're clipping. You've completely run out of headroom and each time this note hits, it will distort.

Your stereo track output should have the following effects in this order:

- Equalizer then compressor, or
- Compressor then Equalizer
- Maximizer
- Limiter

There are two different schools of thought whether to put the compressor before the EQ or vice versa, and the answer is *whichever sounds right to you*. Also, you aren't limited to only using the effects listed above in your signal chain but remember this: your compressor or EQ should always be first and your limiter is always last. Any signal manipulation after the limiter will result in it not doing the job you placed it there for.

I highly recommend that if you always cross-reference your mix between your monitors and your headphones to be objective.

Now let's address your performance track in regards to any vocals that are embedded in this recording.

When your CD was recorded in the studio, or when you recorded it at home, you most likely brought the vocals to an optimum level to sit in the mix for your final product. If you didn't have the foresight to prepare a performance track, you will run into additional problems with clipping.

Once again, this is a headroom issue.

Your vocals have a unique frequency signature. When you speak, each word that you enunciate will reside in the same frequencies each time you repeat that word. You can view this on a spectrum analyzer or a good EQ plugin that has this function built in. When you sing over your vocal recording, these frequencies sit on top of each other and the result is as if you took the EQ post for each spot where your voice resides and raised that frequency, eliminating any headroom that you had and once again exceeding 0dB. Another way of increasing volume is by raising the individual frequencies in the equalizer.

So here's the fix:

Rap artists that I've worked with have asked to have the vocals suppressed in the mix where they're only audible enough in the background to enhance their live vocals, or they have them removed altogether.

Whether your performance track contains suppressed vocals or is only an instrumental, you should leave enough headroom for the sound engineer to do his job, which is mix.

If you leave anywhere from -3.0 to -6.0db of headroom after your track's final mix and give that to the sound guy, you'll leave enough headroom for him to mix your live vocal performance with the music and still have plenty of room to raise the master stereo output fader without it clipping. In any mix, be it live or in the studio, the individual tracks should never be louder than the master stereo output track.

Following these simple guidelines will result in you having a nice, clear, and discernible performance.

INEXPERIENCED SOUND ENGINEER

Audio engineering is not only a skill, but a science. There are many things to take into consideration when mixing live music just as when mixing studio music. You can't just have anyone run sound. Besides the engineering part, there's a lot of technical troubleshooting that is involved should the speakers or the monitors not work, and it can involve searching through a spaghetti bowl of cables to find the problem.

Furthermore, if you have someone controlling the live sound that isn't familiar with the board itself, he may miss certain essential functions such as if your channel is muted.

If this is the case, you don't want to go through a whole song with no vocals. You need a guy who can mix on the fly, and sitting back there spinning knobs is not what I'm talking about.

Have the right guy for the job, and treat him with respect because he can single-handedly destroy your sound whether it's intentional or not.

Now I know that this chapter provides a huge amount of information that can potentially cause some finger-pointing when things go wrong, but that wasn't my intention. In order to truly analyze a problem correctly, you need to observe it from every possible angle.

Most importantly, you need to step up and look at what you're doing first and foremost. Don't approach someone else about an audio problem until you're sure that you can rule yourself out as the cause.

INNER EAR AND HEARING DAMAGE

Earlier in this chapter I mentioned inner ear damage; I felt that it is extremely important to follow up with you on this subject, as your hearing is something that can't be replaced and if damaged will greatly diminish your quality of life in your later years.

There is a common medical condition that many live working musicians suffer from known as *tinnitus*. The symptomology of this condition is experiencing or hearing a constant ringing or similar noise in your ears. This and diminished hearing are the result of being exposed to high decibels for prolonged periods of time.

Protect yourself, understand when your ears are getting fatigued, and know your limitations.

CHAPTER TWENTY-SEVEN
VIOLENCE AT THE VENUE

Concert violence has been a well-documented fact for some time. Crews have historically been an established part of many music scenes for some time, and it seems that as time progresses, so do the severity of the problems. Call it strong-arm respect, call it whatever you'd like, but there will usually be someone in the crowd who's got a beef with someone else and the result is usually going to be the same.

If you're a band and this is your crowd, you'll eventually wear out your welcome and another venue will be rejecting your shows due to the violence associated with your group. A club or booking agent will associate you directly with the company you keep—your fan base—which may just happen to be a bunch of assholes.

There are a lot of good bouncers out there who tolerate this shit to an extent and can dismantle and diffuse a situation before it gets out of hand. This usually involves tossing at least one person out of the club, but sometimes the person who gets tossed—or is on the receiving end of a well-whooped ass—can't accept this and things escalate.

I live in Chicago, and I can remember fighting at shows dating back to the mid-1980s and early '90s in well-known clubs such as the Cubby Bear and the Metro, which stopped having hardcore shows for a period of time due to the show violence and shenanigans that happened at some of these live events.

Now, three decades later, this city has graduated from having brawls at venues during punk and hardcore shows to full-scale shootouts at underground rap concerts. The old "us versus them" skirmishes between two separate music subcultures or two different crews has now been replaced by gun violence at the hands of opposing street gangs.

Recent events such as the December 5, 2012 shooting at the Ultra Lounge in Logan Square, which resulted in four gunshot victims, and the March 21, 2013 shooting at Mr. G's on Chicago's south side where seven people were shot at a music video release party is setting a precedent amongst venue owners that is going to work against you and all independent live performing musicians in general. The end result of this, which we can already see being implemented, is going to be the refusal to allow your group—or groups from your genre—to perform at their establishments.

This problem isn't indigenous to Chicago either. In 2012, multiple incidents happened at rap concerts nationwide. Thirteen people were shot in Tempe, Arizona outside a Nipsey Hussle concert, Maino was shot at his own concert in New York, and many less notable events led law enforcement to take a more aggressive stance against concerts for this genre of music.

Chief Keef was at the center of controversy (once again) when a brawl at one of his concerts led to the revocation of the liquor license for the already embattled Congress Theater in Chicago.

Eddie Carranza, who had just recently put an additional $2 million above his initial investment into the aging theater, is now tangled up with court dates and legal fees and may lose his capital investment because of the Congress Theater's failure to report the violence associated with this artist's performance, which escalated to a point where the police and fire officials shut down Milwaukee Avenue, the street that the Congress is located on, for several blocks in both directions.

This incident happened on (oddly enough) Friday the 13th of April 2012, only three days before a Deleterious Impact/Public Nuisance hearing was scheduled based on complaints from neighbors and area residents. These complaints began in March 2012 following the rape of a concert patron who'd been turned away from the venue that New Year's Eve.

After three intensive hearings, the Liquor Commission's Hearings Commissioner Robert Nolan ruled to revoke the theater's liquor license.

According to Nolan's ruling, the Congress "failed to report promptly to the police department illegal activity" and that "within 12 consecutive months five separate incidents occurred… involving acts that violated a state law regulating narcotics or controlled substances."

Carranza has stated that they will appeal the decision but as of today, the rumor is that the Congress Theater is done. Although no official statements have been released, there are no upcoming shows at this venue and the phone number has been disconnected.

Mr. Carranza's ability to recover his assets may only be by selling the venue itself.

I'd like to make myself perfectly clear by saying that concert violence is not just a rap music problem. Fights occasionally break out during events in all genres, but as long as gun-toting gang members are shooting up live music events, the rap genre will remain at the forefront of what's wrong with the live music aspect of this industry and will be used as a prime example of how violence at shows has an impact on the music community as a whole.

The venues that house these concerts may have 20 or more performances a month from a wide variety of acts. This volume of people itself is difficult to control, and any skirmish that the bouncers and hired security staff are unable to handle themselves results in a call to local law enforcement. These calls are cataloged and a record is kept regarding the amount of complaints against a particular address. In the case of a bar or a concert venue, these complaints are reported to the city's liquor commission, which holds in its power the ability to revoke a liquor license and shut a music venue down indefinitely. After enough complaints to a particular establishment are on file, the commission moves to revoke the establishment's license.

A club owner's number one priority is his business, which is his livelihood. So when he faces the possibility of losing the revenue stream that feeds his family if he takes the risk of hosting a concert that brings with it the potential for gun violence, can you really blame him if he says no?

Liquor license revocation, wrongful death lawsuits, legal fees, loss of revenue, foreclosure, and bankruptcy are the things that this owner has to think about. Once this live concert venue is closed, there's a possibility that it will remain closed for good, and nobody wins here.

An example of this can be seen in the chain of events that unfolded on February 17, 2003 where 21 people died and 95 were injured when a security guard used pepper spray to disband a melee between about 15 club patrons in the E2 nightclub in Chicago, which was packed five times over capacity on the second floor, which the City of Chicago had ordered closed by judicial order prior to this tragic evening's events.

This was 18 months and six days after the World Trade Center was attacked on September 11, 2001 and America was still very much in the height of the terrorist paranoia that ensued after that tragic event. It is reported that someone spread a rumor that the club was hit by a terrorist attack and that poison gas had been released after witnessing the symptomatic after-effects of the pepper spray that was used on the unruly patrons.

The fast-spreading rumor combined with the noxious fumes sent a stampede of more than 1,500 people down one single staircase in an effort to quickly evacuate the building.

The doors at the bottom of the building were built to open inwards, which caused a backup of panicking patrons all the way up the stairs.

This resulted in people being trampled to death and smashed against the doors with the weight of 1,500 people on top of them all due to a chain of events triggered by a brawl that consisted of less than 20 people.

Criminal charges of involuntary manslaughter and criminal contempt were filed against club owners Dwain Kyles and Calvin Hollins Jr. along with the promoter, Marco Flores, for their roles in the tragedy. The involuntary manslaughter charges were eventually dropped, but they were sentenced to two years in prison as a result of criminal contempt charges. The owners ultimately agreed to a settlement of $1.5 million to compensate the families of those who were killed in this incident, which could have and should have been avoided.

Although having a club packed five times over capacity and having the front doors of the establishment open inward are both fire code violations, it was the blatant refusal to follow the court order to keep the second floor closed that led to criminal contempt charges being filed against the defendants.

The conviction was appealed; however the appellate court upheld the lower court's ruling.

In 2008, the City of Chicago proposed a live concert promoter ordinance to prevent a disaster like E2 from ever happening again. This ordinance would require a $500 to $2,000 licensing fee depending on the size of the venue and $300,000 in general liability insurance for all concert promoters operating within the city limits. It was extremely unpopular among the independent music community because it had additional layers of restrictions for venues with an existing Public Place of Amusement license that had less than 500 fixed seats.

It also had required an additional license and fee for any independent promoter bringing in a show, which made the risk far outweigh the potential reward.

In November 2010, then-mayoral candidate Rahm Emanuel was asked about his feelings regarding this ordinance and was quoted as giving this answer:

"There is a balance to be struck—we should go after illegitimate underground promoters operating in Chicago, but we should not regulate to the point of choking off our vibrant small music venues."

Ultimately, the ordinance got tabled. Emanuel also won the mayoral election and has since proven to be a patron of the arts. He has initiated a plan to revitalize a live music district on the city's North Side near the Riviera Theater and Aragon Ballroom, and on September 20, 2013 introduced the first annual Chicago Music Summit; a conference and series of panels, workshops, and live events coordinated by the city government's Department of Cultural Affairs and Special Events. However, with the violent events over the last few years I would say that there remains the possibility of this ordinance being reintroduced to the city council.

The ball is actually now in the court of the promoters and the entertainers. If the powers within the music community can prevent violent or catastrophic incidents from happening at concerts, it will reduce the possibility of this ordinance from being reconsidered.

In regards to the illegitimate underground promoters, you're running the risk of having your event shut down every time that you have one if you're hosting an event at a location that doesn't have a public place of amusement license. You're still just as responsible as any other promoter for crowd containment and control whether you're having an illegal showcase or not.

Your actions, along with the actions of your patrons, affect the music community as a whole and you'll run the risk of stiffer penalties being implemented on yourself and everyone else in the profession if you happen to make yourself the subject of the next newspaper headline.

It's also very likely that you'll be made an example of because of your blatant disregard for the rules in the first place. So before you become the poster boy for violence erupting at illegal showcases, maybe it's time for you to evolve and start doing this professionally.

Either we exercise some personal responsibility before, during, and after the live events we engage in or we musicians will inevitably become isolated and locked out of the live venues and halls of which this entire industry is built upon because we didn't grasp ahold of a situation that is spiraling out of control and make a positive effort to reverse it.

If you're a band or an artist that has a bad element that travels with you, the word is going to get around amongst venues and promoters and you may find yourself unable to perform live, which in this industry is pretty much the equivalent of showing up for work. If you're not able to perform live on a consistent basis, you're pretty much fucked and your career will go nowhere.

You create the environment in which you exist.

CHAPTER TWENTY-EIGHT

LIVE PERFORMER ETIQUETTE

One of the most overlooked things in today's world is human decency.

ENTER THE ROCK STAR PSYCHOSIS

In a world of psychotically egotistical self-centered and self-righteous insufferable douchebags with an unquenchable sense of self-entitlement, you come to quickly realize that there is a large amount of performers that have a bad mental reaction to fame and develop an immediate psychosis when they feel that they are on the receiving end of some attention.

It seems as if certain performers just can't be put in front of people for the very first time without something changing drastically inside them in a Dr. Jeckyll and Mr. Hyde manner.

Their brain chemistry's reaction to crowd exposure is so transformative and overwhelming that it is as if they placed the entire audience in a crack pipe and smoked them or put the attending concertgoers in a syringe and shot them into their neck, because the exposure goes straight to their head.

Often early on, all attributes of humility, dignity, and human decency vanish from their persona, and they become an unsociable supercilious fame monster.

For the people who work in this industry, event management can be a very unrewarding place. Being forced to deal with people like this, along with the myriad of other psychological character disorders that a concert promoter or talent buyer has to encounter on a daily basis, can make one wonder if they really want to continue doing this for a living.

So let's look at some of the bullshit that bands and artists pull that pisses off promoters and the people who work at the clubs and venues.

SHOWING UP LATE

As a performing artist, the first impression you give says a lot about you, especially if you show up to a gig late.

There really is no excuse for this.

Shows are planned well in advance, and the sound check is set up not only for the headlining band's benefit, but to also troubleshoot the audio chain for bugs and glitches, along with allowing the ample time needed to backline all of the equipment for the bands that will be performing that night.

If you can't make it on time for sound check, and have the audacity to show up in the middle of a show that's already in progress, don't think that they will stop their production schedule and adjust everyone's time slots to allow you to get your equipment out of a van and three other cars. If you think this club or this promoter owes you something, you are sadly mistaken.

I have seen bands lose their time slots altogether because of this, and no matter the size of the parking lot temper tantrum they throw, they still have been told to go fuck themselves and that they should have been on time in the first place.

Unfortunately many of these artists usually have a very fragile self-image and don't handle rejection well. They're apt to pull immature stunts such as fighting with other artists' fans outside of the venue or calling in bomb threats before they go home and pout.

Live shows run on a production schedule that usually allows only 10 to 15 minutes between performances. During that small window of time, one band is removing their equipment from the stage while another is setting up.

The promoter and the stage manager's job is to make an effort to make sure that everything runs smoothly and on time.

Any delays on the behalf of the opening acts can affect the time slot for the headlining act and potentially push the performances back too close to last call or closing time.

As it so happens, there always seems to be someone in the group that's next up to perform that usually tends to wander off with a couple of "his people" and go self-medicate before getting onstage. Of course this is never done within the 15 minutes that's allotted between performance sets either. So when this band member eventually does float back in and is met by an angry promoter who did a stage call five times, you shouldn't get upset that he cuts every minute that you were late off of your set.

ENTOURAGE

The groups that pull this shit are usually the same groups that almost always have more than 10 people with them drinking and getting high in the parking lot who are their "entourage" and need to get in for free because "they are with the band."

This puts the promoter in a bad position because he has guarantees that need to be met, and a club and its staff that need to be paid. Bands and artists that do this have no respect for the show or the promoter who has put them on the bill and are so clouded in their own sense of self-entitlement that they don't even begin to realize it.

The same performers who insist on having their entourage get in for free are also the same artists that bitch at the end of the night because they aren't getting paid.

This almost always results in an argument where they need to have it explained to them that no one paid admission to come see them, and it is most likely because the only people that attended the show for them were the people that they let in for free and those people didn't purchase any alcohol because they were going in and out all night and drinking the beer they had stashed in their cars in the parking lot.

The economics and accounting practices of live events are simple; if the door makes no money, and the bar makes no money, then YOU make no money. Get it?

As a performer, you need to have some respect for the promoters who put you on the bill and realize that this is the equivalent of showing up for work in this industry. Be on time and don't make a spectacle out of yourself and your friends by turning the parking lot into a trailer park for the few hours before you perform. All this does is make the club owner and staff view you and the promoter in a bad light with and create an open invitation for the arrival of law enforcement.

CANCELLING SHOWS OR NOT SHOWING UP AT ALL

This is the number one dickhead move that you should not do under any circumstances.

After all the begging and crotch juggling some of you assholes do to get booked on a show, nothing— I mean nothing—says you're a piece of shit more than cancelling a show last-minute or not contacting the promoter at all to do so.

In actuality, once you confirm your ability to perform on a show, it's a bad practice to back out. Once promoters lock a show, they move on to the task of generating flyers and posters and mailing local publications with the lineup for the evening. Your band's name appears on all of this material, and quite possibly on the tickets too.

So once the promoter provides you this type of visibility, and may even be receiving some revenue because people have paid in advance to come see you, it would show zero professionalism on your part to back out of the show.

As someone who booked a large majority of my bands' shows, I can tell you that this is my number one pet peeve with other bands, and if they had a reputation of cancelling often, it's also the number one reason that I refused to book them on events that I had scheduled.

Last, but not least, this is a standard that I held other members of my own bands to as well, and if they had a problem with attendance, they were removed or replaced. I have also seen this scenario play out time and time again with members of other bands that I know personally.

The sad irony is that there are countless musicians out there who all use the common phrase:

"I was in that band before they got big."

Well guess what, asshole?

The reason they got big...

...is because they got rid of you.

THE DOUCHEBAG FACTOR

Just because you are performing at a club—and God forbid your name is lit up on the marquis—you still need to realize that it's not all about you. There are other people involved in making this performance happen from front to back. Many of these people show up for a job that doesn't pay incredibly well to make sure that you are able to get on stage and do your thing. No matter who you are, nobody wants to deal with your bullshit, so please, for the sake of humanity try to act like you were raised with a shred of decency and have some redeeming morals.

Realistically, if you are realizing that you are guilty of most of the things that have been outlined in this chapter, you may now realize why you haven't been asked back to perform at these clubs a second time.

If you are some small market act with a big swollen head that can't make the club money then you will blacklist yourself because people will quickly get tired of catering to your unrealistic expectations and your sanctimonious sense of arrogance and pomposity.

Unfortunately, some of the artists that have the ability to pull in big numbers at the door are void of any sign of moral decency and have developed a reputation for pulling shit like this on a repetitive basis.

It's saddening to see news feeds about major label artists who leave their fans waiting in crowded and uncomfortable sold out venues for more than an hour during the hot and humid summer months before coming on stage after everyone is infuriated that they paid an overly inflated ticket price just to get treated like cattle at a stockyard. On occasion, this level of discomfort is only exasperated when the artist does eventually take the stage and cuts their performance short due to some negative fan interaction that happened solely as a result of this artist's deliberate postponement of the show and ends up walking off stage after only a few songs, refusing to finish his performance.

As a performing musician I never pulled this shit, and none of the bands that I've supported in my life have ever pulled this either.

The artists that treat their fans like this obviously don't give a fuck about them, and if you are a fan of an artist that has a reputation of pulling this shit and you are continuing to support them, then not only are you getting what you pay for, but you are also encouraging this artist to treat the people responsible for his or her success like shit. If someone pulled this shit with me, I can guarantee that I've purchased my last album from that artist and attended my last show of theirs.

Artists who do shit like this show zero respect for the fans that have put them where they are. I have stressed the importance of maintaining your fan base since the earliest chapters in this book because without these people buying your music and paying to see you, you are nothing.

So if you ever find yourself in a position where there is an arena full of young star-struck people waiting to see you, you will need to decide how to interact with a crowd whose sole purpose was to come out to see you perform that night.

How you decide to govern yourself under these circumstances is entirely up to you, and what you do will say a lot about who you are as a person.

CHAPTER TWENTY-NINE

HATERS

I was a kid who grew up in the inner city and as a mechanism of survival I've been analyzing human behavior on a daily basis for the better part of 40 years.

It is with almost absolute certainty that I can tell you that you'll eventually witness the exact same psychological and sociological disparities between people with positive and negative mental attitudes as you're about to read in this chapter.

There are many ways to try to get a read on a person, but for the purpose of opening this chapter I'll break this down to one simple question that you can ask yourself in order to clearly understand the genuine character of the people you associate yourself with:

Do the people that surround me support my endeavors wholeheartedly or do they comment, criticize, and attempt to undermine my efforts?

It's a well-known fact that successful people encourage each other and help each other along. Nothing more needs to be said here to elaborate on that point.

Negative people, on the other hand, will try to discredit your actions or achievements.

You have talent, and you're going places. The people around you will start to see that you're achieving more than them or that you have the potential to achieve more than them.

This will generate feelings of envy and jealousy amongst some of your peers, which is by far the nastiest combination of human emotions ever listed in religious text or in clinical handbooks.

But don't let their negative feelings discourage you.

The fact is that these people need to criticize you and they need to discredit you.

Why?

Because your actions and achievements remind them how unsuccessful, shiftless, and miserable they are.

Envy is a very vicious and childish emotion that remains with some people throughout their adult lives. It's been a plague on humanity since before the earliest of our world history was ever written.

From a philosophical standpoint, Aristotle defined envy "as the pain caused by the good fortune of others."

From a clinical standpoint, Mary C. Lamia, Ph.D stated in *Psychology Today* that when you experience jealousy or envy, you've measured your sense of yourself against your image of another person and arrived at a conclusion that was motivated by the biological signal of the effect of shame.

In haters' minds, talking bad about you makes them look better, because at least for the short period of time that they're talking about you, the attention is shifted away from them and their shortcomings.

The underachieving, aimless, and insecure people in your life will go to great lengths to make harmful and libelous statements against you in an effort to make themselves feel better. These statements do little more than show the ignorance and pettiness of the person or persons slandering you and will have zero bearing on your success.

The only way that these statements can affect you is if you internalize them.

So don't.

If you do, then you're just exposing your own weakness. This will encourage them to continue to attack you, simply because they know that they've gotten to you. Misery loves company, especially when it feels that it's being left behind. The best course of action is to just stay out of these people's negative, pathetic, and dramatic lives.

It's been said that a single tongue is such an evil, malicious, and nasty part of your body that it needs two sets of teeth to imprison it.

Let's look at what happens when it breaks loose.

Throughout my life, I've discovered a sure-fire method of immediately determining if people have a history of making vicious and slanderous statements about others.

When they talk, look at their mouth and count how many of their front teeth are missing. Almost every person who I've ever met that habitually runs off at the mouth has had a few of his front teeth knocked out. Most often, the only way to stop a person from continuing on one of these shit-talking tirades is to physically put a sock in it. Once this happens, you'll have a window to observe that nasty tongue thrashing and flipping around in its jail cell and you'll come to appreciate what's been written here.

Try to eliminate negative people from your contact list altogether; they carry a negative energy and vibe with them that consumes them. These people appear to have a storm cloud that happens to follow them around everywhere they go. There is *ALWAYS* something bad or controversial happening to them or around them, and they rationalize it as normal because they're so used to dealing with calamity on a daily basis that they don't know what normal is any longer. Their lives are summed up as maneuvering around catastrophe and implementing damage control.

Bertrand Russell, considered one of the founders of analytic philosophy, said that envy was one of the most potent causes of unhappiness. Not only is the envious person rendered unhappy by his envy, but he also wishes to inflict misfortune on others.

Russell sums it up well, and I'd like to add that it's been my personal observation that negative people who harbor envious feelings have a tendency to be at odds with the whole world in general. They seem to usually have a long working list of accumulated enemies due to a result of their own negative interactions with others. These people are confrontational in nature and are quick to act on their emotions instead of

309

acting on rational thought. Should they take a step back and reassess their situation, they may one day realize that the only real enemy they have is the one that looks back at them from their mirror.

St. James the Apostle further reiterated this point and committed it to religious text in his Epistle when he said, "*If you have bitter jealousy and selfish ambition in your hearts, do not boast and be false to the truth. This is not the wisdom that comes down from above, but is earthly, unspiritual, and demonic. For where jealousy and selfish ambition exist, there will be disorder and every vile practice.*"

If you're in the company of habitually negative and envious people, *it will affect you.* You don't want this contaminating your positive relationships, so you may as well disregard these negative people altogether.

The sooner you do this, the better.

As a rule, you should try to involve yourself with people whose achievements and standards you need to climb to, not people whose level and standards you need to lower yourself to.

Nurture the healthy positive giving relationships you have and acquire because they'll keep you moving in a forward direction. Hold onto these relationships no matter where and when you come across them on your path to success because finding people with PMA (Positive Mental Attitude) can be very challenging and genuinely good people don't come along every day.

Earlier in this book, I shared with you the statistics of how many artists will actually make it.

You'll be on your own path, and if you manage your career correctly, you'll surpass many of the people that you meet.

This is natural selection.

It's Darwinism.

Only a select group of people have an increased ability to compete, succeed, and survive in this industry or in any field for that matter.

When people talk about you, don't let it bother you. Whether it's good or bad, if people are talking about you, it means that you're doing something right; and every time your name falls out of their mouths its free advertising.

CHAPTER THIRTY

BANDS,

CHEMICAL DEPENDENCY AND DRUGS

There's a long laundry list of musicians who have died of overdoses or are currently making headlines for their substance abuse problems, and they're in a competitive abundance to the artists who are making headlines for positive endeavors.

For me to dedicate this chapter to listing each and every artist who met an untimely demise at his own hand would be a disservice to you. As unfortunate as their deaths are to the music community and the people around them, they made a choice, and this choice ultimately affected those close to them.

There's a large percentage of drug use in this industry and I'm no person to judge how each individual handles his own personal consumption of substances. What I am here to address is how full-blown addiction can affect your band and your career.

Addiction affects people in many different ways; changes in behavior, personal detachment, irritability, problems making and keeping appointments, money problems, dereliction of health and hygiene, and engaging in dangerous behavior are the most commonly listed symptoms.

Here's a quick look at how each of these symptoms can affect your project and a few possible results of how they affect the overall health of the band:

SYMPTOM 1: CHANGE IN BEHAVIOR

Let's say that *Band member A* is chemically dependent. Recently, he's been spending a lot of time with other people outside of the group's usual social circle, and it appears his enthusiasm is gone along with his positive disposition.

Result – An overall feeling of discomfort seems to settle into the band because the overall dynamic has changed. The natural harmony of the group is not as cordial as it once was, which places a sense of uncertainty in the air. This new vibe not only has the group off of its mark, but others close to the band's inner workings, such as mangers, promoters, investors, and support staff pick up on the vibe that something has changed.

SYMPTOM 2: PERSONAL DETACHMENT

Recently, this band member's priorities seem to be shifting and he isn't carrying the amount of duties and responsibilities he once did. He's becoming more difficult to get a hold of when he is needed, either for studio time, interviews, or to confirm his availability for live events.

Result - You become unable to confirm appointments with promoters and other industry professionals because your internal communication has broken down.

SYMPTOM 3: IRRITABILITY

This band member's brain chemistry is imbalanced and he may be also feeling the symptoms of physical withdrawal from anything from an alcohol hangover, lack of sleep from cocaine use, opiate withdrawal, or a combination of all three. His personal discomfort makes him prone to lash out at band members and management and makes him intolerable to deal with.

Result - Productivity is compromised at band rehearsals, and recording sessions become a chore. People walk into sessions with a negative attitude because they predict that they'll be entering into an uncomfortable situation and this ends up being embodied in the performances on the recording, resulting in a less-than-great album.

Management, booking agents, and promoters soon become tired of dealing with this guy's negativity and stop booking your act and working with you.

This member's irritability and shitty disposition can cost the group dearly at a live event. Being in public with this chip on his shoulder can end up resulting in making a bad impression on an important industry professional or can be the cause of a physical conflict, which nowadays may end up involving weapons. This can be a problem, because when the shit hits the fan, you're a member of his band and therefore may be the target of someone's misdirected anger as well.

SYMPTOM 4: PROBLEMS MAKING AND KEEPING APPOINTMENTS

As your band member's addiction progresses, he'll begin to spend more time trying to obtain drugs, more time consuming drugs, and more time recovering from drugs. Hangovers and coke binges do not work well with early morning appointments.

Also, erratic brain activity can impede a person's ability to make an immediate decision and commit to it.

Memory lapses due to intoxication and deteriorating organizational habits result in forgotten appointments and unexplained absences

Result – Deadlines fail to be met. There is a load-in time for concerts and specific slot times that promoters and production managers adhere to, so not being punctual can result in your group's inability to play at all. Also, if you're on a tour, and *Band member A* goes on a binge with some fans and falls off of the grid, you'll need to spend the limited time and resources you have trying to locate this guy in an unknown city or unknown country. If you aren't in control of your own tour production, there's a possibility that he'll get left behind and need to find his own way to the next city that you're playing. From a logistical standpoint, tour busses or any form of transportation will need to leave at a preordained time in order to meet the deadlines in the following city and for the following date. Contrary to your band member's drug-inflated ego, the tour does not solely revolve around him.

SYMPTOM 5: MONEY PROBLEMS

Getting high costs money. As addictions progress over time, so does a person's tolerance to the substances that he's consuming. In short, getting high is getting more expensive. Bands on tour are always on a budget. If your bandmate becomes a full-blown coke fiend, he's going to try to acquire money to get high one way or another. Letting this bandmate have access to your money box is a mistake. He shouldn't be in charge of collecting guarantees or allowed to relieve the person at the merch table. Leaving him near cash will result in your revenue being short. He has a monkey on his back that needs to be fed and is screaming at him because it's hungry; it's not a matter of if he will steal money, it's a matter of when, how much, and how often he will be stealing.

Result – The band needs to cut corners on all essential expenditures, including, but not limited to food and fuel. The band begins skipping meals to stay within budget, which affects their overall health and energy levels and they're unable to muster up the kind of strength they usually have when performing live. Enthusiastic fans become disappointed because the group delivered a sub-par performance and the word spreads through the gossip vine. The band is also forced to skimp on the amount of gas they can put in the tank resulting in their tour vehicle running out of gas in the middle of nowhere...

Should you encounter stealing from any band member, please take this important point into consideration:

It may seem a manageable indiscretion for this band member to take a few dollars here and there (usually $20 or $40 because that's the going cost for a bag) but in reality if this goes on unchecked, you may be training this guy that stealing from the band is acceptable.

The big picture is this: if he can't be trusted around small amounts of money, what happens when the stakes are raised and you're making $7,000 to $12,000 a night in cash? How much money will he entitle himself to then?

Remember: *A thief does not only steal one time and a liar does not lie only once.*

SYMPTOM 6: DERELICTION OF HEALTH AND HYGIENE

Some people have a tendency not to nourish themselves while binging. Failure to rehydrate with anything except for alcohol and the absence of any meals for an extended period of time can wear someone down drastically and be potentially fatal. Also while binging, this person may be too intoxicated to remember to bathe and the offensive smell of this person perspiring the alcohol that his body is metabolizing may become quite overpowering. Furthermore, lack of solid foods in this person's stomach and negligent to non-existent oral hygiene can cause a repugnant, putrefying halitosis.

Result – You get stuck in a van with no air conditioning for 16 hours with a drunken coked-out chatterbox whose oral hygiene makes it seem that his mouth is no more than a rectum with a set of teeth. He keeps brushing up against you with skin that is greasy to the touch, creating a heightened level of discomfort in already cramped quarters. Road trips become extended because of multiple stops for bathroom breaks and routine in-fighting amongst band members including the occasional stop necessary to give this asshole a tune-up. All of which results in less time to meet show deadlines and sound checks, and adds to everyone's stress level overall.

SYMPTOM 7: ENGAGING IN DANGEROUS BEHAVIOR

It's no secret that your judgment is clouded while intoxicated. Intoxication can lead to unpredictability, emotional episodes, periods of feeling low self-worth, unmanageability due to a drug-inflated rock star ego, intravenous drug use, traveling to dangerous areas to obtain drugs, acquiring drugs from dangerous people and much more.

Result – This Pandora's Box full of problems can result in anything from missed engagements, tour cancellation, band member incarceration, prison time, trips to the emergency room, surgery, overdose, and death. These problems can obviously interfere with your band's success from start to finish.

This is just a short summary of a few examples of things that can easily go wrong. You can use your imagination and realize that this list of problems can become quite large and far-reaching.

Your efforts approaching a person who has this condition and encouraging him to stop or change his behaviors will be an exercise in futility and a complete waste of your time.

Although you may care about this person's sobriety and how it affects your group overall, there's absolutely nothing you can fucking do about it. This person's addiction will have to run its course. Until the addict is ready, willing, and able to exorcise his demons, you'll either need to deal with it or cut this guy loose and get him out of your life.

There's no amount of intervention, detox, rehab, counseling, or support groups that will effectively get this person to quit before he's ready. It will be on his time and on his terms—if you can't come to terms with this and recognize it for what it is then you are a fool.

I feel obligated to end this chapter with a hard dose of reality.

Opiates seem to have an allure on certain people. Keep in mind how many people in this industry are DEAD because of this. A bag of heroin costs $10 and that will be the price you pay to sell your soul to the devil.

Junkies don't recover. Junkies are found cold and blue in abandoned buildings with needles still stuck in their arms.

The *live fast, die young* mentality is nothing but a path to your own self-destruction. That being said, before you consider experimenting with this drug, please take the time to consider how your family will feel when they come to the medical examiner's office to identify your body after the rodents and maggots have been feeding upon your bloated corpse.

So if your idea of a good time is sharing a rusty spike with a homeless, hepatitis- and AIDS-ridden prostitute in an abandoned building, then be my guest.

But know this:

Every person I've met that's done heroin is either trapped in the lifelong ongoing living hell of addiction or has only kicked the habit and remained drug-free because they're in a casket.

Nobody ever said the truth was going to be pretty.

Play at your own peril.

♩♪♫ *"Just a spoonful of heroin makes the rockstar go down…"*♫♫♪

CHAPTER THIRTY-ONE

RAP AND MIXTAPES

The whole process of getting your music out to the masses is very time-consuming and in the end costs you money. You should constantly review and refine what you're doing to make sure you're achieving the maximum impact that you desire.

MARKETING DOs AND DON'Ts

I see aspiring rap artists standing in traffic intersections trying to sell mixtapes at red lights. This isn't how you market your music; in the larger scope of things, this is merely aggressive panhandling.

Getting your word out on the street is important, and maybe up until reading this book that was the only way you knew how to market yourself. But ask yourself this: is this method effectively hitting your target market? Is every single person that drives down that street a fan of your genre of music or a fan of you as an artist?

The answer is no, they aren't, and how many times have you heard the distinct sound of an automatic door lock being engaged while practicing this marketing technique?

How many times have you pulled up to a red light yourself and thought, *"Ahh shit, here comes somebody trying to sell me something again."*

Whether it's peanuts, factory-defective socks, a window wash, or mixtapes, this is not the approach you want to take.

I've also seen some rap artists in Chicago's Loop—the central downtown business district—walking up to people that they don't know with a pair of headphones and a CD player. Although their intentions are commendable, this is time-consuming for the artist and also for the potential customer, who may not want to run the risk of an ear infection because the earbuds have been in the dirty wax-covered ear canals of half of the people on State Street.

Well, at least these guys were asking people to listen to their music, because the next group of assholes we'll discuss just decided to force people to listen to their music.

PLAYING YOUR MIXTAPE ON PUBLIC TRANSPORTATION

First it was blasting mobile devices as loud as they could go, then it was connecting a battery powered bass-bullet to the phone, and now I have even seen kids placing a powered studio monitor in their backpack and connecting it to the phone.

A lot of kids (and grown men) today are doing this while singing along to rap music on the train to a song that no one else seems to know but them, and it's probably because it's their mixtape.

There are really only two possible reasons why anyone would be doing this:

- Either you are a complete fucking asshole who refuses to buy a set of headphones,
- Or this is a severely misdirected way of trying to promote your music.

If you have practiced this technique, you really need to ask yourself if it's ever even worked for you.

Take the time to look around you and read the faces of the people on the train. Do they look frustrated, inconvenienced, or pissed off?

Well, this is most likely because the minute you got on the train, you changed the whole atmosphere from a quiet and peaceful one to one where people have no choice but to deal with the kid who has zero respect for anyone else around him.

If this is you, you should think about this for a minute, because instead of engaging people you are rubbing them the wrong way.

All of the techniques that I just mentioned are overly aggressive, intrusive, potentially harassing, and somewhat misdirected.

I'm sure every city and every region has its own unique methods of hustling, but perhaps your time marketing and promoting your music would be spent more efficiently if you utilized the things that you've read in the chapters on building an online presence and marketing and promotion and tweaked what you're currently doing.

That being said, let's put a little bit of a customized spin on what we covered in the chapter on marketing and advertising:

Since you can't assume that every person listens to your genre of music, you need to figure out how to identify who does. If I was a rap artist, the first thing I would do is profile my consumer, who more likely than not, would be a lot like me. If I'm promoting a release and am involved in my own street-level promotions, I'm going to approach people who follow the same urban fashion trends as myself or other rap artists. In other words, I'm going to give the guy with the lined-up beard, big oversized watch, and fresh pair of sneaks my promotional material, but I'm not going to waste my time handing my flyer to a guy with a leather jacket and green spiked Mohawk because he obviously listens to punk rock and will most likely put my flyer or mixtape in the garbage.

As I stated in the chapter on marketing, *hitting your demographic or target market in these campaigns is critical to their success.*

Seeing that I've been putting 808's and other serious trunk-rattling percussion and de-tuned synths in my music, I'm going to target consumers who have professional audio installed in their vehicles because my music is tailor-made for amplifier-driven kicker boxes. So I'm going to leave my promotional materials and perhaps my mixtape in places where people go to buy and install custom pro audio systems in their cars, along with places that tint car windows, sell chrome rims, and install chrome highlights and after-market custom add-ons to vehicles.

Then I'm going to go to the place where everybody gets faded up and give the barbershop a copy of my music to play during work hours; I'm going to leave promotional material there, too.

If I can't go to a busy well-known barbershop that's located in an area I'm not welcome in—perhaps because it's in hostile gang territory—I'm going to find someone that isn't in a gang and that can get my flyers and music in there. And I'm going to do this in every neighborhood I can get to, and every neighborhood where I can send somebody.

Next on my list would be my tattoo artist. Music plays all day in these shops, so it may as well be my CD that's playing in the background while the place is open for business.

In a nutshell, and regardless of what genre of music it is that I perform, I'm going to get my flyers and posters in every establishment that reflects my lifestyle, including the smoke shop. This is how I intend to hit my target market and create exposure for myself and my music to people that I don't know personally or who are out of my extended network.

There's no point for me to mention that you need to put your promotional materials in the record stores, because if you didn't figure that out a long time ago, then you're way behind the curve.

POSTERS AND STREET LEVEL MARKETING

Another great way to brand yourself in your city is by putting posters up on lampposts at intersections. These oversized posters are usually stapled back to back with the pole in the center, taped up, or put up with wheat paste by street teams or promotional companies that specialize in this specific type of marketing.

This is already a common practice and this material is much cheaper when purchased in bulk. Although I personally would attempt to concentrate my efforts to business and live music districts along with school campuses, placing these things everywhere gets the word out on the street.

I feel it's important to mention my observation that more often than not, the printed media that these artists are manufacturing only includes their Facebook and Twitter info, with no mention of where the music can be purchased, be it online or in a local record store. This tells me that they are committing a sizeable budget to market a mixtape release which in turn will create no revenue, therefore making this a foolish business expenditure.

If necessary, you can do your street-level marketing by yourself. If combined with the use of DJ pools and the other marketing techniques that have been provided to you in this book, you should have no problem creating the awareness and visibility for yourself that will get you out of the underground market and into the next arena.

In order to obtain this type of visibility, you need to cover a lot of neighborhoods, a lot of business districts, and you need to network with a lot of people.

But even if you're hitting all of these locations, this still doesn't even scratch the surface.

You need to start to view your market as more than just an intersection, a neighborhood, or even your hometown or city. You need to look at things from a global perspective and educate yourself on what's happening in this world on an international basis if you want to achieve any real success.

At the time of this book's publication, the independent rap movement is undergoing quite a noticeable growth spurt including a large amount of new artists; and is a resurgent developing music scene. However, just as when any market becomes flooded with new occupants, there are obstacles that need to be overcome and unfortunately there are problems that need to be addressed, some of which I've already pointed out throughout this book.

So let's look at some ways we can overcome the obstacles you'll face as an underground or independent rap artist who's just stepping into the game, and look at a few ways that you can facilitate some personal growth.

DISSECTING THE MIXTAPE

Mixtapes have always been the tried and tested method of creating awareness for underground rap artists, while playing live and touring have always been the tried and tested way for underground bands to make a name for themselves.

Maybe you've been selling mixtapes and you feel that you aren't getting as far as you like.

How much money have you sunk into this effort? Are you spending more than you're making? If so, how do you justify this? Are you stuck doing the same thing that everyone else is with the same limited or non-existent results?

If you're giving everything away free of charge, there's no way to justify this—not from a business perspective and certainly not from a music business perspective.

I expect at this point for your response to be that you're doing it for visibility.

Well, so is everybody else.

Flyers, posters, and ads in magazines are for visibility; they advertise the product. In this case, your product is the music, which should be for sale because it is the foundation of all the revenue sources in this industry.

I've mentioned the need to get a return on your investment earlier in this book. Keep in mind that this is not only a financial investment but also one of your *time*, and time is also very valuable commodity.

There's no doubt that mixtapes have worked for many a rap artist in the past, and I'm not privy to whether any of these artists had a plan B or an alternate comprehensive marketing strategy, but even though the mixtape has worked for them, you need to ask yourself: has it been working for you?

Now I'm not completely out of touch with reality, but I don't believe that this method by itself is going to make you successful any longer. Rap music is the most oversaturated market in the industry; there are just too many of you doing the same identical thing as the next guy.

And it's not about what the next guy is doing.

Those moves have been done already, and every single artist that lacks any originality whatsoever is following those same played-out moves to the letter, resulting in a huge crowd of artists that no one clearly sticks out of.

I've been at rap concerts and festivals alike where every single person is handing out a flyer or a shitty-looking mixtape that's basically a blank disk with their name, track list, and contact info written on it with a marker. Many of these get discarded by the end of the night and when the club is closing you look at all the promotional materials and CDs that have been discarded and left behind and realize how much of this stuff actually ends up in a landfill.

To figure out how many of these CDs actually turn into garbage, I did a little research and found that ECOcoalition.org estimates that over 100,000 pounds or 45.359237 metric tons of unwanted CDs get disposed of every month.

If it's your CD that's getting disposed of, this happens at a cost to you. Why did this happen? Who knows, maybe there was just too much free music being passed around at the event. Maybe the packaging made it look like it wasn't worth listening to. Maybe you have terrible social skills and haven't established yourself as a known figure in your local rap community and you don't stick out of the crowd.

Be innovative, be different, and do everything imaginable to try to stick out of that crowd without looking like you're crying for attention.

THE MIXTAPE DJ

Perhaps you should try this option. Have you tried to have a professional DJ with a solid reputation and well-established network host your mixtape? This is historically what the correct definition of a mixtape is anyway and this has had proven results for people, even very recently.

A3C mixtape marketing panel at Criminal Records in Little 5 Points Atlanta Oct. 2011(From L to R) DJ Chuck T, Tef Poe, Mike Repel, DJ Burn One

In October 2011, I was asked to speak on a music marketing panel at the A3C Hip Hop festival in Atlanta. The panel also included an artist named Tef Poe from St. Louis, DJ Smallz from Miami-based Southern Smoke Mixtape series, and award-winning DJ Chuck T of the Carolinas, among a few other heavy-hitting mixtape DJs.

Tef Poe had DJ Smallz host his mixtape *War Machine 2*, which soon obtained visibility from both *The Source* Magazine and *XXL*. This marketing method obviously worked for Tef Poe, who has since remained relevant in his area. The circumstances related to this mixtape release may have been the tipping point that created his heightened level of public awareness.

Tef Poe invested in a DJ to host his mixtape. That in itself was a wise move, but the visibility from that mixtape wasn't going to last forever, and it appears that Tef Poe knew that all along.

He was grinding long before the arrival of this mixtape and he has continued to do so afterwards. This is an independent artist who has realized the importance of self-reliance and continues to make his own moves even though he has been building a team around him.

The DJs who host mixtapes specialize in breaking records. They have an established network of purchasing consumers who frequent their websites and their name carries some weight behind them. This in itself will create visibility for you to a listening base to which you don't already have access.

DJ Chuck T mentions that at this time in his career there's not much he needs to do to create visibility for his mixtapes. He has a store, he has an e-commerce website, and he just launched a DJ crew. This alone will create a decent amount of exposure for an artist, but he also mentions the need for an artist to have a comprehensive marketing campaign of his own.

Everyone on that panel agreed that as an independent artist you still have to put in your own work.

Don't pin all of your hopes solely on the DJ and his network; pick up the ball and market that mixtape yourself as well, which will create a doubled effort and another layer of visibility.

Tef Poe reaped some limited success from marketing his CD with a well-known host DJ, but this was just a hinge pin in his other activities as an artist.

Keeping up his visibility, he not only stays active in his hometown's music scene, but also has created his own festival and was recently handed the key to the city from the mayor of Pine Lawn in St. Louis County. Tef has also become a weekly writer for the *Riverfront Times* music and entertainment section in St. Louis.

I've met countless independent rap artists who are directionless and will never climb above the pile of artists that are all doing the exact same thing as each other. But based on what I've seen from Tef's activities, I believe this is an artist to keep an eye on, because after being a part of several music scenes spanning several genres and several decades I can say that he's really one of the few and only independent rap artists that I've met that truly understands what it means to be an INDEPENDENT artist by making his own moves and not waiting for a helping hand.

Too many of you underground rap artists seem to be waiting for that major label lifeline to fall out of the sky and pull you up out of your local market. Unless you start climbing the ladder on your own, you'll never reach this hypothetical "lifeline."

In this industry, you need to create a domino effect for yourself. This is going to involve shooting at multiple angles at once; your market is way oversaturated and there are too many people doing the same thing as each other. If you keep pulling the same moves as everyone else, you're not creating your own lane and your hard work will get lost in the herd.

THE PROBLEM WITH MIXTAPES

Even though the mixtape has become the rap music industry standard for breaking new artists, it is not without its own set of flaws.

What many of you are selling is music that you don't even have the rights to use.

Jacking beats off of Soundclick, sampling others' music, or just doing a full remix of a well-known artist's song and putting it out on your mixtape is a daily practice in the rap industry and it's also against the law.

From a legal perspective, what you're selling is plagiarism and is also a Digital Millennium Copyright Act (DMCA) violation.

Many artists would respond to this by stating that they're giving it away for free and therefore not breaking any laws.

To address this, we must look at actual definition of Title 17 of the United States Code, Sections 501 and 502 which provide severe civil and criminal penalties for unauthorized reproduction, distribution, or digital transmission of copyrighted sound recordings without the permission of the owner. The courts have repeatedly upheld decisions where it has been made clear that uploading and downloading copyrighted music without permission is a violation of Federal law. Copyright law provides full protection of all registered sound recordings regardless of what medium they are embodied on or in. In other words, whether you distribute copyrighted material by giving away CDs or even by simply emailing a copyrighted song to someone, you are guilty of copyright infringement.

So you need to ask yourself: would this cash have better served you if you just purchased all of the music that you were using for this album outright and had it professionally mixed and mastered?

First of all, owning the music will allow you the ability to remove those annoying "tags" or "drops" that producers put in their songs. That is such an unnecessary and unprofessional distraction that you should try to distance yourself from that practice altogether.

What a noble concept;

Since you are already using the producers (composers) music – Just **fuckin' pay the man already!**

After all, he didn't spend hours in the studio exercising a talent which in itself is far superior to wordsmithing so you could spend a few hours rapping over his hard work and musical craftsmanship free of charge.

Most of you rap artists talk about how you're making big money, so put your money where your mouth is and pay the man.

Think about it;

Isn't it also a good business practice for you to insulate yourself from any bullshit that can arise right from the start? Your options for what you're able to do with this music would immediately increase if you owned all the rights to your recordings and would also shield you from any type of DMCA violations or copyright infringement prosecution that could arise in the future for using music for which you don't have the rights.

Legally owning the music also puts you in a position to sell it on every digital online retail store like iTunes, Amazon, and more. Additionally, it allows you to license your music for use in movies, video games, commercials, and other opportunities.

After copyrighting your material and sending the music and the album cover artwork to a pressing plant, you would have an abundance of professional-looking CDs to sell.

And why wouldn't you? Don't you stand a better chance of being taken seriously if your music is packaged professionally in a jewel case or eco-pack instead of the flimsy transparent envelopes with the one-panel insert that have become the mixtape standard?

Do you really want to hand a CD that you wrote on with a marker to a rep from a major label?

Couldn't you also use the added benefit of having your music available on an international basis where people can discover you in every country? Isn't it time to stretch out and give your music some room to breathe instead of having it suffocated in your oversaturated local market?

Where does it say that you need to play by everyone else's rules and continue to give your music away for free anyway?

DJ Quik said it best when he immortalized the phrase, *"If it don't make dollars then it don't make sense."*

This has to be the most sound business advice to ever come out of your genre. It not only applies to every economic market across the globe but also to the music industry as a whole, yet as artists, an alarming number of you seem to have discarded this concept altogether through your proliferation of free mixtapes.

Utilizing the things you've learned in this book, you could be selling your own CDs and merch at the shows that you've booked yourself and you could run a successful marketing campaign for the release of your *album*—not your mixtape, but your album.

The difference in how you present your product verbally also is a significant factor on how people will perceive your release. If you have a release where you own the rights to the music, using the word *album* as opposed to *mixtape* sounds much more professional—just as I would rather have a band try to sell me their *EP* rather than their *demo*.

Your next move from here would be to implement the techniques that bands use and book yourself dates to perform often and tour in as many different places as you can effectively market your music.

For all practical purposes, this should become the point where you aren't an underground artist anymore; you're an independent artist with a lot of work to do because you now have a direction in which to travel.

And that direction is up.

You are the product that you've been tirelessly investing in. Now you need to start creating revenue streams for yourself. Successfully doing this will give you a working budget to reinvest in yourself.

Besides the obvious benefit of being able to fund the visibility you'll be creating for yourself through the marketing and advertising that you're doing, there may be additional positive scenarios that arise because of these revenue streams you've created.

Once you can show that you have earning potential, you will stand a better chance of procuring investors, sponsors, management, and labels. Giving away music for free does not prove that you have potential to earn money. Your download numbers don't mean shit when everyone in the industry knows that you can pay to have those numbers boosted.

Once you can reach this realistic and obtainable level of success, you'll stand a better chance of attaining the dreams that I tore apart in the introduction of this book and you can start working towards making them a reality.

IMAGE

For many of you—and I mean a lot of you—up until this point the sum of your career has been nothing but smoke, mirrors, and complete bullshit.

Rap music embodies and emphasizes the need to have a physical appearance that emulates success. The media has spoon-fed you the idea that you need to present yourself with a wealthy successful image that parallels the major artists in your field to the point where some of you are living way outside of your means.

The moment that your desire to get rich quick or create the illusion that you are already successful takes precedence over the importance of creating great music is also the moment that you fail as an artist.

Projecting a false image is bullshit; keep that in mind.

For those of you that care to disagree with me, let me ask you this:

While you were purchasing Movado, Gucci, and Prada, how much money did you spend on developing your career? Have you purchased the rights to a single or a series of songs that you have released? Did you hire a professional mixing engineer to produce your song? Have you sent it to an established mastering house? Have you done any professional photo or video shoots? Have you hired a publicist? Have you launched a guerrilla marketing campaign to create visibility for yourself, your music, and your video? Have you paid to have your video hosted on a popular rap website? No?

Well then, you're all dressed up with nowhere to go, aren't you?

Maybe you should try a career in modeling designer fashions because you're way off-target on your marketing necessities and you need to start prioritizing if you intend on making it in this industry.

Instead of focusing on the need to dress for success, perhaps you should adopt a mentality that demands that success should be dressing you.

By the way, when you were shopping, did you get the real designer stuff or are you wearing the knockoff bullshit with the plastic diamonds?

Fake it till you make it; I understand.

Now I'm not saying that you shouldn't look presentable. What I am saying is that you need to have a balance. If you're presenting yourself as something that you are not, then people will eventually see you as a fraud. This is a reality, and once you're pegged as a poser all your credibility that you've been working for goes down the toilet. Keep this in mind, because you're in a market where other rap artists will be quick to jump behind the mic and expose you for your flaws. Furthermore, if your taste for the finer things in life is interfering with your ability to keep your phone and Internet bill paid, then booking agents and people providing opportunities won't be able to contact you.

I've met people that have invested more than $50,000 on artists and have had zero to show for it. Instead of using that money wisely on developing media or advertising like I've mentioned above or spending it with a purposeful direction, the money was wasted on renting stretch limousines to show up at open mic nights and on other image-related extravagances.

Obviously there's a "go big or go home" mentality that exists within your genre, so if you're going to commit to renting a stretch limousine for an evening, you'd better have the foresight to hire a professional photographer and videographer as well so you can document this and use it for promotional purposes later such as for flyers, album covers, or music video footage.

If you don't use this as an opportunity to create media for yourself then you aren't spending your money efficiently. Every dollar you spend and every action you make should have more than one purpose behind it. Therein lies the strategy. If I spend money on A, then I can do B, which will result in C and D.

There is also a large majority of you that would not hesitate to spend thousands of dollars to have a popular rap artist featured on one of your tracks. So let's say that you've spent the money to do this; was there an equal or larger amount of money left in the budget to promote and advertise this song? Because once you have this artist featured on your track, how are you going to get people to hear it? How are you going to get people to buy it?

Without having a solid marketing plan in place to create revenue from the substantial expenditure that you've incurred in this matter, this is just a monumental waste of time and money. So if doing something like this isn't in your budget, perhaps you should focus on building up your own reputation instead of riding on someone's coattails. And perhaps having a featured artist on your album would be completely unnecessary and your music would gain more traction on its own if you followed the songwriting and composition guidelines mentioned earlier in this book and simply wrote better music.

So have you, in fact, been spending a large amount of money?

If you have, did you create solid revenue streams with it to receive a return on your investment? Do you have an e-commerce website developed?

Have you developed a product line of merchandise related to you and your music?

During this whole time did you even develop a fan base that purchases your music? (This, by the way, costs nothing.)

Maybe you haven't, because if you're fronting too hard there's a distinct possibility that listeners can see right through your façade and they can't identify with you on any level because you talk about things you've never owned, a lifestyle you never had, and your songwriting is based on nothing but your own personal delusions and lies. People in general don't want to be lied to and they want to have something to believe in. If your message is true to your lifestyle then others will recognize that and believe in you because your songwriting talks to them on a personal level. It's really as simple as telling the truth; this is how you connect with people and this is how you will get fans.

Real fans support real artists. Your real fans are the people who are purchasing your music and merchandise and are paying to see you perform; they wholeheartedly want to see you make it. The people who aren't your fans, on the other hand, are all the people who tell you they support you but haven't purchased your music or your merchandise and will not pay to see you perform live. Please learn to differentiate between the two.

Once again, if they won't purchase your music, they aren't fans. It doesn't get any more cut and dried than that.

If you've had a lot of downloads from music that you release for free on DatPiff, don't kid yourself into thinking you actually have a fan base, much less one single fan. Those numbers don't mean shit.

YOUR MUSIC WAS FREE. Just because they downloaded it does not mean they are converts. And if you're spending money to boost numbers of something that is available for free then you're one sad case and you cannot extrapolate any real analytic on exactly how many people actually are listening to your music. The amount of listeners you have or plays you receive is meaningless unless there is a sales conversion.

Renting limousines in four-hour billing cycles and creating this false image of major label level of success while you haven't even sold one single copy of one song or album means that you're a joke.

You aren't only perpetrating a fraud to everyone you meet in the industry, you're also lying to yourself and spending a lot of money keeping yourself fooled.

You oversaturate the market with music that you have no rights to copy, use, distribute, or sell in any form. Many of you have songs about unrealistic things that you never had and will most likely never have the ability to obtain because over the last several years all of you rap artists combined have inadvertently destroyed the purchasing power of your so-called fan base by cramming volumes and volumes of free music down their throats to the point where they are now conditioned to expect free music from every developing artist.

The RIAA reported that rap music had sales that made it climb to the second largest revenue-generating music genre in the year 2000. But, according to *Billboard* Magazine, rap sales have declined 44 percent since 2000. That is inexcusable in a music genre where studies have shown that 65 percent of all kids aged eight to 18 years old are listening to rap music on a daily basis.

But once again, many of you have raised and groomed your consumers since their earliest musical experience with the understanding that music is meant to be free.

So now that you're personally responsible for altering the business model of the entire music industry, please tell me where the revenue is now going to come from. I and other soon-to-be starving artists would like to know.

Are you aware that rap music is the only genre of music where artists continually give away their music for free?

Nobody else is doing this.

(Some) bands may give away an initial four- or six-song EP, but that's it. After that, they're packaging their music and selling it at shows from their merch table because they value their product and understand the need to create revenue streams.

I don't even remember the last time I've even seen a merch table at a local independent or underground rap concert. The lack of its presence is tantamount to the lack of fan support that exists in your industry on the independent level.

Furthermore, there's an underlying attitude in your market that it's okay if the bootleg man is selling your music because it means that you're getting big and that this is additional exposure for you. This is nuts, and this is also revenue that you'll never see. Piracy of rap music is far worse than it is in any other music genre. This is another contributing factor to why hip hop sales consistently decline. It seems that many of you will shoot yourself in the foot for visibility and exposure rather than slowly building a dedicated fan base who will be eager to continually purchase your music one CD at a time over an extended period of time.

If you think that I don't fully understand your market, I'll tell you that I don't think that you fully understand the business aspect of the independent market. I'll also tell you that another thing that I understand is inefficiency, and you can see in this book that I have no problem speaking up about it either.

Give yourself some sales history and you will give yourself some professional leverage in this industry.

So while you've been exuding a false image of success, you've given up your strength as an artist and devalued your market by giving away your music for free and paying to perform.

Many of you are continually being pimped by promoters for the money you bring to live events to pay for a performance slot and realize no revenue or monetary compensation for your work that evening.

That statement alone should infuriate you, and if it does, good; because now maybe you'll have the drive to wrestle back your value as a live performing artist by booking your own shows and hopefully you will have the integrity and moral compass to pay your peers fairly. If you feel that you must put out a mixtape, you need to ask yourself to what end you're

338

doing so. What is the purpose of your mixtape? Are you just doing this to get known for your free music? If that is the case, then from a business perspective your expenditures don't justify the lack of revenue you'll receive from this endeavor.

Perhaps you should consider using this mixtape as a free advertisement for the upcoming album that you'll be selling on iTunes. Load the mixtape with references to the upcoming album, including its name, release date, and references to the song titles and topics and turn it into a 40-minute commercial for your upcoming album. This takes your manufacturing and recording expenses and rolls them right into your marketing campaign. Every free download of this mixtape will keep pounding the message of your next album's title into the listener's head until he's programmed to buy it on the release date that's stated in your songs.

If you disagree with what I've written in this chapter then you need to ask yourself if you think that following the advice in the other chapters of this book may possibly create a more viable path for you than what you've been doing for yourself up until now.

If the current landscape of your genre makes you feel like the cards are stacked against you then it's time to walk around the pile.

Dare to be different. Stop being a part of the status quo and have the fucking balls to be a trendsetter, not a trend follower.

At the time of writing this book, I've been involved with the rap genre for more than four years. I've been looking at the independent side of the rap market from a grassroots level and up. I've seen everything that you artists are going through in the many stages of your development and I've been doing so with an objective set of eyes because I've been a part of other music scenes and different markets, which gives me the ability to compare and contrast what I witness from genre to genre and region to region.

Even though I openly criticize industry practices, I do so with your success in mind, which I take seriously, because if you fail to find a more successful avenue for yourself within the pages of this book then I've failed in writing it.

On the flipside of that coin, if I have indeed provided you with a more successful avenue to pursue within the confines of this book, but you've failed to implement and follow it, then you've failed yourself.

CHAPTER THIRTY-TWO

REVENUE RECAP

Let's face it, this entire lifestyle is not the same as the one that your normal run of the mill 9-to-5 cubicle critter has.

While Dilbert and the worker bees have the comfort of a steady paycheck every two weeks and a 401k, you're going to need to hustle.

Long nights, big crowds of people, and constant networking night after night and city to city is a demanding lifestyle that requires you to keep up a certain pace. It's also going to cost money to keep this machine humming along.

If you don't have an entrepreneurial side to you or a history in retail sales (*whether it's store or street corner sales, it makes no difference here*) you may have some difficulty monetizing your product in the beginning.

Should you be lacking in your salesmanship qualities, then now is the time to develop them. You may want to even consider getting a job in retail to help condition yourself towards customer interaction and the art of closing the deal.

There's a salesman-like mentality that you'll need to adopt if you want to make it in the music industry, and that mentality is:

I got it, and I'm gonna sell it.

Repeat that to yourself as often as you can until it's all that you know and all that you believe.

These life skills are a must-have for you; whether you're doing something as simple as selling your product at shows, or if you find yourself engaged in professional situations where you're selling yourself to a booking agent, promoter, label or sponsor

You need to be a *go-getter.* This industry has no place for the timid. You must be assertive if you want to be successful.

So if you have problems casually approaching strangers and interacting with people that you just met, you'd better get your mind, your heart, and your balls wired together quickly or you will fail in this business.

There are even times where you may show up to a performance completely prepared but nothing happens, even though the place was packed and you rocked the crowd. Let me give you an example of what I'm talking about.

I did a show one night that didn't have a designated merchandising area in a well-lit or highly trafficked area near the door. We hung our T-shirts and hoodies behind the table with a price list and had a wide variety of other merch and our CDs on the table as well. We staffed the table with two attractive young women and still had a minimal amount of traffic to the table, resulting in dismal sales.

After my band performed, I went to the bar to grab a beer, which was where a few of my friends had chosen to take residence for the evening. While I was grabbing my beer, they asked me if I had any CDs with me, I told them yes and they asked for five copies.

I ran back to the table and grabbed five copies of my CD and didn't get more than 15 feet away from my merch table when people saw me walking through the crowd and recognized me from being on stage a few minutes earlier.

Once they saw that I had CDs in my hand they asked me if I had any for sale. I politely informed each person who approached me that we had professionally packaged four-song demo CDs that we were selling for $5, and double-sided single color T-shirts for $10 at the merch table with the girls.

This resulted in over $350 worth of sales for one evening that I wouldn't have received if I wasn't visible in a general area immediately after performing in front of everyone. This was our sales total before we even counted the total from the door.

Sometimes you just need to work the crowd. There isn't a single more effective salesperson that you can have other than yourself. You are the performer; you are the one that stands on the stage and underneath the lights. You are the person that people identify with your music and many times people will also ask you to sign the CD that they buy from you, so have a marker handy as well. This is one of the things that I've been referring to throughout this book when I mention the need to be proactive in your career: **Because simply having cute girls at the merch table doesn't sell records, simply having your music on iTunes doesn't sell records, and simply getting signed to a label doesn't sell records, but;**

Engaging your audience and interacting with the crowd; That is what sells records.

If you are unsure of how to price your product, I've always used one simple equation and I know many others who use this same pricing structure.

- Demos or EPs are $5.
- Full-length CDs are $10.

So there you have it, one night out for a band that's prepared with music and merch creates revenue from three sources in one location and they might even be eating and drinking for free if they worked that out with the club or the bar in advance. If you don't ask for these perks from a club then these things won't happen for you.

And if you don't inform your crowd that you have music and merchandise for sale then you may not sell any merch. You cannot ever assume that people know that you have these things available even if you have a table set up somewhere in the club. The best time for you to make an announcement about this is while you're still on stage right after your last song just before you put down the microphone.

Keep in mind that *only the squeaky wheel gets the grease.*

As an independent artist, you have multiple sources of revenue available to you from very early on in your career. So to summarize how we'll get paid as musicians let's take a brief overview of the various revenue streams that we need to create in order to make this happen:

- Physical music sales
- Digital music sales
- Ringtones and Ringback tones
- Streaming
- Sync licensing
- Performance royalties
- Digital performance royalties
- Live performances
- Booking and promoting events
- Merchandising

I've addressed every single one of these items in this book. If you've put the necessary foundations in place then you'll have given yourself the ability to *make money.*

As a breaking artist, you aren't going to see massive amounts of cash coming in through these sources in the beginning of your career; you'll see one sale at a time, per fan, per listener, per performance or broadcast.

Over time, as your popularity increases and as you add releases to your discography you'll utilize these same outlets to monetize your music. You may have to get as far as your third album to reach a tipping point in your career where everyone starts discovering who you are. Once this happens, all of these sources become active and will not only provide you revenue from your latest album, but will also most likely create revenue from your prior releases because people are now finding out about your earlier albums and purchasing them as well.

It costs you money to create music and your talent has value. You need to understand this and you need to put a price on it. First and foremost, you need to cover all of your expenses. Secondly, you need to make money doing this. In order to grow as a musician or as a band, you need to continue to reinvest in yourself and you can't do that if you haven't created viable revenue sources.

Some of you die-hard scenesters from very underground music scenes may beat your chest and say, "that's selling out, man!" Well, no it's not. It's called preparing yourself to be successful in life, which is a concept that many of you need to get on board with.

Oddly enough, and as timing would have it, just before the release of this book, this exact scenario just played out where the Samuel Adams Beer company licensed a song titled "I'm Shipping Up to Boston" by Dropkick Murphy's for use in their "30 years of Boston Lager" commercial.

This was met immediately by punk rock bellyaching on social media about capitalism and the establishment with statements like "just because you have a cool song in your commercial doesn't mean I'm going to buy your beer."

Well, the fact of the matter is that this person probably has never bought Sam Adams anyway much less any other beer that costs more than PBR does, and I don't recall the punk community going into an uproar when this exact same song was used in Martin Scorsese's 2006 movie "The Departed."

Although punk's not dead, it's getting older and probably has a mortgage to pay by now. So instead of complaining about bands selling out, you should be happy and proud that a band from your music scene has grown to the point where they were able to command a sync licensing fee which very well may have been up to $3,000 for their original music. These guys are adults and have bills to pay. They have made their imprint on the world and deserve to be paid accordingly.

I do, however, commend music scenes in niche markets like punk rock for not becoming homogenized and having a die-hard spirit that vehemently sticks to its roots, but if the ideology of your scene remains so exclusive to the point that you're restricting your growth then you also run the risk of having your music scene retract in size over a period of time. I can't say in good conscience that this is good for the bands or the movement overall if the same rigidly held beliefs that keep your music pure are the same ones that keep you from obtaining widespread success. If I were you, I would do everything in my power to ensure the growth and survival of my genre as an art form and I would try to direct as much attention to it as I would be trying to divert listeners away from the bullshit that the mainstream media is force-feeding everybody.

It's true that the contraction and expansion of music scenes is cyclical in nature, and this may be simply due to older scenesters fading away due to becoming adults that are married with children who eventually do conform to society, and its growth spurts could be due in part to the fresh new blood that enters the scene as the next generation comes of age and brings new and younger musicians along with it.

Either way it goes, in order for you to be a band that will withstand the test of time you'll need to follow the concepts of development that I've laid out in this book. If you have good music and brand yourself correctly in your genre and have created these realistic sources of revenue which will remain open during times of inactivity in your career or in your music scene, then you will not only sustain yourself on residual income but will also remain relevant while transcending the next generational gap.

CHAPTER THIRTY-THREE

BECOME INFORMED

ENTERTAINMENT NEWS *IS NOT* MUSIC INDUSTRY NEWS

An alarming number of you wouldn't know music industry news if it was printed daily and thrown at your fucking head every morning by the delivery boy.

So many of you are so caught up in gossip and the stories of the lives of celebrities that you haven't allowed yourself to learn jack shit about what is actually happening in this industry.

The superficial, self-serving shenanigans from artists that make the news have zero to do with the marketplace and will only perpetuate your ignorance and pettiness. Don't become caught up in the daily lives of these celebrities who, for the most part, do not qualify as role models anyway.

- Which celebrity's titties popped out in a photo shoot last weekend?
- What rap artist was dissing other artists during a live interview last night?
- Who just purchased a new yacht?

The answer to every single one of these questions is: ***Who gives a fuck?***

For many of you, your understanding about wealth, fame, and fortune is limited to the gossip columns that you read and to the ignorant shit and socially unacceptable behavior that you hear about celebrities doing.

What is even more problematic is that some of you are really just mindless fucking sheep who follow these behavior patterns thinking that it will get you in the spotlight quicker.

What will more likely happen is that you will alienate yourself from many of the people that can help you move forward and you may blackball yourself or possibly even get locked up.

But again, that's only going to happen if you really are a stupid fucking moron.

I have gotten to the point that I am blocking news feeds from people who constantly post material from TMZ and similar sites. This shit is always negative to some extent and has become such an energy-draining waste of time.

Entertainment news and celebrity gossip will not provide you with any tools to succeed, so if you are one of the many people who tune into this brain-melting chatter, you are hurting yourself more than helping yourself.

And how is it that I have become so sure of this?

Because you are allowing yourself to become distracted by meaningless garbage that doesn't affect your daily life or your career goals in any shape or form whatsoever.

You have allowed this bullshit to consume your time and it is not allowing you to focus on setting goals and accomplishing tasks.

WHAT *IS* MUSIC INDUSTRY NEWS

You can obtain information about what is happening in this industry from a wide variety of reputable news sources that provide stories which focus on changing trends within this industry that you should keep abreast of.

This is an unregulated industry that changes and adapts very quickly, and in order to keep your finger on the pulse of what is happening in this business you should start visiting some of the following sites and subscribe to their newsletters:

1. Ascap.com/news-and-events
2. Billboard.com/biz
3. DigitalMusicNews.com
4. Hypebot.com
5. Soundexchange.com/blog
6. Theguardian.com/business/musicindustry

CHAPTER THIRTY-FOUR

WHAT THE FUTURE HOLDS

At the time of this book, we've just started coming out of a sluggish and retracted global economy, there's always the potential of getting involved in another foreign war, and the geo-economic scenario frightens everyone from conspiracy theorists to Warren Buffet.

Plunging stocks, rising gas prices, and rising taxes all affect people's disposable income. With music deemed a non-essential item, these external factors will more than likely have a continuing detrimental impact on the annual sales overview of the music industry. These problems coupled with the rampant piracy and file sharing in what is a digitally dominated marketplace has permanently affected how music is bought and sold.

From within the industry, the streaming model has already had a negative impact on artists' and labels' ability to make money from sound recordings. It has decimated revenues for artists and labels by paying amounts far less than $.01 per stream and has also come into direct competition with downloading sales.

Throughout 2012-2013; artists, labels, and distributors alike have all voiced their frustration regarding the massive amount of line items that their accountants need to process now just to show revenue that equates to that of one single download for the same song.

Although it appears that an artist's song activity is up across the board due to streaming, his revenue is being driven down immensely by this same activity because now consumers aren't purchasing music to own.

PANDORA LOBBIES CONGRESS IN 2012

In 2012 the music streaming giant Pandora petitioned Congress with the Internet Radio Fairness Act (IRFA) (H.R. 6480/S. 3609), complaining that they aren't making enough money and believe that artist revenues from streaming should be reduced by 85 percent. They told Congress that they run the risk of having their business fail if they remain obligated to pay the artists what they're currently paying them for the use of their music.

And what artists are currently getting paid from Pandora is $0.0012 per play. For a corporation to attempt to reduce such an already miniscule amount by another 85 percent is grossly unfair and cripples the financial sustainability and security of all emerging artists and independent labels.

To address the current amount that Pandora pays to artists, we look at David Lowery's (the singer from Cracker) blog from June 2013, where he states:

"As a songwriter Pandora paid me $16.89 for 1,159,000 plays of "Low" last quarter. Less than I make from a single T-shirt sale."

I spoke to Lowery before completion of this book and he clarified his post by conveying to me that

"As a songwriter that was my share of the royalties ($16.89), as a performer I made approximately $152…the blog is in the larger context of my fight to equalize performer and songwriter royalties… and of course raise all the rates."

So, for you to clearly understand the economics of streaming, the payout that Lowery received for a song that was once a number 64 hit on the U.S. *Billboard* Hot 100 chart, and which still garnished a notable 1,159,000 plays in the last three months of 2012 only paid him an approximate total of $168.89 for the same quarter. If Pandora was to be successful in reducing its payouts by 85 percent, that would mean that Dave would have only received $25.33 for almost 1.16 million streams of this song.

Now if fans had downloaded these same 1,159,000 songs for $0.99 on iTunes instead of streaming them, Lowery may have actually made somewhere in the ballpark of $860,557.50 after iTunes took their standard revenue share, which is on average about 25 percent of sales.

Now you should take into consideration that the figures listed above are for an artist who has realized major market success. As an independent artist who may only have a few hundred people that even know who you are, and your revenue share will obviously pale in comparison. Not to mention you have just been given an example of how streaming is undermining your ability to make money from your music.

TAKE ACTION

I personally, along with many others, took the initiative to get involved in a fight to secure a future for ourselves in this industry. I contacted my congressman, state representative, and state senator on several occasions to express my frustration with this bold revenue-crippling move by Pandora and its detrimental effect on independent labels, as well as independent and underground artists' ability to move up in this business.

Michael Huppe, the president of SoundExchange, also testified before the Senate judiciary committee on November 28, 2012 in an effort to keep the bill from passing.

This bill was voted down, and at least for now, the small amount of money you make from streaming will remain intact.

However, as it appears, this is a fight that is far from over.

Pandora has already shifted its focus and its tactics towards finding another way to resolve this issue in their favor.

In the spring of 2013 Pandora executive Tim Westergren sent out a personalized email to artists and rightsholders that use their service asking them to sign a petition to support IRFA.

What the letter didn't state was that in signing this petition artists were also supporting an 85 percent pay cut in the revenue share. This resulted in a huge outcry from the music community, accusing Pandora of padding its own bottom line by tricking artists to support their own pay cut through an eloquently worded letter.

Should Pandora use this petition as evidence of overall artist support while reintroducing the bill to Congress and is successful in having it pass, it would mean that an artist's music would have to stream all day, every day for several years before that artist could afford to buy a cup of coffee.

Pandora is a company that has a net worth of more than $5 billion, and had more than 72 million active users in August 2013 alone.

This is a company that would not be able to exist had it not been for the content creators, which includes new and up-and-coming artists. Yet as with many corporations, the need to maximize profitability supersedes the fair payment of the person providing the content—or in this case, the copyright owner.

If you want to be made aware of any additional developments with the IRFA, you can place yourself on the mailing list for Music First on www.fairpayforartists.com or join the mailing list of your performing rights organization. You can also keep abreast of information related to this subject by staying on top of breaking music industry news.

Should you want to get involved and fight for your rights as an artist, you can make a difference by emailing your congressmen if you don't agree with certain developments in the music industry that require the approval of Congress. You can find the contact information for your congressman and state senator online.

The only way to change a system that you don't approve of is by getting involved in it.

Don't ever underestimate the power of your one, single voice.

In September 2013, I and other songwriters, content creators, and copyright owners banded together with ASCAP and sent a petition to Pandora's new CEO, Brian McAndrews, which gave him our thoughts on the matter of his company's current efforts to reduce what they pay rightsholders. My contribution was similar in content to the points that I have presented in this chapter and was summarized by this question I asked Mr. McAndrews:

"How would you like it if Pandora's revenue was reduced by 85 percent?"

One should take note on how large corporations across the board drive a stake between the customer and the content supplier. What Pandora is doing is no different than what Wal-Mart has done.

Create a massive expanding platform to sell a commodity at a bargain price, sell it cheaper than your competition, and pay the manufacturer next to nothing, making massive profits in doing so.

Musicians get paid little or close to nothing for streams, just like the factory workers in third world countries get paid little or close to nothing for manufacturing goods. Existing businesses are forced to close down because of a huge company's new method of doing business that is too large and too widespread to compete with. Just as your local family-owned hardware store and electronics store went out of business when the big box store moved in, so may iTunes and Amazon MP3 lose the ability to compete one day.

There you have it. Music the Wal-Mart way.

SoundExchange hasn't limited the scope of its fight for the fair payment of artists to just Pandora alone, either.

SoundExchange has recently made allegations that SiriusXM satellite radio took a number of impermissible deductions and exemptions in calculating its royalty payments between 2007 and 2012. If SoundExchange is correct in these allegations and is victorious in the underpayment lawsuit they filed on August 26, 2013, they'll recover between $50 and $100 million in unpaid digital artist royalties and pay the artists and the labels what they are rightfully due.

It's very disheartening to see that multiple corporations are simultaneously attempting to expropriate small revenue amounts from unknowing and unsuspecting independent artists and labels, resulting in their inability to grow and thrive or realize the correct amount of revenue that they are due without a third party stepping in.

SPOTIFY IN THE HOT SEAT

Next on this list is Spotify, who has also recently become the target of heated criticism.

In a country where streaming holds 89 percent of the market share of all music industry revenues, Spotify is realizing massive profits while the payout to rights holders for a single play of a track is between $0.006 and $0.0084.

The entire Swedish Musicians Union, which is comprised of over 5,000 artists in the strongest stronghold of streaming, is beginning to question if Spotify even has a right to use their music:

"We're saying that labels aren't even allowed to give out this digital content to begin with. So we want our music deleted, from every streaming platform. That way, we can start from scratch and start re-negotiating and see where it lands."

A large portion of artists are becoming outspoken in their disapproval of this business model overall.

Zoe Keating, who has been publishing her criminally low streaming royalty statements for years, said this to the *New York Times* in January 2013:

"In certain types of music, like classical or jazz, we are condemning them to poverty if [streaming] is going to be the only way people consume music…"

David Byrne of the Talking Heads criticized streaming as *"unsustainable as a means of supporting creative work of any kind."*

Beck was quoted as saying, *"If I tried to make my albums with what Spotify pays me, I wouldn't make them. I couldn't hire other musicians or someone to master it; I'd have to do everything myself."*

There's even conjecture among a growing number of musicians that suggests that streaming will be the overall death of the music industry. This sentiment was echoed by Thom Yorke of Radiohead when he described Spotify as *"the last desperate fart of a dying corpse."*

It can be argued that this business model isn't good for anyone but the streaming service. It's destroying revenue shares for distributors, labels, and artists and has threatened to impact iTunes' bottom line due to the fact that listeners can now stream instead of buy (download).

Apple's only viable way to compete with this has appeared to be with an "If you can't beat them, join them" attitude towards business manifested by their move in the Fall of 2013 with the creation of iTunes Radio, a platform which by 2015 failed to remain competitive against Pandora.

TIDAL FAILS TO MAKE A RIPPLE

Tidal was launched in March of 2015 by Jay Z as the first artist-owned company to deliver high fidelity CD-quality music to the consumer.

Alicia Keys pomped the launch of the streaming service as *"a powerful moment that will forever change the course of music history."*

However, not much history was made here—because contrary to what the general public might think—Jay Z didn't start a new business with Tidal.

Tidal was actually a digital service provider named Wimp, which was an imprint of Aspiro. And as its name may insinuate, Wimp never did become a digital music powerhouse; as a matter of fact, it only held about 1 percent of the market share as a digital music streaming platform. This makes you wonder why Jay Z shelled out $53 million to purchase and re-launch a bottom-of-the-barrel music platform.

After rebranding this company and re-launching it under the Tidal moniker, the first public mention of this involved an all-star cast of limited partners who were given approximately 3 percent ownership of the company in exchange for an agreement to pre-release their music exclusively on Tidal before it was available elsewhere.

These limited partners included Madonna, Rhianna, Deadmau5, Daft Punk, Alicia Keys, and Nicki Minaj, and the service wanted to convince independent artists everywhere that it understood the plight of independent musicians and wanted to create an avenue that would pay them more.

Or, as Keys put it:

"The goal is simple; we want to create a better service and a better experience for both fans and artists, and that is our promise to the world."

All of this was done at a cost of $19.99 per month to the consumer with no free platform available.

In its first few weeks after launching a "premium" instead of "freemium" platform, Tidal seemed to alienate people and actually push them towards Spotify, which moved to the forefront of the streaming app market.

Spotify's numbers went up, and some believe that Tidal's launch actually created awareness for Spotify's free platform to people who were previously unaware of the service *(and who subsequently also thought free was a much better deal than 20 bucks a month).*

Jay Z may have tried to connect with the *up-and-coming music artists*, however, what Tidal and its fees failed to do was connect with the *consumers.*

However, artists across the board have been slamming Tidal as just another platform to make the rich richer, and none have done so as eloquently as Ben Gibbard of Death Cab for Cutie who told the *Daily Beast:*

"… I think they totally blew it by bringing out a bunch of millionaires and billionaires and propping them up onstage and then having them all complain about not being paid.

"There was a wonderful opportunity squandered to highlight what this service would mean for artists who are struggling and to make a plea to people's hearts and pocketbooks to pay a little more for this service that was going to pay these artists a more reasonable streaming rate, and they didn't do it. That's why this thing is going to fail miserably."

Again, I'll reiterate a point that you must keep in mind as an artist:

As long as you opt in to these services, you'll be paid next to nothing while these corporations realize massive profits, and as long as your music is available on these services it will compete with your download sales and drive down your revenue—not substantially, but massively. It's argued that the exposure is good, but is it worth the tradeoff?

Looking at the corporate imprint in today's music market, I can't help but think back to 1988 when Ray "Raybeez" Barbieri, the lead singer of the New York City hardcore band Warzone, stated during the intro of the title track of his band's debut full-length album Don't Forget The Struggle Don't Forget The Streets,

"In our minds and in our hearts we feel that hardcore music should stay out of Big Business and stay in the streets, where it belongs..."

Ray appears to have left us with a premonition of what we're seeing unfold today, and it's starting to seem that he couldn't have hit the nail more squarely on the head. In actuality,

independent music has remained primarily true to its roots and never really did gravitate towards big business; it didn't have to, because big business came to it.

During the last decade, companies such as Tunecore have become the go-to place for indie musicians. Tunecore started in 2006 with good intentions by Jeff Price, Gary Burke, and Peter Wells. Price had a vision of making things easier for musicians and wanted to provide them the services that they previously relied on labels for. In his own words, his vision was to change the global music industry for artists for the better by serving, not exploiting, them.

Tunecore did change the industry, and at least for independent artists, did so insanely well.

So it came as a shock to most of the industry when Tunecore Inc. fired Price and Wells in 2012.

Mike Masnick, the Founder of Techdirt.com, an award-winning blog that provides insight on technology corporations and government policies, had tried to get Gill Cogan of Opus Capital, the main venture capitalist behind Tunecore's original funding, to comment on the ouster of the founding members but was unsuccessful.

Although it's unclear exactly what happened, Price raised his own personal concerns about the future of his former company to Masnick and shared his observation about what happened when John Sculley came in as CEO of Apple during their discussion of Tunecore's future.

"Neither Peter [nor] I are even remotely in the league of Apple or Steve Jobs, but you look at what happened to Apple when John Sculley came in as CEO. He changed the Apple vision from making "insanely great easy to use products" to one of "making money at any expense."

This unfortunately appears to be the fate of many startup companies. A great idea or product, with a solid belief in the customer, starts doing well enough to attract the interests of an investor or venture capitalist, and then the visionaries eventually sit down at the opposite side of the table of the financiers and have a meeting. Once a merger or acquisition happens, the original vision of the company eventually becomes eclipsed by the financiers or board of directors' profit margins and bottom line and the original intention and direction of the company changes from one of customer service and satisfaction to one of maximizing profitability.

Price also explained the importance of vision to Masnick:

"It's the vision that drives the success and revenue, not the other way around. We did everything we could to instill the vision as deeply as we could. We just hope it sticks."

I personally cannot be certain that it has stuck.

Price stated that he has no faith in the company's ability to succeed and has recently slammed Tunecore as being directionless with no current CEO to keep it from falling off of a cliff. In an October 2012 interview with *Digital Music News*, he made this statement:

"I wish I could provide a simple clear explanation, I can't. It's getting close to half a year since [cofounder] Peter Wells and I were pushed out and still no real reason has been provided. As far as the three original founders, advisors and investors know, there is no new CEO, no interim CEO, no plan, no vision, no leadership and no innate understanding of the music industry or the needs of artists at the top of the company.

From what we can tell, a venture capital banker with no true, solid experience in the music industry, no experience in digital distribution, copyright, licensing, digital music services or the overall emerging digital music market place is running the company. He has few or no connections or relationships with anyone in the industry and can't speak to and understand artists."

Needless to say, I'm in full agreement with the point that's been made here about the lack of understanding about the music industry on the behalf of outsiders. Inserting a person with no extensive knowledge base into a decision-making position cripples a company's natural evolution by destroying its ability to refine and improve upon its existing products and services.

I see it often, and no matter what division of the industry it comes from, whether it's distribution or live concert promotion, the scales are always way off balance when the knowledge base and experience is not present.

When talking to these people, it always seems like it's the first day of school and the outcome always appears to be detrimental to the artists and the industry as a whole.

Tunecore has since appointed Scott Ackerman as Chief Executive Officer.

It's reported that Ackerman's resume includes working for eHarmony, Orbitz, CheapTickets.com, Lodging.com, American Airlines, Northwest Airlines, and US Airways, but he appears to have zero music industry experience.

What this means for Tunecore's future overall remains to be seen, but it seems to read like this:

Banker hires travel agent to manage rapidly growing market share of artist-owned, retail-ready digital music.

...They're turning fire red to money green.

Musicians now have more tools at their disposal than ever before in the history of music.

The ability to create, replicate, and distribute music is readily available to all that have talent and/or the desire to create.

Artists from prior generations seem to have placed a higher value on music, and it was a very big deal for an independent artist to release an album on vinyl and have it distributed to record stores. Vinyl manufacturing and closed-door distribution helped add to the value of music overall because these albums weren't easily replicated and bootlegged. Yes, it did happen, but not at the rampant, out-of-control pace that it does with CDs or digital music.

THE RETURN OF THE VINYL RECORD

Vinyl for quite some time had pretty much gone the way of the eight-track with the exception of some limited pressings that bands released to appease the record-collecting portion of their fan base. However, in today's independent market we're beginning to see a resurgence of the vinyl release, which is known for its superior high-fidelity sound quality that digital recordings just can't compare to.

Growth in vinyl sales was up 32 percent in 2013, and grew an additional 47.5 percent in 2014 to a total 6.074 million units per Nielsen SoundScan.

The uptick in sales for this format could mark the beginning of a new trend where artists begin making money while simultaneously giving people music in tangible form once again, instead of this invisible bullshit that they are buying and therefore don't associate value to.

I know a lot of bands that are planning on making their next release a vinyl one and I encourage you to get in front of the curve here as well. You will want to get yourself involved in this market before it blows up again.

People with a keen sense of business get involved in things early on. It's always better to be a trailblazer than a trend follower.

As of the summer of 2015 vinyl pressing and cutting plants are operating with a six month backlog in order fulfillment. If this does not give you a snapshot of where this is headed then I don't know what will.

CD manufacturing is cheaper than vinyl pressing and even though CD sales are on the decline *(during the first six months of 2014, only 62.9 million CDs were sold, which is less than half of 2009's six-month total of 136.4 million)* with digital sales outpacing it and stores reducing rack space almost on an annual basis, it still seems to be the favored medium amongst artists who are selling their music on the street and at live events. But overall—and with the exception of vinyl—there has been a massive decline in sales in all markets over the last decade, both physical and digital.

THE DEVALUATION OF MUSIC

Today, artists are creating volumes of work at a rapid pace. The amount of artists and new music is creating an oversaturated market and artists are shying away from traditional time-proven trends in marketing and releasing music such as some of the scenarios I've presented in this book.

I believe what artists are missing today is the ability to effectively market and promote one full-length album to massive amounts of people. To the contrary, it seems that artists today are providing massive amounts of music to a limited amount of people, and in many cases they're doing it for free.

Giving away your band's demo for free is a common practice; a limited release of six songs or less is not a bad way to engage potential fans. On the other hand, if you're releasing multiple full-length "mixtapes" or albums and giving this music away for free, you're conditioning your consumer to expect music for free. Combine this with file sharing and piracy and you see a growing trend where music consumers will feel that they're not obligated to pay anything at all for music.

This is really an issue that you need to explore as a musician. When you started reading this book, I mentioned the bright lights, the huge stage, and the vast amount of fans packing an arena that you picture yourself arriving to in private jets and limousines. How do you realistically expect to achieve this level of success when you're giving away all of your music free of charge?

Once you eliminate an entire generation's desire to purchase music, there's a good possibility that it will be gone forever and so will your hopes for obtaining vast amounts of wealth.

The devaluation of music is happening now, and if you're flooding the market with free music, then you're the one who's responsible for it.

When you devalue your music, you devalue your worth as an artist, and you devalue this industry overall.

Gone are the days of the huge cash advance. Some artists believe that they need to hold out and wait for the big break that's never going to happen instead of taking their career into their own hands and making the proper steps to get noticed. This all-or-nothing mentality plays directly into the instant gratification frame of mind that so many of today's youth are beholden to and is the exact thing that will greatly diminish their potential for success.

Sitting on your hands and biding your time is not a habit of successful people. One thing that's clearly evident about time is that it eventually runs out. You'll either be a person that turns around and says, "I did everything I could for myself over the last several years to get where I am now," or you'll look back and say, "I've waited for my big break for years and nothing happened."

Some of you may feel that giving away large amounts of music is a necessary step before you release your music through a distributor. Even if you choose to distribute your music though a digital distributor, a lot of your content will now be streamed instead of downloaded, which will have a detrimental effect on your sales revenue.

While you've been concentrating on giving away your music for free, you haven't been paying attention to the fact that the percentage of money that some corporations want to pay you for your music is being decreased.

AND THE DAMAGE BECOMES BLATANTLY EVIDENT…

Pointing a finger directly at illegal downloads, file sharing, and streaming as well, **it comes as no surprise that in the first nine months of 2014, not one full-length album has gone Platinum**. This is actually the first time that this has ever happened since RIAA implemented the rating system in 1976, and it is a foreboding sign of what is to come.

This can be directly tied to the change in how music is consumed. Beyoncé and Lorde both released albums in 2013, neither of which were able to surpass 800,000 units sold by the end of Q3 in 2014. This also held true for Coldplay and Eric Church's 2014 album releases, which both sold less than those of Beyoncé and Lorde.

Digital single sales, digital album sales, and CD sales all took a beating in 2014 and the ongoing market share reduction for these formats is showing no sign of letting up.

ITunes may have had its heyday, but we are living in different times now and the streaming giants have one very powerful tool in their corner: the fact that *after years of piracy, file sharing, and artists giving away free songs, people just don't want to pay for music anymore*.

So I will reiterate what I said before in this book. Develop a fan base and maintain a relationship with them, because their support is where your revenue is going to come from. If they're not buying your music embodied in a physical product or your merch, you will be very disappointed with your streaming revenue.

You need to actively control these small revenue streams from direct fan contact as best as you can, because technology and business are retooling the way that music is consumed and the amount of revenue that all artists receive.

Whether you are an underground artist, and independent artist, or even signed to a major for that matter, you're not ever going to make the same kind of cash as the rock stars and rap stars of the 80s and 90s did.

To make things even worse, the streaming giants have undermined the market share of paid downloads and physical album sales and have been fighting Congress to wrestle more money out of your pocket

And they are getting help too, from the people at…

THE DIGITAL MEDIA ASSOCIATION

The Digital Media Association, or DiMA, was founded in 1998 to defend corporations and other businesses against artists like YOU.

DiMA publicly lists its policies on its website, one of which includes *"defending against songwriters' efforts to legislate "double-dip" royalties."*

It appears that DiMA's position on copyright law is that the law is outdated, is not updated often enough to keep up with modern times, and has an antiquated approach to how intellectual property rights relate to the businesses that are involved with them.

They are also focusing on challenging existing laws so that businesses can move forward (*make more money*) and they want to *modernize music licensing and promote innovative business models*. It doesn't take a genius to realize what this will mean for your publishing revenues.

The Trichordist also lists three specific current DiMA policy positions that are directly in opposition to artists and songwriters rights:

- DiMA supports Pandora buying a terrestrial radio station in an effort to lower the royalties Pandora will pay to songwriters.
- DiMA is opposed to the Fair Pay Act, which would pay performers a terrestrial radio broadcast royalty.
- DiMA is opposed to The Songwriter Equity Act, which would allow songwriters the ability to negotiate fair market rates for their work.

We have now come full circle, my friend, because as I stated in Chapter One:

"The music industry seems polarized due to the fact that it's occupied by two completely different forces that can't work or even exist without each other. The sometimes free-spirited views of the artists and their desire to write, create, and just get out and play sometimes hits a wall because of the business side of the industry."

And as you can see, the music business will continue to become less of a place you can thrive in. Why is this? Because that's exactly what it is—a fucking business, something that I can say with all honesty that many of you just aren't cut out for. So I encourage you to start approaching your career as a businessperson if you are truly serious about making a living at this.

Otherwise, you are fucked.

Corporations were once nickel and diming you to get out of paying you your statutory royalty rate of 9.2 cents per song.

Now they are trying to fuck you out of fractions of one penny.

When we are at the point that we are fighting over amounts that equal less than one penny we are very close to the end of having any realistic expectation of getting paid anything at all.

My friends, the well is about to run dry.

This entire chapter is to let you know that your hopes, dreams, and realistic ability to make a living as a musician are being compromised; sadly many of you are just finding all of this out now as you read this book.

As a musician, you face challenges on all sides. Will you rise up and face these challenges?

Or are you the type of person that will lay back and get rolled over because you assume that there's someone else out there who will fight these challenges for you? If so, all you're doing is exercising the mentality of failure.

If you've chosen this lifestyle as a career path then it's your obligation as an artist to mold the future of this industry for yourself and those that come behind you. What legacy are you going to bring an industry that has fulfilled some people's wildest dreams? As you can see, it's becoming more and more difficult to fulfill these dreams. So will you become actively involved in it or will you sit idly by until the whole system burns to the ground?

It's high time you start implementing some measures to unfuck yourself, Junior, or you'll become one starving motherfucking artist in a very short period of time.

Get involved, not only in your career, but in the industry as a whole. Do things one step at a time, and bigger opportunities will eventually come your way without you needing to force the hand of fate. Once you have experience and wisdom in your corner, take the personal initiative to create and fill the much-needed leadership and mentoring roles that this industry needs.

Don't ever underestimate the power of your sole independent actions.

FINAL THOUGHTS

The biggest enemies you'll face in the music industry and in your own life are ignorance, ambivalence, and laziness. In other words:

- Not knowing,
- knowing and not giving a fuck,
- or knowing and being too lazy to give a fuck.

If these apply to you, then you're not only going to go nowhere in your music career, but you're going nowhere in life, either.

Oftentimes people blame their surroundings before ever realizing their own role in their lack of success. The fact of the matter is, no matter how dire or impoverished your situation is, no matter how broken down your family system is or how violent your community is, no matter what degree of depression or addiction you may have, there are vehicles and mechanisms you can use to get out and away from that oppression. But you need to seek them out on your own and fight for your way out by yourself because nobody gives a flying fuck about you.

People in general are too concerned about their own self-absorbed lifestyles to take the time to focus on your problems because they have problems of their own. Even if they're trying to pull themselves up out of the same gutter as you, don't expect them to throw you a lifeline, because they're probably carrying all the weight that they can handle already.

They've also embraced an unpopular concept that cannot be taught to others because it's so widely rejected by the average and less-than-average majority of the population, which is that hopelessness is only a state of mind.

People that suffer from hopelessness have been led to believe that it's a social condition. However, their social condition is merely a reflection of their mental condition.

The ability to overcome this condition is not only a key element to your success and growth, but to your long-term survival as well. It's an ongoing battle that you must fight with the intention to win as if your life depends on it, and your life does indeed depend on it. Because you only live once and time is NOT on your side.

This fight is yours and yours alone and it starts with you having the inner strength to raise up your fists and combat your inner demons, because nothing will ever change around you until things change within you.

The harder the circumstances, the stronger the person will become.

If you step into any of the potholes or pitfalls that society has placed in front of you, it's really nobody's fault but your own. If you were unable to avoid peer pressure or steer clear of something that you knew was wrong in the first place then you've gotten what you had coming.

You placed your thoughts, beliefs, and gut feeling aside and gave in to outside influence. You lost your stance and you folded.

You failed. Period.

This may sound like a harsh reality but it's the truth, and if you haven't figured it out yet, this book wasn't made to coddle you; this book was made to EMPOWER YOU.

Self-empowerment is a direct result of self-awareness, and you'll only become empowered once you make a fearless search of yourself and confront your issues and your weaknesses head on.

Some of you may think that there are invisible walls that will keep you from achieving success. Unfortunately, if you believe in walls that aren't physically there then you have conceded to defeat before you even started.

Unlock your mind and escape this imaginary prison without walls. If you can't see or touch a barrier that you believe is in your way then it doesn't exist.

Yes, there are challenges you'll face and there are people and practices that you should avoid, but at the end of the day nobody walks through life in your shoes. This is your life and it's your journey. No one has the power to dictate the path you choose in life other than yourself.

If you do fall down on this journey—whether by your own dereliction or the influence of another—it's critical that you get back up again, because you're measured by your successes in life, not by your failures. Without having a list of any accomplishments or milestones in your life, your total is zero, which is exactly what people will refer to you as—a zero.

Your time on this earth is limited. If you're going to do anything at all, I suggest you make a whole-hearted effort to move forward on your chosen path in life, and this needs to begin now if it hasn't already.

With that being said, what personal successes can you claim as your own as of today?

To gauge what direction you're going in, I want you to answer these two simple questions:

- What are your current short-term goals?
- What are your current long-term goals?

If you can't answer these two questions with an immediate response then you really don't have any viable prospects on the horizon, do you?

Sometimes being on the right path can be attributed to in part by who we choose to surround ourselves with.

If you haven't had mentors or role models in your life then you're without a doubt a part of the wrong social circle, and are most likely surrounded with people that only have the potential to drag you down instead of bringing you up.

I've observed a lot of things in life that could either determine a person's personal success and systematic rise up the corporate ladder or his systematic detachment and cultural dissimilation from organized society along with his utter failure and self-destruction. If you keep your eyes open, you'll see that the behavior traits from both of these classes of people read like a book and aren't that difficult to figure out.

So when I say *personal* success, I mean that it starts with you and you alone. Success is something that comes from within you and spreads outward, not the other way around.

369

Successful people are extremely competitive, responsible, hard-working people who are eager to learn new things and are extremely tough on themselves. They're creative, focused, quick on their feet, and have the ability to plan things out.

Start exercising these traits and these are the people in whose company you'll eventually find yourself.

If you have negative, inspiration-draining people in your life, or are surrounded by people who are bringing you down in general, it's time to get rid of them. In order to keep a clean house, you need to take out the garbage every day.

Just as most parents continually try to instill a value system in their children—and as yours may have tried to instill in you—you need to break any bad habits you have and become a self-starting, self-motivated person.

Whatever you ultimately do with your life, if you don't apply yourself, you will fall upon hard economic times. This, my friend, is something that I can guarantee you.

Even with a limited education, if you can embrace the concept that hard work and dedication will take you to your destination in life, you will be light years ahead of those that surround you.

Success is a steady consistent climb; you can't cut out the front and the middle. The end result is built upon and supported by the foundation that they provide.

I can't even count the times that I've said to myself, "If I only knew that when I was younger..."

Well, unfortunately experience is something that you don't have until five minutes after you actually needed it, and this is exactly why I wrote this book for you.

Working in the music industry can be a great experience, if you're a performer; a hard day's work may one day only involve stepping on the stage for 40 minutes. Until that happens, realize that the music industry, just like any job, has entry-level positions. You'll have to work your way up the ladder. The sense of pride that comes along with knowing that you've built your career up with your own two hands is just as rewarding as the money you receive from it. But remember one thing:

You have to do the damn work.

The moment you open your mouth and say, "I can't do it," "I won't do it," or, "it's not my job" is the moment that you've exceeded your own level of incompetence. In doing so, you have not only proven this to the person to whom you are speaking, but also to yourself.

This is also the moment where your forward progression ends.

The road to success ends exactly where you stop having the desire to drive on.

The music industry is a competitive arena the minute you step in the door. As you grow, learn, and climb to the top things should get easier but not necessarily; because the better you get, and the higher you climb— although there's less competition—the other competitors that you'll face are the best in their field and have a large team of professionals managing them along with the resources that are provided to them, financial and otherwise.

It's my hope that you've experienced some growth and have become a better, more productive person as a result of reading this book. So if it has seemed to you that some of—or even the entire—context of this book was an accusatory finger-wagging tirade from some guy on his soapbox, well, you were right.

This book was meant to provoke thought, because only until we identify what we're doing wrong will we then be able to address it, correct it and start doing what's right.

Stop thinking success is based on being in the right place at the right time, even if there's a remote possibility that this is true; I can guarantee you that the right place that they've been referring to isn't your couch.

So put down the beer, put down the blunt, put down the game controller, put down the television remote, and detach yourself from the unnecessary time-consuming daily distractions that prevent your mind from achieving its potential genius. It is said that anything that your mind is capable of conceiving, you are capable of achieving.

It's time to stop making excuses and postponing your destiny.

Anything less than total success is total failure, so make sure you cross the finish line.

In closing,

The process of writing this book was by no means an easy task; it didn't happen overnight. It was done by eliminating distractions, and it involved a lot of self-sacrifice in regards to my personal time, but it's a testament to what one single person can accomplish when they set their mind to one specific goal or objective and refuse to give up before the job is done.

Now having this completed, I'd like to say that I'm happy to have been able to take some of my personal experiences and knowledge and commit them to a book for you to read and learn from. This has been a reward in itself. Thank you for reading.

This book was meant to give you a leg up on the things that you need to do when taking your first steps in the industry along with gaining a perspective on the independent market.

Having this knowledge base should put you in a better position than you were before you read this book and people will recognize you for what you've learned. Combine this with some hands-on experience and there's also a good possibility that based on what people now see in you, they may open some doors for you.

This is because now you have the ability to show up for work prepared.

I'm glad to have had the opportunity to show you the moves you'll need to make to get a running start in your career and I've made you aware of some the mistakes you need to avoid.

Keep in mind that all of this information is meaningless unless you have the motivation to put your left foot in front of your right and start moving forward.

I can teach you what I know, but what I can't do for you is fill you with the unyielding personal desire to achieve that which comes only from within yourself.

That's known as passion, and either you have it or you don't.

So if you happen to be a person that's extremely passionate about what you do, then take that fire that burns inside you, fuel it with the knowledge contained in these pages, and rise up, because now is your time.

Only you can turn your vision into a reality.

LIST INDEX

In an effort to make this book more practical and easier to reference for the reader, I have entered this quick lookup index for all of the lists that are in this book.

REFERENCES

CHAPTER ONE

Dischord Records. "History." Dischord.com. http://www.dischord.com/history.

CHAPTER THREE

Fernández, E. M., & Cairns, H. S. (2011). *Fundamentals of Psycholinguistics.* West Sussex, United Kingdom: Blackwell Publishing.

Hodges, Kenneth. "Meter." University of Oklahoma. http://faculty-staff.ou.edu/H/Kenneth.L.Hodges-1/Meter.html.

Inzuna, Victor. "Writing Tips and Techniques for Poets." Pencils.com. http://www.pencils.com/blog/writing-techniques-for-poets.

Tilden, Imogen. "What Pop Music Owes to the Classical Masters." Theguardian.com. http://www.theguardian.com/music/2013/jan/24/what-pop-music-owes-classical-masters. 24 January 2013.

Wikipedia."Muhammed Suicmez." Wikipedia.com http://en.wikipedia.org/wiki/Muhammed_Sui%C3%A7mez.

Smith, Steve. "Odd Meter: Pink Floyd, 'Money' (1973)." Hooks. https://hooksanalysis.wordpress.com/2009/07/02/odd-meter-pink-floyd-money-1973/. 2 July 2009.

CHAPTER FOUR

Internal Revenue Service."Is Your Hobby a For-Profit Endeavor?" IRS.gov. http://www.irs.gov/uac/Is-Your-Hobby-a-For-Profit-Endeavor%3F. June 2008.

CHAPTER SIX

Levinson, Jay Conrad. Guerrilla Marketing: Easy and Inexpensive Strategies for Making Big Profits from Your Small Business. Boston, Massachusetts: Houghton Mifflin Company.

CHAPTER EIGHT

McDonald, Heather. "Readers Respond: Which Social Networking Site is Most Useful to You?" About.com. http://musicians.about.com/u/ua/musicpromotion/networkingpromousersrespond.htm.

Siu, Eric. "24 Eye-Popping SEO Statistics." Search Engine Journal. http://www.searchenginejournal.com/24-eye-popping-seo-statistics/42665/ -. 19 April 2012.

eBizMBA. "Top 15 Most Popular Social Networking Sites: May 2015." eBizmba.com. http://www.ebizmba.com/articles/social-networking-websites.

CHAPTER TEN

Roche, Jason. "The Top 20 New York Hardcore and Metal Albums of All Time." The Village Voice. http://blogs.villagevoice.com/music/2013/07/top_20_nyhc_metal_albums_all_time.php. 9 July 2013.

CHAPTER TWELVE

United States Copyright Office. "Electronic Copyright Office." https://eco.copyright.gov/.

Section 504 of the Copyright Law of the United States of America and Related Laws Contained in Title 17 of the United States Code.

CHAPTER THIRTEEN

BMI. "BMI Live." http://www.bmi.com/special/bmi_live.

SoundExchange. "About Digital Royalties." http://www.soundexchange.com/artist-copyright-owner/digital-royalties/.

CHAPTER FOURTEEN

Holz, Alex. "How You Can Clear Cover Songs, Samples, and Handle Public Domain Works." Ascap.com. http://www.ascap.com/playback/2011/01/features/limelight.aspx. 26 January 2011.
Section 115 of the Copyright Act of the United States of America and Related Laws Contained in Title 17 of the United States Code

Sellars, Andy. "Rethink Music: A Compulsory Sampling License." https://andyontheroad.wordpress.com/2011/04/26/rethink-music-a-compulsory-sampling-license/. 26 April 2011.

CHAPTER SEVENTEEN

Huffington Post. "The U.S. Illiteracy Rate Hasn't Changed In 10 Years." http://www.huffingtonpost.com/2013/09/06/illiteracy-rate_n_3880355.html. 6 September 2013.

CHAPTER NINETEEN

Image screenshot. Statcounter.com

Farrish, Bryan. "Radio Airplay 101." Bryan Farrish Radio Promotion. http://radio-media.com/song-album/articles/airplay69.html.

Lieb, Rebecca & Owyang, Jeremiah. The Converged Media Imperative. (2012). Altimeter Group.

CHAPTER TWENTY-ONE

Cumberland, Robert. "The Money Sponge." Bemuso. http://www.bemuso.com/articles/moneysponge.html.

Rapaport, Diane. "How Record Companies Make Money." Music Business: Producers. http://www.music-business-producer.com/record-companies-money.html.

CHAPTER TWENTY-SEVEN

DeRogatis, Jim. "More Trouble at the Congress Theater." WBEZ. http://www.wbez.org/blogs/jim-derogatis/2012-04/more-trouble-congress-theater-98249. 14 April 2012.

DeRogatis, Jim. "Congress Theater Liquor License Revoked." http://www.wbez.org/blogs/jim-derogatis/2013-05/congress-theater-liquor-license-revoked-107360. 24 May 2013.

Petty, Lauren. "7 Shot at Club during Rapper's Album Release Party." NBC Chicago. http://www.nbcchicago.com/news/local/7-Shot-Club-Rapper-Album-Release-Party-Chicago-199331621.html. 21 March 2013.

Slodysko, Brian & Clauss, Hunter. "Four Shot During Hip-Hop Show at Ultra Lounge in Logan Square." Chicago Sun-Times. http://www.suntimes.com/news/metro/16819805-418/2-men-shot-inside-logan-square-bar.html. 5 December 2012.

TimeOut Chicago. "Promoters' Ordinance." http://www.timeoutchicago.com/things-to-do/93929/promoters-ordinance. 10 November 2010.

CHAPTER TWENTY-NINE

Lamia, Mary C. "Jealousy and Envy: The Emotions of Comparison and Contrast." Psychology Today. http://www.psychologytoday.com/blog/intense-emotions-and-strong-feelings/201307/jealousy-and-envy-the-emotions-comparison-and-contr. 13 July 2013.

Russell, Bertrand (1930). *The Conquest of Happiness* New York: H. Liverwright. P. 90-91.

CHAPTER THIRTY-ONE

Eco Coalition. "Don't Trash Your Old CDs, Recycle Them." Ecocoalition.org. http://www.ecocoalition.org/don%E2%80%99t-trash-your-old-cds-recycle-them.

RIAA. "The Law." Riaa.com. http://www.riaa.com/physicalpiracy.php?content_selector=piracy_online_the_law.

RIAA. "RIAA Releases 2000 Consumer Profile." Riaa.com. http://riaa.com/newsitem.php?news_year_filter=&resultpage=88&id=B2E888D8-6176-9EBD-C163-BEF6735726E3.

Rakoczy, Sam. MH Learning Solutions. "Why Rap is Going Down, Down, Down, Down, Down, Down." Mhlearningsolutions.com. http://www.mhlearningsolutions.com/commonplace/index.php?q=node/5590.

Rideout, Victoria, Donald F. Roberts and Ulla F. Foehr (2005). *Generation M: Media in the Lives of 8–18 Year-Olds.* Menlo Park, CA: Kaiser Family Foundation.

CHAPTER THIRTY-FOUR

SoundExchange. *SoundExchange Soundbyte* Vol 2 Issue 2 October 9, 2013 (PDF) http://www.soundexchange.com/wp-content/uploads/2013/10/Soundbyte-10-9-13.pdf.

Dredge, Stuart. The Guardian. "Spotify Opens Up Analytics in Effort to Prove its Worth to Doubting Musicians. http://www.theguardian.com/technology/2013/dec/03/spotify-analytics-musicians-streaming-music-artists-earn?utm_content=buffer23dee&utm_source=buffer&utm_medium=twitter&utm_campaign=Buffer. Theguardian.com.

Lowery, Dave. The Trichordist. "My Song Got Played On Pandora 1 Million Times and All I Got Was $16.89, Less Than What I Make From a Single T-Shirt Sale!"

Resnikoff, Paul. Digital Music News. "16 Artists That Are Now Speaking Out Against Streaming." Digitalmusicnews.com. http://www.digitalmusicnews.com/permalink/2013/12/02/artistspiracy.

Leon, Melissa. "Death Cab for Cutie Frontman Ben Gibbard Slams Indiana and Talks Divorce." The Daily Beast. http://www.thedailybeast.com/articles/2015/04/11/death-cab-for-cutie-frontman-ben-gibbard-slams-indiana-and-talks-divorce.html. 11 April 2015.

Resnikoff, Paul. Digital Music News. "I'm Jeff Price. And I'm Ready to Talk About My TuneCore Departure." Digitalmusicnews.com. http://www.digitalmusicnews.com/permalink/2012/10/24/jeffpricetunecore.

Masnick, Mike.Tech Dirt. "Jeff Price Pushed out of TuneCore, Despite Tremendous Success in Helping Artists." Techdirt.com. http://www.techdirt.com/articles/20120815/15194320063/inexplicable-jeff-price-pushed-out-tunecore-despite-tremendous-success-helping-artists.shtml.

Fox, Zoe. Mashable. "Vinyl Record Sales Increased 32% in 2013." Mashable.com. http://mashable.com/2014/01/07/vinyl-comeback/.

Anderson, Trevor. "Albums Suffer as CD Sales Decline." The Wall Street Journal. http://blogs.wsj.com/numbers/albums-suffer-as-cd-sales-decline-1569/. 15 July 2014.

eBizMBA. "Top 15 Most Popular Music Websites." eBizmba.com. http://www.ebizmba.com/articles/music-websites. August 2015.

The Trichordist. "Digital Media Association (DiMA) Always Against Musicians." http://thetrichordist.com/2015/05/27/digital-media-association-dima-always-against-musicians/. 27 May 2015.

Digital Media Association. "DiMA's Position on Coppyright and Royalties." http://www.digmedia.org/issues-and-policy/copyright-and-royalties/141-dimas-position-on-copyright-and-royalties. 2015.

ACKNOWLEDGEMENTS

It is with profound gratitude that I thank the following people for their contribution to this book's completion.

Carlos Fournier
Editor
The Music Industry Self Help Guide Editions 1, 2

Hank Pearl – Black Pearl Photo
Photo Contributor
p.iii: Never We See
Scarecrow pictured

Steven Stolper
Photo Contributor
Table of Contents, p.v: Flames of Fury
Angelica Valkyrie pictured

Amanda Nowman
Photo Contributor
Table of Contents, pp. vi-vii: Blood In Blood Out
Jaaron Sanford pictured

Eric Munnings and Victory Records
Photo Contributor
Table of Contents' pp. viii-ix: Emmure

Justin Koteff – Red Flame Photography
Photo Contributor Table of Contents, pp. xi-xii: Warbringer
www.redflamephoto.com

Mr. Sean Taggart
Album Cover Artwork – Chapter Ten, p.117
Agnostic Front Cause For Alarm album cover artwork
seantaggart.com

*Acknowledgements are listed in order of appearance.
Any photographs not credited within the body of this book
were submitted by the author himself.*